Regions Reconsidered

Economic Networks, Innovation, and Local Development in Industrialized Countries

Edited by E.M. Bergman, G. Maier, F. Tödtling

MANSELL

First published in 1991 by
Mansell Publishing Limited, *A Cassell Imprint*
Villiers House, 41/47 Strand, London WC2N 5JE, England
387 Park Avenue South, New York, NY 10016–8810, USA

Reprinted 1993

British Library Cataloguing in Publication Data
Bergman, E. M.
    Regions reconsidered: economic networks, innovation
    and local development in industrialized countries
    I. Title II. Maier, G. III. Tödtling, F.
    330.91722
    ISBN 0-7201-2108-6

Library of Congress Cataloging-in-Publication Data
Regions reconsidered: economic networks, innovation, and local
    development in industrialized countries / edited by E.M. Bergman, G.
    Maier, F. Tödtling.
        p.   cm.
    Includes bibliographical references and index.
    ISBN 0-7201-2108-6
    1. Regional economics. 2. Industrial organization. 3. Regional
planning–Case studies. 4. Industrial organization–Case studies.
5. Technological innovations–Economic aspects–Case studies.
I. Bergman, Edward M. II. Maier, Gunther. III. Tödtling, Franz.
HT388.R455 1991
338.9–dc20
                                                          91-4106
                                                          CIP

Printed in Great Britain by Ipswich Book Co. Ltd., Ipswich, Suffolk

Contents

I   Networks of Firms and Industries

II   Innovative Local Districts and Milieus

6   Maillat: The Innovation Process and the Role of the Milieu   103

7   Garofoli: Local Networks, Innovation and Policy in Italian Industrial Districts   119

8   Hadjimichalis, Papamichos: "Local" Development in Southern Europe: Myths and Realities   141

III Sectoral Dynamics of Regional Restructuring

IV Development Concepts Reconsidered

Preface

It was a beautiful mid-June afternoon on the grounds of a small castle overlooking the city of Vienna. Gathered there were a handful of Walter Stöhr's colleagues from various parts of the world, all of whom continued to debate the many fresh ideas that arose during the course of a small conference on Technology, Innovation and Local Development. Although the formal program had ended, the vigorous discussion of many fascinating points raised earlier continued to stimulate the participants' renewed interest in unraveling regional development questions previously thought too tightly interwoven to grasp fully.

When at last it was time to leave, everyone agreed the contributions were sufficiently original and focused on important questions of regional development that they deserved exposure to a wider audience. This volume is the happy result.

While the purpose of this conference was an intellectual one, its occasion was personal. We had gathered at this conference facility in Vienna to honor the 60th birthday of Walter B. Stöhr, of a man who has contributed more to the conference topic than many others. His 1981 book[1] *Development from Above or Below? The Dialectics of Regional Planning in Developing Countries*, which he published jointly with D.R.F. Taylor, proved to be of particular influence. It was among the first to discuss concepts of "endogenous regional development". Although the title of the book refers specifically to developing countries, Stöhr's ideas have been recognized in the Western world as well. Austria and the EC are among those that integrated these concepts into their regional policies. Another step in the same direction was the 1987 volume on *International Economic Restructuring and the Regional Community*, edited jointly with H. Muegge, P. Hesp, and B. Stuckey. This book collects evidence on the economic restructuring processes of the mid-1980s and the various responses at the regional level. It combines examples from First as well as Third World countries.

In the late 1980s Walter Stöhr's main focus – besides many other areas of research interest which are documented in numerous journal articles –

---

[1]References to work cited here can be found at the end of Chapter 1.

vii

shifted from the regional to the local level and particularly to strategies of local mobilization. This is documented in his most recent book, *Global Challenge and Local Response: Initiatives for Economic Regeneration in Contemporary Europe* (1990). This book documents research undertaken as a part of the United Nations University's European Perspectives Project and it provides a deep understanding of the structural changes occurring at a local level in contemporary Europe.

If they had not known before, many participants realized during the course of the conference how much they are influenced by Stöhr's work and his ideas. Reference to his work can be found in almost all papers of this volume. Moreover, by the time we left the conference we had agreed that the contributions to this conference were so interestingly and stimulatingly discussing regional development issues that we should try to allow a much larger audience access to this material. The present book is the result of this attempt.

We thank all the participants of this conference for their contributions and our colleagues at the Interdisciplinary Institute for Urban and Regional Studies, University of Economics and Business Administration, in Vienna, Austria, for all their contributions to the conference and the book. In particular, we extend thanks to Uwe Schubert for single-handedly organizing this excellent conference and, indirectly, making the book possible. The Editors and participants together dedicate this book to Walter B. Stöhr who provided the immediate occasion for this gathering of interesting colleagues and for the many sustaining intellectual contributions that drew us together on that welcome occasion.

Chapel Hill / Vienna, February 1991

1

Introduction

Edward M. Bergman,* Gunther Maier,**
Franz Tödtling**

At the beginning of the 1990s the regional question poses itself quite differently than a decade or two ago. In Europe in particular the ongoing economic and political restructuring is likely to have dramatic regional impacts. An integrated European Community, on the one hand, will be defining underdeveloped areas and problem regions quite differently from today's nation states. As is clearly visible already, large parts of the Mediterranean will fall into this category forming a large "European periphery", while in some of the more centrally located countries the areas which qualify for economic aid will be shrinking. The shifts in the power structure will probably allow the formation of new regional coalitions; some of them revitalizing ancient ethnic and cultural identities. Obvious candidates are, for example, the Basques in France and Spain, Brittany in France, some of the German states, Lombardy in Italy.

In the countries of the former Eastern Bloc the regained national identity goes hand in hand with increasing regionalism. After the strong grip of international centralism has weakened it is becoming more than obvious that most of the eastern countries are formed from different nations which are now trying to stake their claims for the future. The lethal conflict between Romanians and Hungarians in Romania and the tensions in Yugoslavia and the USSR are just the most brutal variants of this struggle. Ethnic tensions are just one aspect of the internal structure of east European countries. Despite decades of centrally planned resource allocation they display considerable internal economic and social diversity, just like most other countries in the world. Congestion problems in some urban agglomerations go hand in hand with lack of opportunities in rural areas.

*University of North Carolina at Chapel Hill, Chapel Hill, NC, USA.
**University of Economics and Business Administration, Vienna, Austria.

Central planning with its tendency toward big solutions has been very successful in creating the "old industrial" areas of the coming decades, the restructuring of which will probably remain on the agenda well into the coming century.

All these arguments suggest that at least in Europe regional problems and the issue of regional disparities and adequate policy instruments will be even more important in the near future than they are today. Unfortunately, these shocks come at a time when regional science has lost most of its confidence in its ability to understand the regional development process and to guide it by applying a set of policy instruments. While there is a long list of paradigms and policy strategies which the scientific community agrees are inadequate and do not work, the complementary set is rather small. To a large extent this is the result of unexpected trends regional development has displayed in most developed countries since the late 1960s.

In the 1950s and 1960s cities were seen as engines of economic growth for the respective region and the country as a whole. Important questions were economic benefits and costs of agglomeration, the "optimal" city size, and the role of cities in growth generation and its spatial diffusion. In this period problems of less developed areas and seemingly stable core–periphery relations were also major issues of analysis and policy. Locational factors of development such as the density of activities and agglomeration economies, access to transport and communication facilities, and other physical infrastructure played an important role in these concepts. The combination of these factors constituted a "locational hierarchy" which was seen as valid for service as well as manufacturing activities. Infrastructure investment was the most important drug in the regional planner's medicine-chest. It was prescribed for most regional development diseases.

As for economics and policy-making in general, the 1970s were a sobering decade for regional policy as well. The 1970s saw a breakdown or stagnation of some of the former core areas such as regions with a long industrial tradition and large agglomerations. These once leading areas showed an unexpected reluctance to change and some of them were severely hit by the economic crisis. Suddenly new regional distinctions appeared, with former disparities seemingly having been turned around. In the US the stagnating South was transformed into the sprouting sun-belt leaving the industrialized North to be renamed from "snow-belt" to "rust-belt". Also in Europe some of the strong and dynamic industrial agglomerations turned into old industrialized areas. The large industrial units from the English motherland of industrialization around Manchester to the German Rhine–Ruhr region were easily outcompeted by small and flexible companies, most of them located outside traditional industrialized areas. "Small is Beautiful" became the phrase of the decade also in industrial and regional policy. Growth occurred in rural and even peripheral areas while policy was burdened with the large industrial complexes of the old industrial areas. Quite obviously, conditions that were once favorable for them turned to their disfavor. Obstacles for their successful transformation were not only rigid technological structures such as capital-intensive mass production but also organizational factors (rigid hierarchies within the large firms) as well as sociopolitical rigidities. The latter were a high degree of organization of the labor force and – via "labor accords" – a considerable improvement of the work conditions, which were sometimes detrimental to the new demands for change and flexibility (Edwards *et al.*, 1986).

The new growth areas, "intermediate" regions and cities, were less predetermined by economic and political structures successful in the past (Storper, 1986). The new spatial patterns and processes as well as the determining factors became more diffuse and less clearcut than in previous decades. Owing to improvements in transport and communication technologies as well as other infrastructural facilities firms became more footloose in their location decisions. Transaction and communication links became more and more large scale (continental or global), seemingly "annihilating space".

The puzzling turn-around of former development paradigms set off a massive search for the new conditions of success. Some of this is reflected in the current volume. One obvious factor, at least in the late 1970s and early 1980s, was technology. Regions like Silicon Valley, Route 128, the M4 Corridor, Cambridge or Sophia Antipolis served as models for economic success based on technological innovation. The small-scale firms of Silicon Valley which dominated the computer industry of that time and produced numerous spin-off companies within the region fitted the stereotype of the era. In regional policy the breakdown of the old locational hierarchy not only questioned the traditional instruments but the traditional approach as a whole. By the mid-1970s traditional "development from above" strategies were criticized for discouraging less-developed regions and contrasted with a "development from below" strategy for regional policy (Stöhr and Taylor, 1981). The aim was to mobilize the creativity and hidden resources of the region. Regional policy should support and encourage regional initiatives rather than try to solve the problems itself (Stöhr, 1990). The new strategy attracted considerable interest, partly because of the lack of resources for regional policy and the growing skepticism concerning centralized policies since the early 1980s.

The quest for the new conditions of success in the diffuse development pattern led to a large number of case studies. Case studies of firms analyzed their investment behavior, their strategies to adapt to changing external conditions, their innovative behavior, etc. Case studies of regions tried to identify the local factors which stimulated or hampered technological and organizational change, rising employment, expanding production and firm creation. As in other economic disciplines where analysis of micro-behavior also gained considerable importance, most of these case studies focused on the single firm or the local economy, trying to identify the factors that determine success at the place where they are at work. Viewed separately the case studies of course suffered the weakness of the approach. With their small number of "observations" it is very difficult to separate the general trend from the specificity of the location or the firm. Taken together, however, this literature – although loaded with references to the particularity of the case under investigation – provides considerable evidence about the spatial restructuring processes which were going on.

In the 1980s out of a synthesis of the collected evidence new "models" of locational dynamism were appearing (Aydalot, 1986; Aydalot and Keeble, 1988). One is based on the agglomeration of interlinked small firms which are able to serve specialized markets and to react flexibly to emerging market niches. Another is based on the location decision of large enterprises, which under certain conditions may imply more than a mere "branch plant economy". A third is based on the successful transformation of old industrial areas. In all of these cases, the emerging dynamism seems to be linked to technological or organizational innovation, i.e. introduction of new products, processes, and organizational devices, as well as to the "network characteristics" of the local actors and their local "milieu". It is these concepts – networks, milieu, and innovation – and their relationship to regional development which constitute the focus of this book.

Organization of the Book

The present book intends to investigate the relationship between networks, innovation, and milieu on the one hand and local/regional development on the other. The book is divided into four parts. Part I, consisting of papers by Johansson, Kamann, Grabher, and Pedersen, focuses on "Networks of Firms and Industries". In some sense, the network concept serves as a common denominator to most papers in the book. It will be picked up explicitly or implicitly in other parts as well.

"Networks" can be regarded as new institutional devices for firms which help to mobilize resources and information, to increase flexibility, and to reduce uncertainty (Håkansson, 1987; Camagni, 1989; Grabher's contribution in this book). They are in between the traditional institutions in the sense of Williamson (1975), the market on the one hand (for occasional transactions based on the price mechanism) and the intraorganizational hierarchy of the firm on the other (continuous transactions coordinated by command). To the extent that firms and regions are able to participate in networks they are able to gain complementary resources and in particular to increase the level of information and knowledge. In this way they are able to reduce some of the uncertainties which are connected with an increasingly turbulent environment and to gain more control over parts of their environment. Participation in networks usually provides firms with more stability than mere market transactions imply, a fact which is particularly important in the context of R&D and innovation. On the other hand networks – by always having a certain degree of redundancy – provide more flexibility than the intraorganizational hierarchy is able to provide. Thus, network participation increases the ability for innovation and for successful adjustment to changing macroeconomic conditions.

Johansson employs an explicitly economic perspective. He argues that because of the costs involved in each economic transaction, in many cases it is rational for economic agents to establish long-term arrangements with their customers or suppliers in order to reduce these costs. These relationships he considers to be links in a network which lead to relatively stable trade relationships as they are utilized in input–output analysis, and rigidities which are viewed as market failures in standard economic theory. In this sense the agents create the network structure of the economy in a form of self-organization and update this structure through the construction, decomposition, and reconstruction of network links. In Johansson's view this dynamic element mainly results from innovation. Since building up the network structure of a firm uses resources and can thus be considered an investment, existing links can hardly be broken up by competition. Only when an innovation in a product, process or in organization makes a potential new link superior may it be able to break up an existing link. Such network dynamics, Johansson argues, have always been a fundamental element in economic evolution and restructuring.

Kamann in his paper puts particular emphasis upon power and dominance in networks. He argues that there is a continuum of possible power structures in networks, ranging from an egalitarian structure to complete dependency and dominance. Those actors who manage to dominate network relations will be able to consume more of the "synergetic surplus" of the network than others and they are also able to shape and organize the future development of the network to their advantage. Another important aspect of his paper is the notion that networking occurs in different spaces (economic, geographical and sociocultural) and on different planes, leading to quite complex interlinked structures. These linkages perform gateway functions between different planes and networks and transmit shocks through the structure. To the network participants these shocks pose threats and challenges to which they may react in very different ways.

Kamann illustrates his theoretical arguments by investigating two empirical examples: the Dutch Tour Operator-Charter Network and the Dutch Horticultural Complex. Because of dominance and power structures in the network, different relationships to other networks, locational advantages and disadvantages, etc. the various actors play different roles in the network and the networks show different dynamics. Kamann argues that one has to take into account all these aspects of a network and its relationship to other parts of the economy in order to understand the dynamics of a network and its impact upon spatial structure and regional performance.

Grabher, like Pedersen, investigates a specific type of relationship in a network: that between large and small firms. Grabher discusses these interfirm relations "from the perspective of large enterprises" (p. 60) whereas Pedersen explicitly concentrates on the small firm sector. Although he agrees that the turbulent economic environment of the 1970s and 1980s has hit the vertically integrated, self-sufficient large companies particularly hard, Grabher expresses skepticism for some of the heroic hypotheses – "end of the division of labor", "end of mass production" – which were drawn from them in the mid-1980s. The large companies have gone through a massive restructuring process with fundamental changes in their organizational structure as well as in the range of products they supply. Grabher illustrates this transition with the example of the coal, iron, and steel complex in the German Ruhr area. Once the prototypes of the German steel industry, conglomerates like Thyssen, Krupp, or Hoesch now make a considerable share of profits by acting as general contractors, particularly in the new markets of plant engineering and environmental technology. Rather than producing all components themselves, they organize a network of specialized and flexible small firms to deliver the necessary components and assemble the final product. In this way a particular division of labor between large and small firms emerges. The network combines the financial power of the large companies with the problem-solving capacity and flexibility of the small to their mutual benefit. "Knowing the right project partner for each problem" has become an important component in the business of the large firms. With these changes, the large companies of the Ruhr found new opportunities by marketing know-how they had once developed only for internal use. For example, the environmental technology they were once forced to develop in order to meet higher standards now contributes considerably to company sales. Grabher argues that the large companies are not bound to become extinct because they can play an important role in a less hierarchical and more cooperative economic environment as well. By cooperating with small firms in various networks they can benefit from their flexibility and react much faster to changing conditions themselves. That this is important in a turbulent economic environment has been demonstrated quite drastically in the recent decades.

Whether the large companies will react to more stable conditions by returning to a hierarchical form of organization will be seen in the future.

Pedersen approaches network relationships between large and small firms from the contrary point of view. His main concern is the fate of small enterprises in the development process. The major theoretical concepts that try to explain the development process of Third World countries and their relationship to the developed world – modernization theories and dominance/dependency theories – imply that the small firms should disappear during the development process. Pedersen claims that this perspective is wrong and results from a simplistic view of the relationships within an economy. Using data concerning the development of the Danish economy from 1818 to 1975 he demonstrates that the hypothesis contradicts empirical evidence as well. He then contrasts this view by a network approach to the small enterprise which takes into account its relationship to large enterprises and the reproductive activities of the household. Pedersen concludes that in a network approach "the small enterprises are considered complementary to the large rather than alternative" (p. 96). The small enterprises not only depend upon the large ones, but at the same time large enterprises often depend upon a network of small service and production enterprises, an argument put forward by Grabher as well. These small firms occupy market niches and undertake tasks the large enterprises cannot do efficiently because of their large-scale production techniques. Therefore, the small-scale sector of an economy is very heterogeneous. Its specialization is an important ingredient in the efficiency of an economy. Pedersen concludes that only policies that do recognize this role of the small firms can be successful. The network links between firms of different size also link the development processes on a local, national, and international scale. Understanding these links is therefore essential for understanding the interference between these processes.

The four papers in Part I are not the only ones to use a network concept. Papers by Garofoli, Traxler *et al.* and Bergman and Maier also refer to networks in their argument. What distinguishes the papers in Part I is their explicit focus on networks and their attempt to contribute to the theoretical development of the concept. The four papers in Part I are complementary in the way in which they approach this goal.

After presenting the network concept in a rather a-spatial way in Part I, Part II focuses on specific types of localized networks, namely on "innovative milieus" and on districts of flexible production. The questions investigated are:

- to what extent a firm's relationship to local actors and the local environment plays a role in innovation and flexible adjustment of that firm, and

- to what extent might localized production networks of the Third
  Italy type serve as a model for endogenous regional development for
  other regions of industrialized countries and particularly the southern European periphery.

The two central and related concepts are, first, the milieu-fostering innovative activities and, secondly, the local production system of industrial
districts. The milieu approach clearly differs from other innovation concepts: Maillat states that "it is the milieu, not the enterprise, on which
the analysis must focus" (p. 113). According to his view, " the milieu
cannot be defined merely as a geographical area, it must be envisaged as
an organization, a complex system made up of economic and technological
interdependencies. In our view, the concept of milieu refers to a coherent whole in which a territorial production system, a technical culture,
and protagonists are linked. The coherence between the different protagonists lies in a common mode of apprehending situations, problems, and
opportunities" (p. 113). The innovative milieu, defined in that way, goes
beyond the mere local concentration of innovation or high-tech activities
since economic and technological interdependencies are regarded as being
constitutive. It also goes beyond the mere production sphere since culture and other protagonists are involved. To put it in Kamann's terms:
innovation occurs at the intersection of networks belonging to different
planes. The way coherence is achieved (common perception of situations,
problems and opportunities) basically reflects an evolutionary approach
in the tradition of Nelson and Winter. Technological change is seen as occurring in the form of (localized) trajectories which are based on common
views about problems and solutions. Maillat's paper investigates to what
extent the local milieu has an influence on innovation activities of firms.
It is based on the work of the GREMI group in which ten innovative case
study regions have been analyzed (nine in Europe, one in the US). The
empirical section of the paper focuses particularly on the types and the
spatial proximity of links which innovative firms establish and maintain.
It also looks at the extraversion and regional integration of firms and tries
to identify those which show a strong interaction with the local milieu.

The papers by Garofoli, and Hadjimichalis and Papamichos focus on
the question of to what extent the industrial district of the Third Italy
type (local productive systems) may serve as a model for regional development in a more general context. In recent years this model has been widely
(mis-)used, therefore a critical evaluation is highly relevant. Industrial districts (local productive systems) are generally seen as the outcome of the
breakdown of the Fordist production regime: large mass-producing firms
("hierarchies") are substituted or complemented by flexible production
networks of small firms. Defining characteristics of such local productive

systems according to Garofoli are

- a high level of division of labor between the firms which gives rise to close input–output relations;
- a high degree of specialization of the firms and accumulation of specialized knowledge;
- a large number of local agents involved (plurality of protagonists);
- an efficient system of transmitting information at the local level including a dense network of face to face contacts; and
- a high level of skills among workers in the area as a result of a historic sedimentation of knowledge.

In terms of regional development this model implies decreasing importance for externally induced development based on the localization of branch plants or subsidiaries but the fostering of entrepreneurship, small-firm dynamics, and "networking" of small firms. Garofoli furthermore looks at different types of local productive systems and analyses strategic variables for strengthening them. The chapter concludes by drawing policy conclusions: he discusses the local development agency, technology centers and business service centers, as instruments fostering endogenous regional development.

Hadjimichalis and Papamichos have a different approach and a more critical view of Third Italy as a model for regional development for southern Europe. After discussing current changes in the spatial division of labor and in the development policies of southern Europe they analyze "misunderstandings" concerning the appropriateness of Third Italy as a model for regional development. They then proceed to an alternative interpretation of local development characteristics.

Part III raises a broad series of issues concerning economic restructuring, with particular emphasis on old manufacturing areas and sectoral transitions that bridge production regimes from manufacturing and services. Much of the successful economic restructuring of the 1980s was based on the adoption of networks or deep structures of supportive milieu discussed in Parts I and II, but not all regions have made the transition successfully. The eventual integration of eastern Europe into the world economy and nearby continental regions will present industrial transition difficulties far greater than those Western economies faced two decades earlier.

There are of course lessons to be learned from regional restructuring paths followed in Western Europe and North America. Simple stage theory proposed initially in the first third of the century provides rough guides to sectoral succession (see particularly Coffey and Polèse, 1984), but debates about this and subsequent views of development succession

or transition remain unresolved. A detailed empirical account of the unfolding of industrial sectors in urban and rural regional economies of the
US South and Midwest (see Bergman, 1990) provides specific clues about
the variety of development paths paved by industrial restructuring. The
difficulty of capturing the full flavor and policy implications of these dynamics with industrial information only is known to all who study regional
restructuring.

The total involvement of a region's core cultural, social and institutional structures in its economy is difficult to assess, yet wholly pivotal
to a successful development plan. This is particularly the case for older
industrial regions. Better means for planners to grasp these important
factors are addressed in Friedmann's chapter. It lays out five overlapping,
and closely interrelated, regional "environments" that those in planning
and leadership positions must face when formulating comprehensive approaches to regional development. In discussing the cultural environment,
Friedmann argues for a "rooted cosmopolitanism" that retains the capacity to develop from within, yet remains open to the emerging world system. And while the political environment of industrial restructuring often
tends toward "corporatist" decision mechanisms, it is argued that planners should remain closely involved in the processes of mutual learning that
accompany strong, open debate about desired futures. Demands on the
physical environment that invariably accompany economic revitalization
efforts require planners to pay close attention to pollution risks, preservation of natural amenities, recycling existing facilities, and improving
transport/communication with the outside world. The economic environment is faced with tasks of reallocating capital away from non-competitive
to promising new ventures while addressing the new educational policies
and labor–management relations that such reallocations imply. These demanding changes in the regional economy call for much more effective
institutional environments than are presently the case. Referring to an
alternative form of "concerted planning", Friedmann concludes by warning against centralized, hierarchic solutions that eliminate the possibility
of major regional actors linked in a loose network of competence who are
made responsive to the inevitable conflicts and compromise of authentic
interests.

Two chapters track the restructuring of metropolitan areas: Vienna,
Austria and Victoria, Australia. O'Connor's chapter on Victoria stresses
the importance of viewing manufacturing and producer services together
in studying that region's restructuring. Based on a review of the literature (Cohen and Zysman, 1987; Marshall, 1982, 1985) and analysis of
secondary data from the 1980s for the Victoria region, he finds support
for the "manufacturing (still) matters" thesis in that region. In addition to
the interdependent roles played by manufacturing and producer services,

other measures of expenditure on factory construction, fixed capital, and research and development reveal the importance of manufacturing beyond simple changes in employment level so often used in regional development analyses. Taking a page from Friedmann and highlighting Australia's continental expanse, O'Connor argues for greater infrastructure investment in the Victoria region to speed and focus its manufacturing revitalization within the world economy.

By contrast, Vienna has steadily shed its manufacturing role and acquired sufficient depth in producer services to be recognized for that role in central Europe, a role that will likely grow as that historical region becomes economically reintegrated. The chapter by Traxler, Fischer, Nöst, and Schubert goes well beyond the routine documentation of aggregate changes in the regional economy by acquiring primary survey data on distinct producer services (advertising, marketing, management consultancy, electronic data processing, and engineering design), their role in linked networks (forward links to clients, backward links to input suppliers, lateral links to cooperative contacts), and their intraregional location. Among the many findings are the following: producer services of all kinds are strongly interlinked throughout the regional economy; input/backward networks are more regionally oriented than output/forward link networks; engineering services are less regionally linked than other services; all service networks appear correlated and used frequently for backward sourcing, forward sales, and lateral support and cooperation. As producer services become ever more important in the Vienna region (and central Europe), the authors predict beneficial effects for manufacturing revitalization of the region as well.

While earlier sections present newly emerging views of forces now affecting regions or the restructuring of regions along sectoral and other lines, these chapters draw our attention directly to regions as units of analysis and policy. They share the further ambition of exploring some of the concepts introduced in earlier chapters by testing these concepts with evidence from many observations and against one or more established theoretical perspectives. These ambitious research designs encourage the reader to refocus full attention on regions and on the adequacy of available theory to understand their contemporary development.

Chapters by Goldstein and Tödtling collect evidence from business establishments involved in the important processes of innovation: corporate R&D establishments and technology-dependent firms (Goldstein) and firms in sectors that are permeated by advanced communication and microelectronic technologies (Tödtling). Goldstein's chapter is concerned with firms that occupy university-based science and technology parks in the US, specifically two case studies: Research Triangle Park in North Carolina and the University of Utah Research Park. The general response by corporations and firms to global competition and productivity accounts for their attempts to improve the technological position of US business. Since corporations might conduct the necessary research or development "in-house", there is the option of establishing satellite centers in amenable environments (e.g. Research Triangle Park). On the other hand, the growing demand for patents, licenses, and other commercially valuable technology provided sufficient stimulus for skilled personnel in universities and other research facilities to become entrepreneurs and establish high-technology businesses (e.g. University of Utah Research Park). The first model can be characterized as a modern "growth pole", while the second falls generally into one or more categories of endogenous development. Based on survey results from the residents of science and technology parks and high-technology firms in the surrounding region, the chapter concludes with a comparison of development outcomes for both cases.

Tödtling also surveys firms dependent on recent product and process technologies, but he draws his sample broadly from four distinct sectors in five regions of Austria. After reviewing several alternative candidate theories, he relies upon evidence of innovation generation and adoption to detect whether interregional innovative practices are sorted across the type of hierarchies predicted by diffusion and production cycle arguments, or whether non-hierarchical clustering occurs within "innovative milieus", "territorial innovation complexes" or "industrial districts". He finds little support for a locationally deterministic process of innovation adoption, thereby indicating spatial indeterminacy and leaving scope for strategic action by firms and in regional policy.

Bergman and Maier investigate a long-established concept of regional development with a new approach. They rely on secondary data from the US for 250 counties in Arkansas and its bordering states to detect the importance of linked interdependencies in growth of private, non-farm-earned income. Highway networks connecting county centroids and travel behavior of firms and individuals establish basic links and nodes used in the analysis of how counties might affect each other beneficially (spread effects) or detrimentally (backwash effects). While counties are the formal units of analysis, they are in fact simple aggregates of more basic qualities held by their populations: high school or college trained labor, entrepreneurs, consumer demand driven by receipt of other income (transfers, retirement, government, farm), and residence by type of regional agglomeration (central city, urban and rural). By examining the effects that these factors have on their own county's income growth and on that of neighboring counties, the authors show how it is possible to infer the degrees and types of spread vs. backwash effects that operate within spatially defined units and over continuously defined regional space.

References

Aydalot, P. (ed.), 1986. *Milieux Innovateurs en Europe*. GREMI, Paris.

Aydalot, P., D. Keeble (eds.), 1988. *High Technology Industry and Innovative Environments: The European Experience*. Routledge, London.

Bergman, E.M., 1990. *Industrial Transition Paths and the Restructuring of Metropolitan and Rural Economies*, Final Report submitted to US Economic Development Administration. Chapel Hill: UNC Institute for Economic Development.

Camagni, R., 1989. Space, Networks and Technical Change: An Evolutionary Approach. Paper presented to GREMI round table, Barcelona, March 1989.

Coffey, W.J., M. Polèse, 1984. The Concept of Local Development: A Stages Model of Endogenous Regional Growth, *Papers of the Regional Science Association*, Vol. 55, pp. 1–12.

Cohen, S.S., J. Zysman, 1987. *Manufacturing Matters: The Myth of the Post Industrial Economy*. Basic Books, New York.

Edwards, R., P. Garonna, F. Tödtling (eds.), 1986. *Unions in Crisis and Beyond - Perspectives from Six Countries*. Auburn House, Dover, Mass. and London.

Håkansson, H. (ed.), 1987. *Industrial Technological Development: A Network Approach*. Croom Helm, London.

Marshall, J.N., 1982. Linkages between Manufacturing Industry and Business Services, *Environment and Planning A*, Vol. 14, pp. 1523–1540.

Marshall, J.N., 1985. Business Services, the Regions and Regional Policy, *Regional Studies*, Vol. 19, pp. 353–364.

Muegge, H., W.B. Stöhr, P. Hesp, B. Stuckey (eds.), 1987. *International Economic Restructuring and the Regional Community*. Avebury, Aldershot.

Storper, M., 1986. Technology and New Regional Growth Complexes, the Economics of Discontinuous Spatial Development, in P. Nijkamp (ed.), *Technological Change, Employment and Spatial Dynamics*. Springer-Verlag, Heidelberg.

Stöhr, W.B. (ed.), 1990. *Global Challenge and Local Response: Initiatives for Economic Regeneration in Contemporary Europe*. Mansell, London.

Stöhr, W.B., D.R.F. Taylor, 1981. *Development from Above or Below? The Dialectics of Regional Planning in Developing Countries*. John Wiley, Chichester.

Williamson, O.E., 1975. *Markets and Hierarchies: Analysis and Antitrust Implications*, Free Press, New York.

Part I

Networks of Firms and Industries

2

Economic Networks and Self-Organization

Börje Johansson*

1   Introduction

The concept of the network and networking gained considerable popularity in the 1980s (e.g. Johanson and Mattson, 1987). To a large extent the concept has been used in the explanation of how corporations form links to subsidiaries, how suppliers establish links to their customers, how various agents cooperate in R&D projects, and how technology diffuses between economic agents. *Ad hoc* considerations have dominated over efforts at theory formulation.

The present study outlines some fundamental elements of an emerging theory of economic networks. A basic assumption is that the economy is organized by means of different links and couplings between agents. An attempt is made to provide an economic model which explains why networks and linkages are established, and which provides an economic argument for the longevity of such relations. The links are analyzed as capital objects, which are basically sunk costs. Therefore linkages bring rigidity and structure into the patterns of interactions between firms as well as other economic agents as regards deliveries of current inputs and capital equipment, and exchange of technological knowledge. A link between a supplier and customer cannot be broken without a change that makes a new supplier superior to the old one. The new supplier has to overcome the sunk cost advantages of an established link.

The analysis focuses on networks for technology trade and knowledge diffusion. It also examines how existing links are used when new equipment, new systems, and technology are supplied and delivered in the econ-

*Regional Planning; The Royal Institute of Technology, Stockholm, Sweden.

17

omy. Finally it is argued that the formation of new links and the dissolution of older ones constitutes a process of self-organization. This process is identified as the basic force of economic evolution.

2   Networks and Flows in Economic Systems

In the subsequent analysis I will elaborate the following hypothesis: an economy develops and renews itself by forming new structures and by qualitative reorganization. In order to understand changes of this kind we need models of the economy that reflect its structural properties. Hence, we must introduce an approach which will make it possible to treat organizational evolution and structural renewal. The subtle approach to observing this economic structure is to define and examine economic networks.

The subsequent presentation suggests that an economic system should be described as a structure formed by submarkets and other interactive devices which can be ordered according to geographical and temporal patterns as well as by organizational couplings. These submarkets bring into play a variety of network formations and transaction systems. In order to shed light on these phenomena in a systematic way, it is necessary to introduce new concepts and to expand the theoretical language which is used in economic models. This language should allow us to characterize and analyze economic networks including the construction, rebuilding, and disintegration of these networks.

2.1   Micro networks and macro patterns

A basic assumption in a vast majority of economic models is that the micro system consists of the following three basic decision-making units: households, firms, and public authorities. These organizations consist of complex systems with comprehensive internal networks for coordination and production. Such networks include extremities that form links with interorganizational networks. This implies that there exists an intermediate area where internal couplings become linked with market networks. A basic element of economic theory is a strong desire to deduce all conclusions from assumptions about elementary economic subjects. In this tradition it has become natural always to ask: what economic incentives are compatible with a given function or performance of an organization? What patterns of behavior are compatible with incentives? Is it possible to make the objectives of an organization coincide with the behavioral self-interest of individuals (cf. Radner, 1972; Hurwicz, 1972)?

Incentive compatibility may be regarded as a property of mechanisms which makes it unfavorable for an economic agent to violate the rules of the game and cause the system to deviate from an equilibrium. There are many examples of exchange mechanisms for which the incentive formation and the behavioral stability are not easily made transparent. These examples include complicated systems of exchange and gift-giving. The associated rules may be based on ceremonial and ethical imperatives of reciprocal obligations. A classical case of this kind is the trade rings of Papua (Malinowski, 1932). These rules must satisfy reciprocity, at least in the long term, in order to be sustainable. This requirement of reciprocity is necessary also for markets of varying complexity (Belshaw, 1965). In contemporary market economies we find for example how reciprocity rules, agreements and implicit contracts, as well as moral codes, are safeguarded by extra-market conditions. Interacting agents and the pertinent individuals may belong to the same church, club, local community, and other social networks (including family relations and school background).

When smooth – i.e. optimized – flows inside a firm or production unit have evolved so that a stable mode of behavior characterizes the organization, we can observe the firm's routine or system of routines (Nelson and Winter, 1982). It is the existence of such systems which gives the firm an identity. These routines may be thought of as the technique of the firm. In this sense the technique includes all regular and predictable patterns of behavior. An important aspect of these routines is the network of established links for interaction among units of the firm. Where observed, network invariances of this kind also constitute a condition for meaningful aggregation of individual firms to a sector.

The pattern of deliveries into and out of a production unit reflects the interaction between it and other supplier units or customers. When this type of interaction gradually develops into a steady pattern we can observe the network adjusting only slowly to changing conditions. This intransigence is a precondition for the construction of multiregional input–output models with coefficients relying on observations of more or less "local invariances". A fundamental issue in network economics is to investigate and explain how links and interaction coefficients will change when the economic environment is altered, and then to classify the stimuli and impulses which bring about such adjustments. In particular, a main concern is the adjustment speed associated with different perturbations (compare Batten and Westin, 1988).

2.2 Flow invariances and links between economic units

Consider a firm which has established a long-term contract with an input supplier. This constitutes an input delivery link. From the viewpoint of the buyer, it is a purchasing link. Such a coupling is always the result of a resource allocation and should be referred to as an investment. Hence, such a link has in general a capital value. Moreover, this type of investment often represents a sunk cost, since it is specific to the two parties and has no "general value". If the firm contemplates finding another supplier, then the necessary new link investments must be considered and assessed. By sticking to the already established deliverer, the firm can avoid (save) those investment costs. A firm does not only establish links via purchasing agents to its suppliers, it also forms similar couplings with important customers in its marketing activities. Sometimes these customers are middlemen or intermediary agents. Often the links are two-way and designed to be used for mutual communication and coordination. We shall assume that they are based on implicit or explicit contract-like agreements. Economic links are thus assumed to be durable capital. In this sense they share the same features as the road network. A typical situation is when the deliverer and his customer both have committed capital resources on their own behalf, in order to facilitate the interaction and make the resource flow between them possible. Often such a commitment is a durable investment; in other cases it deteriorates fast and has to be repeated many times. In the latter case there is no long-term contract. In the first case there is a mutual dependency which does not have to be made explicit. Moreover, if the basic link capital is the mutual trust and reliability between the two parties, this is usually the outcome of a long process. Hence, the same reliability is not on sale on the spot market; it has a long gestation lag.

The existence of economic networks implies that we should expect to observe stable and invariant flow patterns at different levels of aggregation in an economic system. Take for example a Swedish firm, with a subsidiary firm in Denmark and a customer in England. The macro invariances present themselves in the form of delivery patterns between sectors and the structure of trade flows between urban nodes and between countries (compare Balassa and Bauwens, 1988; Batten and Westin, 1988).

In a later section we shall focus on networks used in R&D activities. We shall also examine the importance of various types of economic networks for the diffusion of production and market knowledge, and for technology trade. At the same time, we may learn about the properties of these networks by examining more well known examples of economic links. Such investigations show that contracts and property rights explain the existence of many invariant flow patterns. Individuals' daily commuting trips between their homes and workplaces are based on two kinds of contracts, one with their employer and the other with regard to their dwelling. As time goes by these contracts break up and new ones are formed. Usually these adjustments are rigid and the transition tends to be slow even when perturbations are strong. Disequilibrium gaps which develop are usually closed only gradually.

3   Networks of the Market Economy

3.1   Contracts, agreements and links

More than 200 years ago, Adam Smith created the ideal design of a market economy. The free market is driven by economic competition which is governed by an invisible hand that confidently guides market interaction towards an equilibrium state. During the nineteenth century, a new legal framework for economic life was created in many European countries. This development provided the foundation of the market institution in the industrial economy. In the 1980s and 1990s, European policy-makers are once again being reminded of the old rule that market institutions must be constructed according to laws, rules, and a system of supervision. The new institution under construction is the fully integrated EC market.

The interaction between economic agents is usually based on some form of agreement which can be enforced by compulsion, or through the exercise of power. Even if the power of one party is substantial, the agreement can still be interpreted as an economic contract. Every exchange, e.g. every delivery that takes place in return for an immediate payment, is based on an explicit or implicit contract, often concluded by no more than a handshake. The contract becomes especially important when the deal comprises a long-term relation and when the time span between the delivery and payment is considerable. The trade expeditions during the seventeenth and eighteenth centuries are illustrative examples of contractual links over delayed transaction periods.

Examples like the East India companies in Europe of the eighteenth century show that a reliable agreement must be capable of distributing risks and options between the contractual parties. The contract must also provide incentives for the agents involved to fulfill their mutual obligations. A modern form of long-term contract is represented by the link between the typical European firm and each employee. Durable agreements between a buyer and a seller are usually motivated by the fact that one (or both) of them must make an investment which is transaction-specific. A firm which regularly receives inputs from a supplier must often invest in a technique that makes it possible to use the deliveries optimally in its own production. If the customer in such an agreement cannot establish a long-term contract, he is obviously trapped in a weak future negotiating position. Moreover, variations in delivery conditions and preferences may make it both difficult and uneconomic to formulate complete contract texts. Instead these links have to be supported by other forms of social ties, mutual trust, and confidence relations (Hart and Holmstrom, 1987).

3.2   Transaction costs

Economic theorists have spent much effort analyzing the economic implications of complete contracts, while incomplete contracts have been somewhat neglected. A complete contract specifies the obligations of each agent, contingent upon circumstances evident at the time of contract formulation. This is still a mild requirement compared with the omniscient contracts made possible by the perfect market as prescribed by Arrow (1973) and Debreu (1959). Vast resources would be necessary in order to establish this type of contract. As a consequence we rarely observe complete conditional contracts. The resource consumption necessary to establish contractual agreements have been called transaction costs. The higher they are, the more important social norms, business ethics, etc. become as a means to compensate for incomplete contracts.

Transaction costs appear when a transfer of ownership or other property rights takes place. These costs include search costs, communication costs, and other costs for exchanging information. When formulating a contract, the property (i.e. an exchange object in the form of good or service) must be described, inspected, assessed, as well as weighed and measured whenever this is possible. The property to be transferred must be examined and accepted. Other causes of transaction costs are negotiations, consultation of legal advisers, and documentation of agreements.

Because of this complexity, standardization of the interactions can reduce transaction costs considerably. Standardization is a feasible tactic for transactions that occur frequently and with different agents. Rental and leasing contracts provide examples of markets where we can observe highly standardized transactions alongside non-repetitive individual agreements. Another method to reduce transaction costs becomes available when the delivery between supplier and customer is repeated. When this is the case they can form a joint delivery link. This is based on mutual investment in rules, procedures, and trust, which together brings down the transaction costs. This solution makes use of "staged" scale economies in the form of a long sequence of repeated transactions and transfers between the two cooperating parties. This form of link-specific scale effect should not be confused with the scale consequences obtained through market-wide standardizations as described earlier. In concrete terms, the latter type of market organization involves standardized networks of middlemen, brokerage firms, distribution companies, and mediating agents.

Analyses of transaction costs have been concentrated on institutional arrangements and long-term agreements between interdependent agents

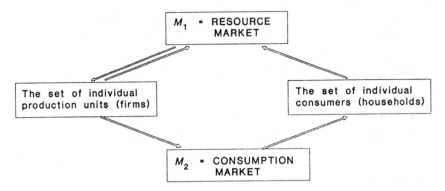

Figure 2.1: The thin network of a perfect market economy.

such that the size of transaction costs can be significantly reduced. Within this tradition we also find attempts to explain the formation of firms as a reaction to high transaction costs (e.g. Alchian and Demsetz, 1972; Williamson, 1979). From this viewpoint, a firm is mainly a logistical device for continuous coordination of resource flows. Continuing this argument, we may say that uncomplicated resource coordination problems remain a market task. When the complexities and subtleties increase, the firm becomes a superior institution (Coase, 1937). We can thus think of the firm as ultimate form of an interaction network, in which the various delivery links have been internalized by one organization (Yarbrough and Yarbrough, 1988). All these processes of formation, remolding, and decomposition of firms are essential parts of the economy's network evolution based on self-organization principles.

3.3 The transaction system of a perfect market

As economists became more skillful in developing models of market economies during the 1950s and 1960s, many started to perceive real markets as incomplete reflections of an ideal market. A fundamental characteristic of the latter is that every equilibrium is Pareto efficient. Simultaneously it became popular to talk about market failures. The latter signifies that the economy does not manage to reach a Pareto-efficient equilibrium.

We may envisage the economy as a timeless system, or as a sequence of markets. In either case, to be in a perfect state it must satisfy strong separability conditions in the sense that every transaction between any pair of agents must be mediated by the market, i.e. trading agents have to be decoupled by the market institution. Classic causes of market failures are the existence of externalities and public goods. In both of these cases, the failure rests in the existence of strong couplings between two or several economic subjects. A perfect market cannot allow any links of this kind.

In Figure 2.1 the market institution is divided into two parts M_1 and M_2, where M_1 refers to the market for resources and production factors, and M_2 refers to the consumption market for household commodities. In the ideal market every firm buys resources from M_1 without any direct contact with any other firm. It sells its outputs to both M_1 and M_2, but never directly to an individual economic agent. Each household sells resources (e.g. its labor force) to M_1 and buys consumption goods from M_2. The perfect market requires this extremely purified structure. In case of economic profit, a more complex link pattern is necessary such that the profits are distributed to the households in given proportions.

Economists like Arrow (1971) have argued that large transaction costs explain why market failures become frequent. Arrow mentions three basic phenomena which increase transaction costs:

- *Exclusion* costs which arise when resources are used to make the delivery of commodities private; we may label this "privatization costs".
- *Interaction costs* which are caused by necessary communication and information exchange between buyer and seller; collection of information about alternative sources of delivery also generates interaction costs.
- *Disequilibrium costs* which emerge as prevailing prices are not equilibrium prices. Decisions based on these prices are "system biased". This forces the agents to use more resources for the search for alternatives.

3.4   Competition and investments in transaction links

In order to understand transaction costs we need to be able to identify and classify different transaction techniques. One technique is the establishment of a transaction link, shared as joint property between two parties. An example of this is relational contracting, where the agreement between two or several parties is supported by extra-market relations that bind the parties together, and make the contract self-reinforcing. A motive for this solution is a desire to stimulate continuing interaction. When a relation like this becomes durable and complex the two parties have to develop and renew their respective administrative mechanisms for solving problems in their joint business. Ultimately this relation can take the form of vertical integration.

Transactions may be characterized with regard to uncertainty, frequency, and the size of transaction-specific investments. The latter estab-

Table 2.1: Delivery links and transaction between firms and production units

THE BUYING FREQUENCY OF THE CUSTOMER*	*SALES INVESTMENTS MADE BY THE SUPPLIER*		
	General investment in sales systems	Partially customer-specific links	Completely customer-specific delivery links
Occasional non-repeated purchase	Delivery of standard equipment and standard services	Delivery of customer-adjusted equipment and services	Design and construction of a plant, factory or a large system
Intermittent purchase (of rare occurrence)	Recurrent sometimes scheduled delivery of replacement equipment etc.	Delivery of new equipment, etc. in response to technical improvements	Scheduled and quasi-periodic deliveries: (1) Delivery of of equipment designed for a particular customer in response to replacement needs
Recurrent repetitive purchases	Delivery of standardized inputs; current input flows	Delivery of customized current input flows	(2) Maintenance, trimming and repair of a customer's system and system components

* Customer signifies an economic agent (firm, production unit, etc.) which receives a delivery from a supplier firm.

lishes a type of link capital. Table 2.1 classifies different types of sales investments that a supplier can make. These investments include transaction methods and general transaction systems which may be used for a large set of customers. At the other extreme we find customer links which are specific for each single customer. The investment options should be evaluated against the size of every delivery and the frequency of deliveries to the same customer.

Table 2.1 is organized to shed light on the economic motives behind

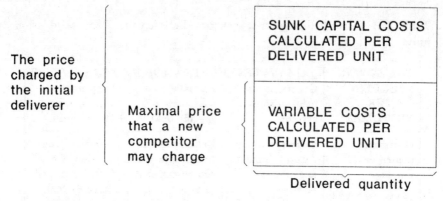

Figure 2.2: Monopoly effect of an established customer link.

the formation of links between production units and firms. Once a link has been established, new reasons to keep it intact arise because of sunk cost conditions. Often the users of a link develop joint knowledge and a transaction-specific language through time. In addition, both parties have usually invested in special equipment and production arrangements which are directly motivated to make the link function properly. This includes special training of the personnel.

The importance of sunk costs associated with a transaction or delivery link may be illustrated by Figure 2.2. The price level in the figure is set in such a way that the initial deliverer receives compensation for (a) variable costs (including a potential mark-up) per delivered unit, and (b) capital costs associated with the sunk costs of the link investment. A new competitor has to invest heavily in the link in attempting to compete while the established supplier may be prepared to relinquish the capital cost compensation if price competition should start. A potential competitor may therefore hesitate to make any initial investment.

The existence of monopoly effects (rigidities, associated with customer links) has fundamental consequences for the dynamics of a market. Figure 2.2 demonstrates that a potential deliverer cannot conquer an existing deliverer link except when (a) the old deliverer has insufficient capacity, (b) the new deliverer has an improved technique (including lower factor costs) which makes it possible to transfer the product at a lower delivered price, or (c) the new deliverer has new products with attributes which are superior in view of the customer's preferences. These attributes include not only characteristics of the product *per se*, but also features of the method of delivery and the associated service. To summarize this argument it can be said that in general an old delivery link is outrivaled by a new link as a consequence of an innovation that makes the new link superior.

4 Restructuring and Self-Organization

4.1 Economic links, competition and technology diffusion

With the beginning of industrialization in the late nineteenth century, agricultural products became less important in the export economy and experienced disruption of their pertinent cycles. The Swedish solution to that difficulty was based on a national agricultural producers' cooperative society. The firms of this society established purchasing links to the farmers and sales links to the retail organizations.

The monopsony links of the cooperative society provided the farmers with secure delivery channels and safe, regulated prices. The same network also developed into an efficient system for the diffusion of technical improvements and associated new equipment. Part of its success was based on the fact that the society controlled the farmers' technique and product mix, the food processing technique, and, to a large extent, the price pattern of final products. Hence, the market and the production system were connected.

The example above has at least one general message: suppliers of new techniques and sellers of new equipment frequently try to use already established economic networks as a means to make contact with potential technology customers. It has for example been observed how the network within a large corporation often functions as an arena for innovation diffusion (Karlsson, 1988). The networks have two distinct roles. First, the seller of technical systems and production knowledge must supply products which are designed specifically for each customer, or which can be adapted to fit the demands of the buyer. Hence, the seller needs the existing links as channels through which it is possible to find alert customers who also have sufficient purchasing power to pay for the necessary customization. One should emphasize that the customers are, in fact, carrying through their own innovations – although a lot of imitation may be involved. Second, the delivery of new equipment and installation of new systems are processes that frequently take a long time to perform and require intense interaction between the deliverer and the receiving firm. In this process both parties need a reliable link for their co-production, which may include joint development, instruction and education activities. These observations combine into the following model of innovation behavior in economic networks:

- Established networks for economic interaction are important vehicles for diffusion of technological solutions. The delivering and receiving parties make contact via direct and indirect links of such networks.

Second, those channels facilitate the pertinent knowledge communication. Networks play this role partly independently of their initial use and rationale.

- The ability of a firm to improve its production, distribution and other techniques depends crucially on its capacity to build new links to suppliers of knowledge and equipment. Network formation is equally important for a firm which tries to establish collaborative efforts with other firms in order to renew and develop products.

In a deep sense, the above suggestions are related to our earlier conclusions about how and when a supplier becomes able to conquer a delivery link from a competitor. Two cases were identified as basic. First, owing to a process innovation the supplier can deliver the same (partly standardized) product as the competitor at a lower price. Second, the supplier has carried through a product innovation and as a consequence can deliver a product with superior attributes. In both cases the role of innovation is stressed. The innovation gives the intruder the means to overcome the advantages of the initial supplier. We have shown that such advantages to a large extent can be explained by sunk costs of link investments.

4.2   Innovation networks

In the subsequent analysis we distinguish between process and product development. Moreover, the term product is used to denote both goods and services. In the case of product development the innovator has to ask: how large is the potential market for this new product, and what is the potential market price? Moreover, is the number of potential customers large enough that the innovation can give rise to a product cycle which can expand, become standardized, and be distributed via regular market channels? The answer to these questions and the nature of the necessary technical solutions determine how different types of economic agents may cooperate to develop a new product or a new process solution. In a study by von Hippel (1988), three basic categories of innovators are identified:

1. The development is organized and performed by the firm which intends to use the new technical solution.

2. The development work is organized by a firm which intends to produce and sell the new product to a group of customers or to a regular market.

3. The innovation is made for and introduced to a single user or a group of customers by a company which will get a larger sales volume of its original products when the customers start to use the complementary innovation.

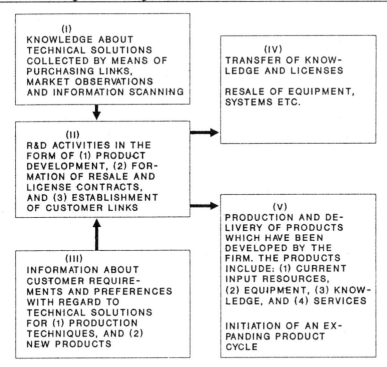

Figure 2.3: Sources, saddles and sinks in an innovation network.

In all three cases we normally observe that the innovation work proceeds from information and interaction links between developer, user, and other actors in a knowledge network. In general, innovation networks revolve around the category of firms which sell new technical solutions, new equipment and knowledge to customers in a contact-intensive interaction. Such firms are also often involved in the transfer and selling of licenses and services which support a given R&D activity. They function as knowledge and technique suppliers. Their most important customers are other firms.

Firms with a central position in an innovation network use their competence, knowledge, and network resources to combine information from two sources of knowledge. They probe for technical solutions which exist in the world economy, and confront the requirements and preferences with regard to technical solutions found among their customers. In Figure 2.3 the world market is described as a basic source of information about technical solutions (I). The potential set of customer links (III) constitutes a source of information about existing product requirements, preferences for product attributes, and demand for technical solutions. By means of R&D work which leads to product renewal (II), the firm itself becomes a knowledge and innovation source in the innovation network. From a global perspective, the central position in an innovation network (II) is a "saddle node" from which knowledge and licenses (IV), as well as equipment, systems, solutions, and other products (V) are distributed to the sinks of the network, i.e. the demand points in the sales network of the supplier. The sinks correspond to firms which are technology customers, while carrying out their own innovations.

Firms and organizations which base their activity on knowledge transfer and technology trade are frequently located in the central nodes of regional and national innovation networks. Such nodes are usually urban regions with a saddle function. From the viewpoint of the global economy they are knowledge sinks, since they have to collect and import the knowledge resources and technological solutions from various points in the world market. At the same time, they are sources of technology for regional and national customers. Urban nodes and local settlements which are specialized in export-oriented production constitute concentrations of customers *vis-à-vis* the central nodes in an innovation network. It has been argued that the evolution of the capitalistic European economy during the last 1,000 years has been founded on the principles of innovation networks (Braudel, 1982, 1984; Hohenberg and Lees, 1985; Jacobs, 1969, 1984).

4.3   Customized deliveries in innovation networks

Industries which produce and/or deliver technical solutions as well as production and market knowledge have to develop a custom-made product (goods and services) for each individual customer. In this way certain suppliers develop into true multi-product firms. Hence, their productivity and profitability becomes based on economies of scope, a phenomenon described by Baumol (1977) and Bailey and Friedlaender (1982).

The above observation makes us aware of the incentive mechanism behind forward link-formation, i.e. when a supplier searches for new couplings to potential customers. The investment motivation is that such a link has the capacity to generate a quasi-rent or link profit. Therefore, a continuing search for customers to which such links can be established is an important competition strategy. Moreover, as the number of such customized sales channels grows, the sum of link profits is correspondingly increased. Thus, economies of scope become an example of dynamic, forward link-formation.

In the 1980s we can observe how computer power and information technology provide options to continuously adjust the attributes of a product with high precision and at controlled costs. A multi-product firm may for each customer group, g, design a product, h, in such a way that h's characteristics are adjusted to the preferences of customer group g. Based on the bid-price function of every customer group and the cost function of the firm one can specify an optimal combination of pairs (g, h) with $g = 1, 2, \ldots$ and $h = 1, 2, \ldots$ (Andersson and Johansson, 1984; Batten and Johansson, 1989; Lancaster, 1970, 1980).

Obviously, delivery and sales of technical solutions are seldom made in regular markets. Instead, this type of delivery usually requires considerable investment in the delivery link. The standard case is that both seller and buyer have to make investments of this kind. Technology diffusion and technique competition also had this character in the nineteenth century. However, new elements have emerged in the last quarter of the twentieth century. In particular, technology trade, sales of systems, transfer of product ideas, and knowledge supporting the R&D work of firms are all activities that have developed into industries themselves.

The diffusion of knowledge, innovation, and techniques takes place in networks between production units as well as within firms and worldwide corporations. Recent studies of the diffusion of applications of information technology show how the transfer activity makes use of intracompany links when these exist (Karlsson, 1988). Cooperation agreements between companies give rise to other networks which complement the intracompany networks (Hippel, 1988). The environment around the intrafirm networks may further stimulate new combinations. Such environments include consulting firms which are specialized in building and remolding networks, conferences, exhibitions, and fairs exhibiting new equipment (Karlsson, 1988). These activities support the formation of new input and customer links for the purchase and sales of technical solutions and equipment. We may also note that the military-industrial complex constitutes networks of this kind. In that context the links between customer, producer and advisors may even be secret.

The dynamics of the links between supplier and customer often lead to "link catastrophes" such that the deliverer loses his customer to other competing suppliers. Another form of link catastrophe results when a buyer switches from custom-made transfers to standardized deliveries. All the time, technical renewal and choice are forces which decompose old and bring together new links. One form of stability in the dynamic processes is the conservation of established spatial patterns of interaction. Such patterns tend to remain intact although individual links are changing and spatial product cycles develop over time. The physical network infrastructure is an attractor field which stabilizes and helps aggregate flow patterns to return to their initial structure after they have been disturbed by link catastrophes. Such a link catastrophe may take many forms for an urban region. The supply of a given product can disappear, and entire industries can cease to exist. Johansson (1989) describes how during the twentieth century the few metropolitan nodes in the Nordic region have repetitively renewed and kept alive their roles as technological saddle-points, through which new knowledge and equipment have continued to be imported and redistributed to technology customers in the export nodes in the network of Nordic urban regions. This innovation network has remained sustainable while facing fundamental structural adjustments in the form of changing product composition and substitution of production technologies. In particular, many export nodes have changed their export specialization profoundly several times. In spite of this the aggregate pattern of interurban flows has tended to return to its initial form after each disturbance (Johansson, 1990; see also Hohenberg and Lees, 1985).

5   Conclusions

All observations and arguments in this essay have been collected to support the following theses: construction, decomposition, and reconstruction of delivery links constitute strategic evolutionary activities of agents in a market economy. In this context, it is fundamental to distinguish between standardized and customized deliveries, as extreme cases on a continuous scale. When products and their mode of distribution become standardized, the degree of prize competition must increase, the price elasticity grows, and the orthodox image of how a market functions becomes more relevant than it is for markets with product differentiation. Higher price sensitivity also means that there is a greater risk for price and sales fluctuations. Hence, large firms try to counteract the sensitivity to shocks in this part of their environment by constructing market networks based on various types of power. The regional–national–global hierarchical networks of the largest oil companies in the world are organized with exactly these motives.

The above statement refers to mature oligopolistic competition. Such enterprises impose their hierarchical system on segmented markets in order to safeguard monopolistic quasi-rents. In this sense link formation has a similar motive for both young and mature markets. The possibility of obtaining quasi-rents forms an incentive for product development, innovation activities and associated search for customer links. Customization and pertinent product adjustments is a basic strategy for firms that want to attract customers away from established deliveries and to form new markets. In this perspective it is natural to see network dynamics as a fundamental element of economic evolution.

In the presentation of innovation networks the importance of economic links is stressed. Many scholars have observed that successful innovation activities are frequently supported by a rich variety of "non-economic" networks for interaction (Stöhr, 1987). In the framework presented here, these constitute an environment that facilitates knowledge creation, as well as formation of deliverer–customer links and other economic couplings.

Which type of research conclusions can we draw? First, theoretical studies will have to direct a lot of effort to experimental modelling approaches, in which model simulations are used to generate "empirical observations" of network dynamics. Second, such efforts need support from empirical micro-investigations of economic links and networks. Third, aggregate analysis of interregional and intersectoral flows can be used to test the conclusions that can be drawn from a more strictly formulated theory of economic networks. The most profound reason to develop models of economic networks is that every network is a structural phenomenon. As such it is a prerequisite for analyzing evolution and structural adjustment.

References

Alchian, A.A., H. Demsetz, 1972. Production, Information Cost and Economic Organization, *American Economic Review*, Vol. 62, pp. 777–795.

Andersson, A.E., B. Johansson, 1984. Industrial Dynamics, Product Cycles and Employment Structure, *IIASA WP-84-9*, International Institute for Applied Systems Analysis, Laxenburg, Austria.

Arrow, K.J., 1971. Political and Economic Evaluation of Social Effects and Externalities, in M.D. Intriligor (ed.), *Frontiers of Quantitative Economics*, North-Holland, Amsterdam, pp. 3–31.

Arrow, K.J., 1973. *Essays in the Theory of Risk-Bearing*, Markham Publishing Company, Chicago.

Bailey, E.E., A.F. Friedlaender, 1982. Market Structure and Multiproduct Industries, *Journal of Economic Literature*, Vol. XX, pp. 1024–1048.

Balassa, B., L. Bauwens, 1988. The Determinants of Intra-European Trade in Manufactured Goods, *European Economic Review*, Vol. 32, pp. 1421–1437.

Batten, D.F., B. Johansson, 1989. Dynamics of Product Substitution, in Å. Andersson et al. (eds.), *Advances in Spatial Theory and Dynamics*, North-Holland, Amsterdam, pp. 23–44.

Batten, D.F., L. Westin, 1988. Modelling Commodity Flows on Trade Networks: Retrospect and Prospect, *CERUM Working Paper*, CWP-1988:30, Umeå University.

Baumol, W.J., 1977. On the Proper Cost Tests for a Natural Monopoly in a Multiproduct Industry, *American Economic Review*, Vol. 67, pp. 809–822.

Belshaw, C.S., 1965. *Traditional Exchange and Modern Markets*, Prentice-Hall, New York.

Braudel, F., 1982. *The Wheels of Commerce*, William Collins, London.

Braudel, F., 1984. *The Perspectives of the World*, Harper & Row, New York.

Coase, R.H., 1937. The Nature of the Firm, *Economica*, Vol. 4, pp. 386–405.

Debreu, G., 1959. *Theory of Value*, Cowles Foundation, Yale University Press,

New Haven.

Hart, O., B. Holmstrom, 1987. The Theory of Contracts, in T. Bewley (ed.), *Advances in Economics Theory*, Fifth World Congress, Cambridge University Press, Cambridge.

Hippel, E. von, 1988. *The Sources of Innovation*, Oxford University Press, Oxford.

Hohenberg, P.H., P.M. Lees, 1985. *The Making of Europe 1000–1950*, Harvard University Press, Cambridge, Mass.

Hurwicz, L., 1972. On Informationally Decentralized Systems, in C.B. McGuire, R. Radner (eds.), *Decision and Organization*, North-Holland, Amsterdam.

Jacobs, J., 1969. *The Economy of Cities*, Random House, New York.

Jacobs, J., 1984. *Cities and the Wealth of Nations*, Random House, New York.

Johanson, J., L.G. Mattson, 1987. Interorganizational Relations in Industrial Systems: A Network Approach Compared with the Transaction-Cost Approach, *International Studies of Management & Organization*, Vol. XVII, No. 1.

Johansson, B., 1989. Metropolitan Nodes in the Innovation Networks of the Nordic Economies, in The Long Term Futures of Regional Policy – A Nordic View, Report of a Joint NordREFO/OECD Seminar, Helsinki, pp. 99–118.

Johansson, B., 1990. Innovation Processes in the Urban Network of Export and Import Nodes: A Swedish Example, in P. Nijkamp (ed.), *Sustainability of Urban Systems*, Avebury, Aldershot.

Karlsson, C., 1988. Innovation Adoption and the Product Life Cycle, *Umeå Economic Studies*, No. 185, University of Umeå.

Lancaster, K., 1971. *Consumer Demand – A New Approach*, Columbia University Press, New York.

Lancaster, K., 1980. Intra-Industry Trade under Perfect Monopolistic Competition, *Journal of International Economics*, Vol. 10, pp. 151–175.

Malinowski, B., 1932. *Argonauts of the Western Pacific*, Routledge & Kegan Paul, London.

Nelsson, R.R., S.G. Winter, 1982. *An Evolutionary Theory of Economic Change*, Harvard University Press, Cambridge, Mass.

Radner, R., 1972. Normative Theories of Organization: An Introduction, in C.B. McGuire, R. Radner (eds.), *Decision and Organization*, North-Holland, Amsterdam, pp. 177–188.

Stöhr, W.B., 1987. The Spatial Dimension of Technology Policy – A Framework for Evaluating the Systemic Effects of Technological Innovation, in Wiberg, U., F. Snickars (eds.), *Structural Change in Peripheral and Rural Areas*, Document D12:1987, Swedish Council for Building Research, Stockholm, pp. 130–143.

Williamson, O.E., 1979. Transaction-Cost Economics: The Governance of Contractual Relations, *Journal of Law and Economics*, Vol. 22, pp. 233–261.

Yarbrough, B.V., R.M. Yarbrough, 1988. The Transactional Structure of the Firm – A Comparative Survey, *Journal of Economic Behaviour and Organization*, Vol. 10, pp. 1–28.

3

The Distribution of Dominance in Networks and its Spatial Implications

Dirk-Jan F. Kamann*

1 Introduction

Local prosperity and economic performance of actors

Local prosperity and well-being are determined by the performance of local firms, local actors. The term actor refers first of all to individual entrepreneurs or firms, including subsidiaries, profit centers or business units belonging to a corporate network. Politicians, trade union leaders, public agents and journalists are examples of non-market actors.

Processes of reorganization such as takeovers and mergers as well as changes in the corporate distribution and organization of production relating to management, R&D, sales, and distribution tasks all lead to reevaluation of locations and the role of individual establishments. Technological changes enable and demand locational adaptations in the distribution of multi-site operations. Such changes will impact on local incomes, career potential, profits, and local linkage multiplier effects. Because of this relationship between economics and geography, there is a growing awareness in these fields of study that firms should not be seen as individual organisms that live their own lives independently from other actors. As a way of examining this, there is emerging a great deal of interest focusing on the networks joining firms, and the process of innovation diffusion between firms. For policy-makers, this means government efforts to stimulate innovative industries by supporting autonomous growth potential, developing

---
*Department of Economics, University of Groningen, Groningen, The Netherlands.

territorial industrial complexes, and encouraging local initiatives.

As a working definition, we will define "networks" here as a class of (dyads, triads, organizational sets and action sets of) actors with different types of relations, some(times) based on trust, some(times) based on opportunism. Actors in networks cannot reach their goals without the active cooperation of other actors, resulting in a degree of mutual dependency.

The major reason for actors to reorganize their activities originates from competitive forces to which they are subjected. There are three major causes for weak responses to competition. In the first case, actors are not aware of the challenge. They perceive safety incorrectly, and by the time they find out they are not safe, it is too late to make an appropriate response. Secondly, actors are aware of challenge, but do not know the proper strategy to follow. In the third case, actors are aware of the challenge, know the proper response but are unable to implement the proper strategy.

The first two cases are information gap problems. The reason for this gap can be manifold. Ignorance, poor information retrieval systems, false routines, inertia, lack of gatekeepers, isolated location, and poor management are examples (cf. Camagni, 1991). However, the actor may also be a victim of deliberate strategic exclusion. Strategic information may be withheld by other actors in an attempt to gain a more advantageous position. As a result of exclusion from information, an actor is unable to seize opportunities or fight threats because external circumstances move beyond his control. Hence, when we want to study the strategic behavior and performance of individual actors, we must also examine the nature of relations (networks) within which a particular actor behaves. Only through the inclusion of network evaluation can one gain a more complete context in which to observe the decision-making process.

The three dimensions of space

The context just mentioned has three major spatial dimensions. They are economic space, geographical space, and sociocultural space. Infrastructure services and urbanization in geographical space influence the behavior and success rate of actors (Kamann and Nijkamp, 1989). In economic space, external network relations with other actors determine the performance of an actor. Finally, we find that actors have to work in a given sociocultural setting. The local sociocultural environment may favor certain technologies, or ways of producing goods and services, e.g. Tayloristic production techniques (Kamann, 1988a), which may hamper other types of production. They favor a particular 'régime d'accumulation', and a particular 'régime de régulation' (Aglietta, 1976). Part of the influence of sociocultural space is the process of socialization and culturalization individuals experience. This creates an internalized value system and behavior and a common personality among the actors, given their biological and genetic inheritance (Kamann, 1988a).

All three spaces show a differentiation. Geographical space is polarized between large metropolitan areas and rural areas. Economic space is polarized for many types of activities, an example being the large multinational versus the small sweat-shop. Sociocultural space is also polarized. "Western" societies, with their emphasis on individual responsibility and action, are juxtaposed to societies with more "traditional" or even feudal value systems. As a result, actors in some societies are better able to cope with Western competitive, decentralized decision-making systems than those in other societies. Even inside Western societies, the large cities with their own life-style show distinct differences with the rural areas, both in sociocultural environment and technology (Kamann, 1988a).

To the differentiation of space we have to add their dynamics because the environment is not static, but changing. Some actors may even have the perception of living in a chaotic environment (Peters, 1988). In the light of present diffusion theories, we may say that these dynamics do not occur at all places concomitantly. Some actors face turbulence earlier or later than others (Kamann and Nijkamp, 1989). Furthermore, some actors will have adapted to the new situation, while other actors are in a state of shock. This will make the latter vulnerable to the former. Additionally, the nature of the environment shows a significant differentiation in geographical space, even apart from the diffusion aspects. Where actors in one area may have a very stimulating environment, other actors in other areas may find their environment very hostile. They use much of their energy to solve the problems arising from that environment.

The spatial differentiation of the three dimensions is a first cause for differences in performance between actors. A second cause can be found when studying the nature of external relations with other actors. We could term this the network performance of actors. The question is, why do actors participate in networks at all?

Motives for network participation

Economic actors must participate in production networks since the interaction of suppliers and buyers is inherent in economic activity. Networking not only consists of cooperative projects, partnerships, and relations based on trust, but also includes contacts with actors one can consider to be "the enemy". Apart from this automatic, passive aspect of network participation, this study will describe the motives for active network participation. One of the most important goals of actors is to maintain or increase market share. Given the information gap discussed above, one finds that a significant part of network participation is directed toward collecting information about customers, suppliers, competitors and their products, prices, R&D programs and policies, new market opportunities, and market trends. Hence, information exchange in networks takes on primary importance.

In his attempting to increase market share, or simply to meet the challenge posed by competitors or newcomers, an actor is likely to run into obstacles when implementing a new strategy. These bottlenecks can occur in any business area. Networking can be used to reduce the shock of such interruptions. For example, actors have become aware that technological developments these days very rarely take place in a single firm. It is an "interplay between different organizations where independent activities are taking place simultaneously in different parts of the network" which leads to innovation (Laage-Hellman, 1987, p. 31). This implies that firms realize that in a number of cases it is better to co-develop product and process innovations with suppliers, buyers, or even competitors. "Different units have different resources and skills which are complementary in nature" (ibid. p. 37; see also Williamson, 1975). The value of the network in this case is the combination of resources and skills which as such is unobtainable for individual actors involved. This network value remains positive, even when the individual actor has to increase his dependency on other actors. Active network participation and distribution of activities enable increased specialization of each of the actors, while increasing the need for interaction because of the required coordination. "The establishment of development relationships may in other words be a pre-condition for increasing specialization of the in-house development process" (Axelsson, 1987, p. 131). Actors start partnerships depending on the bottleneck they experience and the type of specialization they prefer.

We could define network performance as the way an actor is able to use external relations to achieve his goals and to solve bottlenecks. The two questions that follow from this statement are:

- Who are the other actors?
- What is the nature of the external relations?

2   Actors and Relations

2.1   The other actors

Effective networks are created through selecting partners who can provide the latest products, machines, know-how, and information. They must be reliable and trustworthy. To determine who then could be considered for a network relationship, we must first define a selection environment.

The class of entities external to the individual actor and affecting his behavior and performance is known as the selection environment. It has been termed a turbulent field or even chaos because of its dynamic nature (Emery and Trist, 1960; Peters, 1988). We distinguish four subcategories of actors in the selection environment (Kamann, 1988a): friends and family, actors related to locational factors, institutional actors, actors that are specific to the product–market combination of an actor, together with his corporate linkages.

Friends, peers, and family play an important role in the process of socialization. The second category deals with locational factors that make a location attractive or unattractive. Infrastructural services, waterworks, energy suppliers or railroad companies fall into this category. The third category includes trade-union representatives, public administrators, and lobbies. The fourth category of actors in the selection environment we mentioned contains units of the corporate network and competitors, suppliers, customers, producers of potential substitutes or possible entrants (Porter, 1983).

Two organizational (super-structural) elements are included in these categories. They are the organization of the firms and the organization of the built environment (Kamann, 1988a). The first is better known as industrial agglomeration effects in economic space, while the latter is known as urbanization effects in geographical space. Economic and geographical space used to coincide to produce agglomeration effects. Because of improved transport and communication techniques and modes, we find that agglomeration effects in economic space no longer necessarily coincide with geographical space. The widespread phenomenon of the branch plant that is linked to a corporate network of communication, information and transport is a good example from the 1960s. Currently, we find that "just-in-time" deliveries have reintroduced geographical space; they allow for deliveries within a hundred miles, in the Dutch case, between suppliers and their main buyer, even for "vital" parts and components. In spite of this general looseness, we still find examples of agglomeration effects in geographical space (Kamann and Krolis, 1990), even though it is not a necessary condition for survival of the firm. Urbanization effects are also included here. Apart from the usual public services, business services are important as a locational factor for office activities.

We can project the differentiation of economic, sociocultural, and institutional space on geographical space, and add these to the existing differentiation in locational features of the selection environment in geographical space. Together, they show quite clearly the differences in opportunities for existing firms, new firm formation and innovative behavior.

2.2   The nature of relations

Having introduced the potential set of actors, we face the second question: what is the nature of these relations?

Markets and hierarchies

According to Williamson's (1979) transaction cost theory, there is a continuum between markets and hierarchies. The choice between the two extremes (the make or buy question) is based on an optimization process of the organizational form and a minimization of costs. Three aspects play a role:

1. *Asset specificity*: Durable goods and R&D tie up large investments. Commitment of such reduces the flexibility in changing policies. The most common types of asset specificity are site, physical, and human specificity.

   Investments in machines and employees required to satisfy demand of a single large buyer may result in a situation of bilateral monopoly (Groenewegen, 1989); the supplier and buyer are mutually dependent. The supplier has no other alternative demand for his products, nor can he shift to other products without a great loss, while the buyer has no alternative supplier, nor can he make the product himself without heavy investments in machines, human capital and at a cost of lost sales because of transitional problems. Bilateral monopoly is not an exceptional case, although buyers try to prevent it from occurring by means of "dual sourcing". Because of recent technological developments, asset specificity has become a rule rather than an exception in numerous intermediate markets.

2. *Uncertainty about the future*: Like other human beings, actors try to reduce risks, allowing for maximum freedom to alter relations when they become burdensome. The price to be paid is determined by high information, negotiating, and quality assurance costs. The choice between long-term relationships and short-term relationships is a matter of what we would term "relation specificity": investments in mutual trust, knowing each other, understanding each other, and knowing whom to address for information or to fix things.

3. *Frequency*: Transaction chains show a repetitive pattern. This reduces the costs of breaking up a relation, even though this is difficult to quantify. This problem of quantifying costs of a relation coincides with the problem of quantifying the costs and benefits when externalizing certain activities. Quantifying the immediate production-related costs may be quite possible. Quantifying the costs of in-

creased uncertainty in information, quality and reliability is another thing.

The transaction cost theory assumes that hierarchy does not exist in markets, and that markets do not exist in organizations. Real-life experience shows that the opposite is true. Market transactions between completely equal partners, or atomistic actors, are an exception rather than a rule.

Further, it ignores the fact that, as Johanson and Mattson (1984) correctly state, the goals of many actors today cannot be achieved but through other actors. In other words, actors depend on their network partners for the realization of their goals. This implies a minimal mutual trust in relations. It means that actors have to recognize the goals of their partners.

In large corporations, an additional problem occurs when the decision to externalize or internalize has to be taken. Externalizing an activity means that the internal unit that used to perform that activity will lose power. Therefore, that unit is likely to oppose such a decision and will lobby to prevent such. Or, in the opposite case, the unit will give favorable information about its abilities to perform activities that previously were done externally and is tempted to give low cost figures.

Given the fact that spatial differentiation in any space is largely ignored and that knowledge, skills, machines, products, and sites are considered to be homogeneous, one is tempted to declare transaction cost theory to be a neoclassical equilibrium theory (Johanson and Mattson, 1984). Still, the basic question, to make or buy, is valid. When less unrealistic assumptions are included, the theory becomes rather valuable.

Between markets and hierarchies: networks

When focusing on relationships between markets and hierarchies, we find a whole range of exchange techniques. At one side we find completely symmetrical exchange relations between equal partners. At the other extreme, we find the asymmetric relationship of complete dependency or dominance.

The ideal case of a symmetrical transaction relation is the exchange of a product for money between two atomistic actors. An example of a symmetrical relationship is the exchange of production of certain products by independent oligopolistic Dutch dairy companies. Neither partner would reach economies of scale for each of the two products independently produced. When exchanging the production of the two products, each firm produces one product for both partners involved, and gives up producing the other. Thereby both attain economies of scale. An example of the other extreme case can be found in the dual production organization. The Japanese kanban system of a many-tiered hierarchy of subcontractors is a good example. Hence we find a continuum of partnerships:

- Exchange of production between two or more competitors enables all actors involved to obtain scale effects. This may be required to compete with foreign producers.
- The joint venture – a form useful for: (1) development of products and penetration of markets; (2) expansion in markets; (3) consolidation of markets by horizontal integration; (4) retreat from markets.
- Long-term contracts between suppliers and one of their important buyers. They should guarantee timely and reliable deliveries, and enable suppliers to invest in innovations required by their buyer.
- Joint production planning between suppliers and buyers to enable zero-stock inventories and just-in-time deliveries.
- Joint planning of suppliers and their industrial buyers where the latter give active support in R&D and capital.
- Dual production organization; the sweat-shops, subcontractors and other suppliers; here a one-sided monopoly exists. For the buyer it is easy to shift to other suppliers; for the supplier, this is impossible.

License agreements can be part of any of the partnerships mentioned. These include straightforward market transactions without any partnership involved.

Type of dependency

Various activities between network participants are linked together in transaction chains that tend to repeat established configurations. This may induce the following dependencies:

- *Technical dependency*, where products and services fit technically together and result in interindustry standards. A rigid fit between products means that an improvement of the product may upset the fit with products further upstream or downstream and therefore requires close cooperation between actors (Kamann and Strijker, 1991). Actors that operate in a less rigid chain will have more freedom to change their products and also find it easier to leave their network for that reason and enter new networks.

- *Knowledge dependency* means that the supplier has to know the requirements of users of their products, while users have to know what they actually can do with their input materials, machines, hardware, and software.

- *Continuity dependence* occurs when a supplier sells a large share (e.g. more than 10 percent) of his output to a single buyer. The actual percentage is a function of the power of the actors involved, the profit margins, and the profitability of other activities of the firm. Again, there is a reverse side which occurs when producers are dependent on a single supplier for a particular product or service they require. Firms will try to prevent this situation by applying dual sourcing when at least two firms supply the same product. In a large number of cases, increased specialization has led to single sourcing. When producer and buyer are mutually dependent, a bilateral monopoly occurs. The choice to make is whether it is best (1) to take over the actual supplier, thereby ensuring continuity, (2) to switch production in-house, or (3) to buy the product on the market.

- *Social dependency* is the result of normal social group behavior, where participants are likely to cooperate with other similar participants before establishing contacts with actors outside the network. Axelsson (1987, p. 159) uses the term soft distance to indicate the sociocultural distance between actors or entire networks in terms of attitudes, values, norms, or culture. The term hard distance indicates the physical distance.

- *Logistical and administrative dependency* is of increasing importance due to improved information technology, and the strategic role information handling plays. This means that suppliers and buyers have to use the same systems to be able to communicate. Lack of standardization between the various systems means that small suppliers need to use their buyer's system in order to compete effectively, and cannot switch to buyers with other systems.

- *Innovative dependency* exists in three varieties: user dominant, supplier dominant, and research dominant. Increased cooperation between suppliers, users, and research institutes or consultants makes this division less valid today. The new question is who took the initiative for new developments, rather than who actually carried out the development work or produced the product.

- *Financial dependency* has several implications. First of all, profits will tend to be paid as dividends instead of reinvested in new technologies and products to satisfy the demand for a good return on investment and/or to keep shareholders satisfied and quiet. The shareholding actor will obtain strategic information about new developments in techniques, products and markets and will know the actor's strategy. The actor involved may be forced to use licenses, products, or services supplied by the shareholder even at above market prices. These pre-tax costs are common practice of "transfer pricing" under headings such as "Technical Assistance", "Royalties" or just as internal transfer "costs", derived from norms rather than reflecting real costs. This also may occur as part of "tax management" at corporate levels. Sometimes existing actors in the firm's network may be replaced by actors of the shareholders' network. Likewise the actor may be forced to increase his prices for supplies to other actors. When he is in the position of being a bilateral monopolist, his buyers have to increase their prices for final products. The parent company of the initial actor may compete with these final products and does not have to increase prices. In fact, he may use the increased prices to his competitors as a subsidy to decrease *his* prices. By doing so, he weakens the competitive power of his competitors.

Complete takeovers tend to lead to concentration of production activities in a particular location, and centralization of overhead activities in another location. The actor involved runs the risk of being converted into a standardized production branch plant. Even when the actor remains relatively independent as a business unit, corporate planning, investment decisions, and tax management are transferred to the parent company.

The various types of dependency, usually in a user-dominant relationship, may result in a dual production organization (Berger and Piore, 1980). Based on the dual segmentation theory of primary and secondary sectors, large and technically sophisticated corporations are part of the primary sector or core of the economy. They operate in stable, safe segments of markets applying modern, capital-intensive Fordist mass production techniques. In the secondary sector, relatively small firms operate with flexible technologies, catering to fluctuating and risky markets. Companies in the core sector externalize uncertainty and labor costs to the peripheral firms (Piore and Sabel, 1984; Stöhr, 1987). In secondary firms, wages are low, prospects are poor, working conditions are bad. Allan Scott (1985, p. 17) for instance found that many secondary firms in Orange County employ Mexican and Asian workers since these "cannot perceive or are able to demand ... recognition of rights". Although local linkages tend to increase when compared to the situation with branch plants, local firms and segments of the labor market are dominated by the core firms, in a new variant of Myrdal's (1957) cumulative causation theory.

Most of the relations we have discussed so far have been of a dyadic nature. We will now broaden our scope to more relations: the network.

3 The Network

According to Perroux (1955), firms operate on an abstract economic plane where they meet other economic actors. Simon (1957, p. 137) terms this "a surface over which an organism can locomote." In the tradition of Perroux we assume a natural tendency among actors to dominate a relationship and, therefore, a network as much as possible. Johannisson (1987, p. 54) states that an actor tries to exploit his environment. The plane where he meets the other actors is an arena. Authors in the tradition of Lewin's (1951) field theory (Melin, 1983) would state that the position of an actor in the network (the field) is determined by both external and internal forces. Examples of external forces are demand, public policies, new technologies, labor relations, and other participants. Internal forces arise from the organization and are assumed to be non-rational. Such a model, however, tends to underestimate the influence of the individual actor on his environment in his attempts to externalize internal problems and to internalize his external problems. This is a process comparable with negentropic behavior, or the ability to attain stability. In our context, we will use stability in terms of market power, aggregate power, and network power.

Planes in space

Returning to Perroux's description, we see that actors meet on an abstract plane in economic space. For the time being, we will assume that an actor coincides with the entire firm – the holistic concept of the firm. Some actors deal only with actors in their own production column (their upstream and downstream partners). We will label these actors one-dimensional actors. They operate on a single plane in space (Figure 3.1a). A second category operates on a multi-dimensional plane in space. For instance, the transport firm, specializing in transporting cut flowers, operates on a transportation plane, meeting large carriers, car manufacturers, and logistical services. Another plane which this firm faces is the horticultural plane, consisting of large wholesalers, auctions, and state agencies. The transport firm in fact operates at the intersection of the two planes. This type can be called a multi-dimensionally integrated actor (Figure 3.1b). Finally, our third category deals with actors that operate on two unrelated planes. An example would be Philips micro-electronics and formerly Philips-Duphar pharmaceutics. These actors are called multi-dimensional unrelated actors (Figure 3.1c). Because of the current trend to emphasize core activities, many actors of this type are separated into two independent actors.

The effect of being one-dimensional, multi-dimensionally related, or

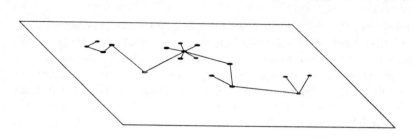

a

b

c

Figure 3.1: One-dimensional and multi-dimensional actors in space.

unrelated is twofold. (1) The performance of one-dimensional actors is determined by the nature and configuration of the network on a single plane. The performance of multi-dimensional actors on a particular plane is determined by the nature of the networks, and the position of the particular actors in those networks on other planes. This implies that an actor may be hampered in pursuing certain strategies on one of the planes it operates on since it has to put all its resources in its struggle for survival on another plane. Or, conversely, an actor may improve his position on one plane because of cross-subsidizing of its efforts with the profits earned on the other plane. (2) Diffusion of innovations may be facilitated from one plane to another plane through bridge actors that operate on both planes. This may give this actor a competitive advantage. It also means that actors not only have to be aware of new innovations or potential substitutes on their own plane, but also on all related planes. This is, for the average small firm, without professional gatekeepers, quite impossible given the limited amount of resources.

Conspiracy, opportunism, and trust

The difference between the various types of clusters that may be found in networks (see Kamann, 1992) is sometimes a matter of the number of relations in the network. In some cases, however, we find an element of conspiracy, which can drastically alter the nature of relations. As with most conspiracies, not every participant will get an equal share of the cake. Given the inequality among the conspirators – inequality in market force, financial strength, know-how, and especially information – the winner may try to take all. This may induce a new series of attempts to conspire more successfully by those who find themselves less privileged than they had hoped. In this case, new conspiracies may arise, with new blood brothers, new promises, new programs, and a new configuration of loyalties, standards, obligations, and values.

The reason for using the term conspiracy is that in our context this is a combination of mutual trust and opportunistic behavior. It is reflected in the cooperation paradox (De Jong, 1987). Actors realize that they need each other to pursue their objectives, but at the same time do not want to become dependent on others. They are fearful that the partner benefits more from the relationship, or is taking unfair advantage of information. This paradox causes cooperative agreements (joint ventures) which are rather unstable. They last until there is a change in the conditions that favored cooperation. This cooperation paradox not only exists in relation to production economics, but rather extends to all kinds of social systems which show such unstable cooperation patterns (Olsen, 1977; Kamann and Strijker, 1991).

In conclusion, we say that actors show opportunistic behavior in some relations, establish mutual trust in other relations and finally mix the two elements in conspiracies with a third set of actors they relate to.

The selection process

The choice of the actual network segment (whether contacts will be direct or indirect, intensive or weak [vide Kamann, 1992]) is a strategic choice. In spite of its importance, this choice is very rarely made with full information about the potential network. The resulting incompleteness is caused by a geographical and informational limitation, which could be improved with government aid as part of an industrial policy (cf. Schenk and Kamann, 1987). This stage of the network selection process is largely determined by the personality of the actor, his business routines, and goals. For a multiple-actor organization with actors in different functions and tasks, each actor has his own personality, while groups of actors show subcultures and coalition behavior. "Individuals are multidimensional and have many roles in the total network" (Hamfelt and Lindberg, 1987, p. 180). This implies that a proper mix of actors is of great importance to the success of an organization.

Activities in organizations differ in their mix and types of internal and external contacts. From research in contact systems in urban areas, we know that some of the external actors are exclusively located in metropolitan areas (Goddard, 1973). This implies that a single-actor firm with time constraints will find it hard to maintain proper network contacts out of the urban areas. A large multiple-actor organization can specialize and distribute the various contacts. Although this requires an internal network, special gatekeepers remain in contact with the environment and provide relevant external information by translating it into the jargon of the internal network. As a result of this, activities that draw their information from the internal network depend less on location in the source area of their relevant information (Kamann, 1985b). Taking into account relocation costs and opportunity costs of missed information, an organization may optimize its location. However, people have a mix of activities and therefore may have different priorities and preferences for certain localities. In an organization with numerous actors, the usual social processes will take place: rather than individual actors, coalitions of power will decide where the total group will locate. These social processes with culturally determined characteristics should be incorporated in an attempt to describe and predict organizational behavior within the network discussion.

4 Power and Dynamics in Networks

4.1 Measuring the distribution of power

When visualizing and measuring relations between actors, we will use the terms manifest and latent relations. Manifest relations are observable. They consist of material relations such as flows of goods, services, capital, printed information, embodied human information, and skills. Manifest relations can also be immaterial exchange relations such as information through personal contacts. Material relations can be visualized by applying input/output analysis or, even better, by means of the expanded filière approach (Kamann, 1988a,b). Immaterial relations can be visualized through contact systems and interlocking systems.

Relations of a latent nature are not directly observable but may be derived or inferred from observable manifest characteristics. Latent characteristics mainly deal with the "strategic value of a relation related to the issue of dominance and performance. Manifest relations are the materialized dimension of latent relations" (Kamann and Nijkamp, 1989, p. 15). Features of latent relations are of three types. Latent relations due to dependency are one type. Instability due to the growth or decline of the individual firm experienced at micro, meso or macro level is another type. Finally, there exist paradigm fixations: "the structure of the network ... will act as a control mechanism ... It makes certain changes easier and others more difficult" (Håkansson, 1987, p. 91). Here, aspects such as inertia (Kamann, 1986) of entire networks may occur (compare Williamson's, 1979, asset specificity). The social aspect of this implies that cities with one activity dominating the social network of the town repulse actors with activities perceived as alien by the rulers in power. These must move to more amenable areas to build their own empire.

Techniques to visualise latent relations

A common method of visualizing networks uses directed graphs and matrices (Aldrich and Whetten, 1981, p. 397, including a discussion on methodological problems involved). Terms such as density, reachability, and hierarchy are utilized. Its static orientation, however, makes this type of analysis less suitable for our purposes. Following the work of Simon (1962) and others, the linking pin theory became a popular object of study. "Having ties to more than one action-set or subsystem, linking pin organizations are the nodes through which a network is loosely joined" (Aldrich and Whetten, 1981, p. 390). The three main functions of linking pin organizations are serving as communication-link between organizations, being a general service provider, and serving as example when dominant.

A popular technique to visualize the structure of loosely connected subsystems is block modeling (Knoke, Rogers, 1979), based on a transaction matrix. This technique is useful for identifying pockets of intense interaction between members, but does not examine relationships between the clusters (Whetten, 1987, p. 242). This makes it less suitable for our purposes.

We propose a triple technique to visualize dominance in networks. First, draw up an expanded filière, containing all material links that the researcher judges to be significant. In order to reach a proper judgment, the researcher should be familiar with the sector and actors involved. Secondly, visualize immaterial links between actors. Compare this picture with the original. In the third step, use the technique of shocks, threats, and challenges (Kamann and Strijker, 1991). Using a dynamic analysis of the network, the enforcement of power and possible shifts in power can be traced. The outcome of this third step feeds back to the first and second steps to check whether all significant actors and their links are included. It checks the initial arbitrary judgment of the researcher. An optional fourth layer could cover the cultural elements of the network.

The distribution of power and dynamics: shocks and turbulence; threats and challenges

In order to operationalize the various types of dependencies, dynamics, and paradigm fixation, we first have to deal with terms such as control, power, and dependency. Power is assumed to lead to an unequal distribution of profit margins among the actors involved. In a static situation, one could use market share or market concentration ratio and aggregate concentration ratio to measure power distribution. Other potentially useful indicators are the share of input or output that an actor accounts for and, related to this, whether a relationship shows evidence of dual sourcing of input versus single buyer of output. In any case, power should be measured in a dynamic context. Kamann and Strijker (1991) describe power in terms of the ability to:

- Prevent a partner from terminating a relation ("no exit power").
- Prevent a partner from duplicating relations with other actors ("power of exclusiveness").
- Exclude potential newcomers from the network or from the market ("no entry power").
- Start and induce innovations in products, processes, and materials used. To alter organizational set-up. Set standards, dictate research agendas, dictate the technological trajectory, or even the entire paradigm.

- Prevent innovations, standards and research projects.
- Internalize external threats to the network without giving up central control.
- Dictate network responses to outside dangers and opportunities.
- Control the interlocking system; to have one's representatives replace representatives of other actors; coinciding with this:
- Increase shareholding and/or board functions.
- Dictate the social paradigm.

An analysis that tries to trace centrality of control – power – must be dynamic. Attention must be paid to the various types of dependencies, paradigm fixations, or relationship shifts.

4.2 Empirical examples

The Dutch tour operator-charter network

A dynamic study of the Dutch tour operator-charter market was used to test the empirical usefulness of terms such as distribution of power and synergetic surplus (Mintjes *et al.*, 1988; Kamann, 1988b, 1992). Financial interests and market shares were used to draw up the network of relevant actors and to trace shifts.

While in 1982–83 a cartel of carriers ruled the network and set the prices, five years later the cartel had lost its power to the tour operators. Cooperation among tour operators, coalitions, and loss in market share of the cartel's own tour operator resulted in a significant increase in network power by the independent tour operators. They managed to create their own pawn in the charter network, creating a threat sufficient to force seat prices to drop 25 percent. In other words, the synergetic surplus shifted from the charter companies, and their owners, to the tour operators.

Another finding was that initially a vertical integration existed between transporters KLM, Nedlloyd, and Dutch Railways which attempted to dominate the entire downstream market. Later on, a diversifying trend became visible. Three of the largest tour operators, Holland International, Hotelplan, and Neckermann, became associated with internationally oriented department store conglomerates (Vendex and Kaufhof, Migros and Karlstad respectively) with European market aspirations. The carriers responded by specializing in flying only; demarcation lines between charter and regular services became vague. KLM increased its number of holiday resorts in the flight schedule at prices only marginally higher than the charter's cheap flights. Transavia recently started a regular service to London (Gatwick) and Martinair continues the transatlantic services to the US and Canada. KLM increased its share in the charter market and took over Netherlines, a Nedlloyd subsidiary. Nedlloyd, meanwhile, came under pressure from Norwegian minority shareholders to specialize in core activities (shipping), and hence had enough problems in setting its course. KLM, meanwhile, was talking with European and US carriers about cooperation, mutual shareholding, or merger. The trend seems a further amalgamation of charter and regular carriers. In conclusion, networks are dynamic, with new entrants and drop-outs occurring. New coalitions mean new situations, new positions, and a new distribution of power. Capital shares and market shares are valuable instruments to visualize networks. It is possible to trace network power. The resulting shift in synergetic surplus was found and even quantified.

The Dutch horticultural complex

The second example describes the analysis of threats and challenges (Kamann and Strijker, 1991) faced by the leading Dutch horticultural complex, the Zuid-Holland Glassdistrict. Since auctions are cooperatives owned by the supplying farms, relations based on exchange of goods and services, rather than financial interests, were used to draw up the initial filières. Actors were clustered into groups of homogeneous economic activities. Next, the analysis of interlocking systems was added to the initial filières. These immaterial relations should give further evidence of the important role of the auctions concluded from the material flows.

According to Kamann and Strijker, power based on influence derived from physical flows of products can only be used effectively when certain other conditions are fulfilled. Two conditions are especially important. First, economic awareness is necessary. Detailed information about what is going on in the market and in the regions has to be available, including information about the socioeconomic environment. Secondly, general influence in the market seems to be important. There should be influence on actors that are not directly dependent on flows of production. These include all kinds of public bodies, both local, regional and national, and firms connected with the farmers, but not so much with the auctions. In those situations, interpersonal contacts are considered to be decisive.

For example, auctions sometimes want to stimulate the production of a certain new crop. It is not enough that farmers are convinced. Many new crops require additional investments, either in new technologies or because of adaptations of existing capital stock. Therefore, any bottleneck in the investment process will hamper a fast take-off of production. This fast take-off is of strategic importance to success in the market. Because of this, it is important for auctions to be able to influence the decision-making processes of industries, banks, and public bodies to prevent such bottlenecks from occurring. From the analysis of interlocking systems, it was concluded that although the auctions were a vital element, the farmers play a pivotal role. Further, the interlocking network of the Zuid-Holland Glassdistrict proved to be relatively flat; many persons were involved, each with a limited number of relations. The interlocking analysis supported the kind of immaterial network to be expected in light of observations about the need to coordinate innovative processes.

A few of the developments that threatened the position of the Zuid-Holland Glassdistrict were analyzed to make the distribution of power within the network more explicit. They were first of all the saturation of markets; secondly, modernization of production technologies; third, negative external effects of concentration; fourth, the rise of competing complexes; and lastly, internal weakening. The ultimate question in the study was how the network actors responded to these threats, particularly who took the first step in instigating a policy, and how or if this individual was able to persuade the other actors to follow his instructions.

One example related to market saturation and ensuing product innovation is the development and introduction of the cherry tomato. The marketing department of the auction was searching for a new variety of the traditional tomato, because it was found that a significant group of consumers did not like the tomato as it was produced in glass-houses. Among other varieties, the cherry tomato seemed very promising. Research institutes were stimulated to do further technical research on this crop. The auctions, organized in the CBT (Central Bureau for Horticulture), were able to stimulate this research because of their many informal and formal contacts with research institutes, and sponsorship of the required research. When the institutes had developed a variety with useful production and marketing characteristics, the auctions created a fund to pay a guaranteed price to a small group of producers that were willing to produce this cherry tomato. At the same time the federation of auctions started a campaign to promote the product on the market. After some years, demand was stable and large enough to terminate the guarantee fund. Now the market forces were strong enough to ensure that the product would be produced by the farmers without subsidization.

Although all actors seem to gain from the successful introduction of the product, this is not the case. The new product takes over part of the market for traditional tomatoes, causing lower prices for that product, and negative consequences for its producers. The distribution of power in the network apparently was such that this last group was not able to block the planned introduction of the new product.

The analysis of shocks (threats and challenges) as done by Kamann and Strijker (1991) shows the coordinating role of the auctions. The study of various situations where action was required in the power structure of the auction revealed that "power" was used through persuasion. When that failed, financial incentives (subsidies, grants, and levies) were used. Finally, regulation was used to enforce policies, while blunt power in the form of exclusions, refusal to accept, etc. was a last resort. In properly functioning networks, power generally should be used as subtly as possible to be effective.[1]

5   Conclusions

Actors do not live in an atomistic world. Their conduct depends on other actors. Because of cooperation between actors, specialization is possible leading to joint projects which alone would not be possible. This network behavior creates a synergetic surplus. The resulting degree of dependence is determined by the nature of the mutual relations between actors. It affects the strategic value of flows of information, goods and services that an actor is able to obtain. Interaction involves the freedom to act in the network at free will, to have some control of the selection of products, processes, and markets. Those actors who manage to dominate network relations or even entire networks will try to consume the synergetic surplus of the network, at the cost of an equal distribution over all participants.

The spatial aspects of networks can be summarized as follows:

- Differentiation in the spatial dimensions of the selection environment causes differences in opportunities which influence the dynamics of rising and dying actors.
- New products and technologies give rise to new networks, possibly with different actors involved. A new network will benefit the area where its actors are located, while the area with actors producing the replaced products will show decay.
- Whether participants of a rising network actually receive an equal share of the benefits or not depends on the power relationship. There is a continuum from equal partners to the dual production organization.
- Whether all activities – managerial, research, production, sales – of the actors involved are located in one area or spread over the globe also affects regional incomes. Relevant is whether actors are part of a corporate network organized in the style of the spatial product life cycle or with business units.

---

[1]The analysis also illustrates the ongoing struggle between the reigning spider and its major rivals, e.g. the large retail chain AHOLD, the latter actor being a good example of a multi-dimensional actor. Finally, the geographical spatial dimension showed how horticultural complexes elsewhere, national and international, were facing attempts of being integrated in the leading complex.

- Takeovers of actors in a region by actors that operate within the same region will result in job losses because of rationalization of production and overhead, but may increase the region's competitiveness with actors from other regions. External control varying from minority shareholding to complete takeovers may in its worst form result in closure of other local actors in the network concerned and loss of jobs and capital. In cases where a large soft distance between head office and local actor is involved, this may have long-term consequences for investments in new activities in the area.

- Areas with exclusively branch plants or with secondary firms operating in a dual production organization are caught in a cumulative causation spiral. Dominance of the social networks by the branch plant managers and core actors may even be a serious obstacle for new activities.

- Although actors may seem to do well in one network (one plane), they may show poor performance on planes that are not related, but may well be of vital importance for survival in the long run. Proper scanning of related planes is therefore a prerequisite for sound management. Since many actors fail in this respect, government support should be given in supplying liaison actors that provide suitable information and act as bridges between networks and actors.

References

Aglietta, M., 1976. *Theory of Capitalist Regulation*, Left Books, London.

Aldrich, H.E., D.A. Whetten, 1981. Organization Sets, Action Sets, and Networks: Making the Most of Simplicity, in P. Nystrom, W. Starbuck (eds.), *Handbook of Organizational Design*, Oxford University Press, London, pp. 385–408.

Axelsson, B., 1987. Supplier Management and Technological Development, in H. Håkansson (ed.), *Industrial Technological Development: A Network Approach*, Croom Helm, London, pp. 128–176.

Berger, S., M.J. Piore, 1980. *Dualism and Discontinuity in Industrial Society*, Cambridge University Press, New York.

Camagni, R.P., 1991. *Space, Networks and Technical Change: An Evolutionary Approach*, Groupe de Recherche Européen sur les Milieux Innovateurs (GREMI), March, Barcelona, to be published by Belhaven, London.

de Jong, H.W., 1987. Joint Ventures, *Economisch Statistisch Bulletin*, Vol. 6, pp. 419–425.

Emery, F.E., E.L. Trist, 1960. Socio-technical Systems, in C.W. Churchman, M. Verhulst (eds.), *Management Science, Models and Techniques*, Vol. 2, Pergamon Press, Oxford, pp. 83–97.

Goddard, J., 1973. Office Employment, Urban Development and Regional Policy, *Office Location and Regional Development*, An Foras Forbartha, Dublin, pp. 21-36.

Groenewegen, J., 1989. Economische organisatie theorieën, in F.W.M. Boekema, D.J.F. Kamann (eds.), *Sociaaleconomische netwerken*, Wolters-Noordhoff, Groningen.

Håkansson, H., 1987. Introduction, in Håkansson, H. (ed.), *Industrial Technological Development: A Network Approach*, Croom Helm, London; Product Development in Networks, id., pp. 84–127; Strategic Implications, id., pp. 210–219.

Hamfelt, C., A.K. Lindberg, 1987. Technological Development and the Individual's Contact Network, in Håkansson, H. (ed.), *Industrial Technological Development: A Network Approach*, Croom Helm, London, pp. 210–219.

Johannisson, B., 1987. Beyond Process and Structure: Social Exchange Networks, in B. Johannisson (ed.), Organizing: The Network Metaphor, *International Studies of Management and Organization*, XVII, No. 1. pp. 3–23; Anarchists and Organizers: Entrepreneurs in a Network Perspective, id., pp. 49–63.

Johanson, J., L.-G. Mattson, 1984, Marketing Investments and Market Investments in Industrial Networks, Paper presented at the International Research Seminar on Industrial Marketing, Stockholm School of Economics.

Kamann, D.J.F., 1985a. Technologie en ruimte: steeds nieuwe paradigma's, in M.T. Brouwer, H.W. ter Hart (eds.), *Ondernemen in Nederland*, Kluwer, Deventer, pp. 171–193.

Kamann, D.J.F., 1985b. Network Dynamics of Economic Activities, Paper presented at the Dutch–German seminar on regional underemployment, Karlsruhe.

Kamann, D.J.F., 1986. Industrial Organisation, Innovation and Employment, in P. Nijkamp (ed.), *Technological Change, Employment and Spatial Dynamics*, Springer, Berlin, pp. 131–154.

Kamann, D.J.F., 1988a. *Spatial Differentiation in the Social Impact of Technology*, Avebury (Gower), Aldershot.

Kamann, D.J.F., 1988b. *Externe organisatie: een inleiding*, Group for Research on Industrial Policies, Groningen.

Kamann, D.J.F., 1992. Actors in economic and geographical space, *Environment and Planning A* (forthcoming).

Kamann, D.J.F., H.P. Krolis, 1990. *Kiezen voor evenwicht en ontwikkeling*, Delft: INRO-TNO.

Kamann, D.J.F., P. Nijkamp, 1989. Technogenesis: Incubation and Diffusion, Research Memorandum 28, Free University, Amsterdam; in R. Cappellin, P. Nijkamp (eds.), *Technological Development at the Local Level*, Gower, Aldershot.

Kamann, D.J.F., D. Strijker, 1991. In Search of the Spider in the Web, *European Review of Agricultural Economics* (forthcoming).

Knoke, D., D.L. Rogers, 1979. A Blockmodel Analysis of Interorganizational

Networks, *Sociology and Social Research*, Vol. 64, pp. 28–52.

Laage-Hellman, J., 1987. Process Innovation through Technical Cooperation, in H. Håkansson (ed.), *Industrial Technological Development: A Network Approach*, Croom Helm, London, pp. 26–83.

Lewin, K., 1951. *Field Research in Social Science*, Harper and Brothers, New York.

Melin, L., 1983. Structure, Strategy and Organization – A Case of Decline, Proceedings of the Workshop on Strategic Management under Limited Growth and Decline, *Report* 83-1, EIASM Institute, Brussels.

Mintjes, B., R. Peletier, P. Rodenburg, R. Sheridan, 1988. De vakantiechartermarkt, Mimeo, Semester course Industrial Organisation and Industrial Policy, D.J.F. Kamann, Department of Economics, Groningen.

Myrdal, G., 1957. *Economic Theory and Underdeveloped Regions*, Duckworth, London.

Olsen, M., 1977. *The Logic of Collective Action*, Harvard University Press, Cambridge, Mass.

Perroux, F., 1955. Note sur la notion pôle de croissance, *Economie Appliqué*, Série D, 8.

Peters, T., 1988. *Thriving on Chaos: Handbook for Management Revolution*, Macmillan, London.

Piore, M.J., Ch. Sabel, 1984. *The Second Industrial Divide*, Basic Books, New York.

Porter, M.E., 1983. *Competitive Strategy*, Collier-Macmillan, London.

Schenk, E.J.J., D.J.F. Kamann, 1987. Naar een ruimtelijk georienteerd specifiek technologiebeleid, in E.J.J. Schenk (ed.), *Industrie- en technologiebeleid*, Wolters-Noordhoff, Groningen, pp. 221–260.

Scott, A.J., 1985. High Technology Industry and Territorial Development: The Rise of the Orange County Complex, 1955–1984, Working Paper Series, No. 85, Department of Geography, University of California, Los Angeles.

Simon, H.A., 1957. *Models of Man*, John Wiley, New York.

Simon, H.A., 1962. The Architecture of Complexity, *Proceedings of the American Philosophical Society*, Vol. 106, pp. 467–482.

Stöhr, W., 1987. The Spatial Division of Labour and Entrepreneurial Strategies; Regional Development Strategies and the Spatial Division of Labour; in H. Muegge, W. Stöhr, *International Economic Restructuring and the Territorial Community*, Avebury, Aldershot; resp. pp. 37–56 and 221–237.

Whetten, D.A., 1987. Interorganizational Relations, in J.W. Lorsch (ed.), *Handbook of Organizational Behavior*, Prentice-Hall, Englewood Cliffs, pp. 238–253.

Williamson, O.E., 1975. *Markets and Hierarchies: Analysis and Antitrust Implications*, Free Press, New York.

Williamson, O.E., 1979. Transaction-Cost Economics: The Governance of Contractual Relations, *The Journal of Law and Economics*, Vol. 22, pp. 233–261.

4

Rebuilding Cathedrals in the Desert: New Patterns of Cooperation between Large and Small Firms in the Coal, Iron, and Steel Complex of the German Ruhr Area

Gernot Grabher*

1 Introduction

We are living in turbulent times; in times of big words and uncompromising diagnosis which can dispense with complicated "ifs" and "buts". At bare minimum, the diagnosis is the "end of the division of labor" (Kern and Schumann, 1984). The "end of mass production" (Piore and Sabel, 1984) seems to be an established fact as well. The prediction of the end of mass production frequently goes hand in hand with a prediction of the end of the large firm. At any rate, while until the late 1970s size was still considered a *conditio sine qua non* for economic efficiency, in the early 1980s the social and economic sciences discovered the "greatness of the small". A decisive impetus behind this profound change of mood was Birch's legendary study "The Job Generation Process". Birch (1979) concluded from his analysis that small and young enterprises make a disproportionately large contribution to the creation of new jobs, and thus that small enter-

---

*Science Center Berlin for Social Research, Berlin, Germany.

prises should be seen as the key to increasing employment and income. In the political arena, this thesis met with a reception that was nothing short of euphoric, not least because of a revival of liberal economic policy. In science, Birch's study soon developed into a veritable research program.

In short, until very recently the scientific discussion focused on the specific strength of particular firm sizes without examining the various interdependencies between firms of different sizes. Consequently, recent employment and structural policy programs have, with a certain regularity, championed the promotion of small enterprises in a correspondingly undifferentiated fashion. However, the limitations of this perspective, which completely ignored the interdependencies between large and small firms, are more and more becoming clear: First, it is evident that in crisis-stricken national or regional economies which traditionally have been characterized by large enterprises such as, for example, the Ruhr area, employment and structural policies without these enterprises, or even against them, are only of limited success (GEWOS et al., 1988). Second, analyses of national and regional economies with a record of successful employment and structural policies (e.g. Japan, Baden-Württemberg) point to specific cooperation patterns that are aimed at a combination of the comparative strengths of firms of different sizes (Herrigel, 1989; Ikeda, 1988).

This essay aims to discuss currently emerging changes in interfirm relations from the perspective of large enterprises. The initial thesis: the increasing turbulence in the economic environment seriously challenges the organizational model of the vertically integrated, self-sufficient large enterprise, which is efficient under stable or predictable conditions. Growing uncertainties related to research, production, and marketing favor an organizational opening of large enterprises vis-à-vis their (regional) environment and vis-à-vis small enterprises as well as public institutions. Starting from this central thesis, I will discuss the following. First, how cooperative relations between large and small firms are organizationally arranged under turbulent conditions: the question of the mode of cooperation. Second, what are the specific contributions of large and small firms to these cooperative relations: the question of cooperative inputs.

The analysis of the mode of cooperation starts from the following thesis: under turbulent conditions, networks are probably superior to primarily price-coordinated interfirm relations as well as to hierarchical forms of coordination. On the one hand, networks are distinguished from price-determined relations primarily by their stability that result from mutual adaptations of the cooperating partners; on the other hand, they differ from hierarchical forms of coordination, which in this context means vertically integrated large enterprises, in having a higher degree of redundancy that results from loose coupling of firms.

With respect to cooperative inputs, the central thesis will be formulated based on the barriers to market entry argument: in industries where barriers to market entry are high, small firms specialize in particular functions of the development and production process, while large firms deal with the control of the development and production process and, above all, with the marketing of the final product. The comparative behavioral advantage of small firms consists in their flexibility in solving specific development and production problems. By contrast, the comparative material advantage of large firms should be seen particularly in their financial strength, which constitutes the essential basis for their control of the development and production process and the international marketing of the final product.

A discussion of changes in the division of labor between firms in the coal, iron, and steel complex of the Ruhr area provides empirical support for these theses. At least on the basis of three considerations, the coal, iron, and steel complex is of special interest. First, until the early 1970s, the organizational concept of the vertically integrated, self-sufficient large enterprise was particularly dominant in this complex. Consequently, challenges to this organizational concept due to changes in competitive conditions should be particularly marked in this complex. Second, the coal, iron, and steel complex is still eminently important for the region (Müller, 1989). Changes in the relations of large enterprises with their environment are thus likely to have important impacts on the further development of the overall regional industry. A discussion of these impacts may help us to understand the spatial dynamics of a change from a self-supporting towards a network-like product pattern. Finally, the discussion of new forms of interfirm cooperation so far has concentrated on sectoral settings (as with the automobile industry) and regional settings (as with industrial districts) in which the preconditions for the emergence of network-like patterns of interfirm cooperation appeared most favorable. An analysis of the coal, iron, and steel complex, however, may help to clarify whether and how networks develop in a regional and sectoral setting which, owing to the dominance of self-sufficient large firms, is characterized by highly unfavorable preconditions.

2   The Changing Relations between Large and Small Firms

2.1   The mode of cooperation

The relation between firms and their environment is typically pictured as a dichotomy of hierarchies and markets. This dichotomy originates initially from Coase (1937) who, breaking with orthodox accounts of the firm as a "black box", conceived of the firm as a governance structure. Coase's key insight was that firms and markets were alternative means for organizing similar kinds of transactions. This notion of the firm, however, did not become influential until it was picked up by Williamson and other proponents of transaction cost economics in the 1970s. The core of Williamson's (1975, 1985) argument is that transactions that involve uncertainty about their outcome, that recur frequently and require substantial transaction-specific investments are more likely to take place within hierarchically organized firms. In contrast, exchanges that are straightforward, infrequent, and require no transaction-specific investments are typically arranged as market transactions.

This orthodox dichotomous view of markets and hierarchies sees firms as separate from markets or, more broadly, ignores the embeddedness of firms in the larger societal context (Granovetter, 1985). Outside boundaries of firms are competitors, while inside managers exercise authority: the firm as "island of planned coordination in a sea of market relations" (Richardson, 1972). Recently, however, more sophisticated amendments to orthodox theory have recognized that the boundaries between markets and hierarchies are blurring. Firms are increasingly engaging in forms of collaboration that resemble neither arm's length market contracting nor the familiar alternative of vertical integration within a hierarchical firm.

Probably, the rigorous market–hierarchy dichotomy always has been as insufficient to an understanding of economic relations as a dichotomy of marriages and one-night stands would be to an understanding of social relations. However, the spread of these intermediate and hybrid forms of organization made a modification of the dichotomous view almost inevitable. Even Williamson is "now persuaded that transactions in the middle range are much more common" than he previously recognized (Williamson, 1985, p. 83). Rather than as exclusive alternatives, markets and hierarchies are more and more looked upon as poles in between which intermediate or hybrid forms of organization, for which the label network has been coined, can be arrayed in a continuum-like fashion: moving from the market towards the hierarchy pole are putting-out systems, subcontracting arrangements, franchising, joint ventures, and decentralized profit centers (Powell, 1990).

From the market pole, where prices capture all the relevant information necessary for exchange, these network forms of organization are distinguished by a higher degree of stability resulting from continuous processes of mutual adaptation. These processes of adaptation follow a basic pattern as described by Blau (1968, p. 453): "Social exchange relations evolve in a slow process, starting with minor transactions in which little trust is required because little risk is involved and in which both partners can prove their trustworthiness, enabling them to expand their relation and engage in major transactions." Through mutual adaptations between the exchange partners, such as the coordination of capacities, of logistics, or the coordination of quality standards, relations within the network are consolidated. As a result of these processes of adaptation, disagreements emerging in the course of the exchange relations are resolved within the relationship rather than by reorganizing relations. In Hirschmann's (1970) terms: "Voice" is given preference to "exit" as a mechanism for conflict resolution. Since with growing intensity of adaptation mutual dependencies increase, so will the costs connected with ending the relations. These costs, in turn, reduce the risks involved in mutual adaptations and in investing in transaction-specific assets.

Through interaction in the context of mutual adaptation, mutual orientation will evolve as well: "This mutual orientation is manifested in a common language regarding technical matters, contracting rules, and standardization of processes, products, and routines. Less overt aspects of the mutual orientation may involve views on business ethics, technical philosophy, and handling of organizational problems. A most important aspect of the mutual orientation is mutual knowledge, knowledge which the parties assume each has about the other and upon which they can draw in communicating with each other" (Johanson and Mattson, 1987, p. 339). This mutual knowledge implies limits to opportunistic behavior and thereby reduces transaction costs. Thus, mutual adaptations and mutual knowledge within networks save the costs of constructing and controlling contracts that, in pure market relations, control for the opportunistic behavior of exchange partners (Lundvall, 1988, p. 353).

However, these mutual processes of adaptation within networks do not culminate in vertical integration of exchange partners within a hierarchical firm. Exchange partners in networks are rather loosely coupled. Loose coupling – and here networks differ from hierarchies – prevents exchange partners from being "locked into" specific exchange relations. Hence, loose coupling preserves a "cultural insurance" to be drawn upon in times of radical change: "In loosely coupled systems where the identity, uniqueness, and separateness of elements is preserved, the system potentially can retain a greater number of mutations and novel solutions than would be the case with a tightly coupled system" (Weick, 1976, p. 7). Loose coupling implies a high degree of functional autonomy of the individual elements, local adaptations to changes in the environment of the system, and decentralized processes of learning and forgetting. Loose coupling provides redundancy which has a function on the level of the network similar to that of "organizational slack" on the level of the individual firm: "Organizational slack absorbs a substantial share of the potential variability in the firm's environment" (Cyert and March, 1963, p. 38).

Redundancy enables social systems not just to adapt to specific environmental changes but to question the appropriateness of adaptation. It is this kind of self-questioning ability that underpins the activities of systems that are able to learn how to learn and self-organize (Bateson, 1972). The essential difference between the adaptive type and self-organizing type of learning is sometimes identified in terms of a distinction between "single-loop" and "double-loop" learning (Argyris and Schon, 1978). Single-loop learning allows systems (1) to scan and monitor significant aspects of the environment, (2) to compare this information against operating norms, and (3) to initiate corrective actions when discrepancies are detected: the intelligence of a thermostat. However, the learning abilities thus defined are limited in that the system can maintain only the course of action determined by the operating norms and standards guiding it. This is fine as long as the action defined by those standards is appropriate for dealing with the changes encountered. But when this is not the case, the process of negative feedback ends up trying to maintain an inappropriate pattern of behavior: "Highly sophisticated single-loop learning systems may actually serve to keep the organization on the wrong course, since people are not prepared to challenge underlying assumptions" (Morgan, 1986, p. 90). Loosely coupled systems are particularly adept at generating new interpretations. As information passes through loosely coupled systems, it is "thicker" than information obtained in the market, and "freer" than that communicated in a hierarchy (Kaneko and Imai, 1987); new connections and new meanings are generated, debated, and evaluated ("double-loop learning"). This is essential for the network's ability to question the appropriateness of behavior and to challenge underlying assumptions.

Redundancy provided by the loose coupling of firms thus prevents the aim of minimizing transaction costs through mutual adaptations from undermining the network's adaptability. Growing intensity of mutual adaptation lowers transaction costs but increases the probability that the network is being locked into a specific trajectory that may turn out to be the "wrong" course. In this sense, networks cannot simply be assessed in terms of transaction cost efficiency. Although redundancy, as well as organizational slack, in a narrow economistic perspective appears as inefficient, it is an essential precondition for adaptability and the ability of learning to learn. Balancing the contradicting requirements of efficiency and adaptability is the specific strength of networks (Lundvall, 1991). Networks combine the transaction cost saving forces of mutual adaptation and the innovation and learning stimulating forces of loose coupling. Thus, networks provide an organizational solution that, on the one hand, is more efficient than market exchanges since mutual adaptations lower transaction costs and, on the other hand, is less prone to "lock in" effects than hierarchical relations.

2.2   The cooperative inputs

Networks, like any form of cooperation, are aimed at gaining access to complementary assets. Complementarities pertaining to scale are probably of particular importance in industries with effective barriers to market entry. Bain (1956) in his classical study distinguishes between three types of barriers to market entry. First, economies of scale are effective entry barriers if competitive unit costs can be realized only with a correspondingly high output. Second, absolute costs may keep firms from entering the market if the costs of establishing production facilities alone are prohibitive, or if the acquisition of know-how on products or processes of already existing firms would be connected with prohibitive expenditures on R&D for new firms. Finally, product differentiation may act as an entry barrier if the products of existing firms are widely known, and new firms have to lay out high advertising expenditures in order to divert market shares from the established firms.

Large firms as a rule are in a better position to overcome these barriers to market entry (Acs and Audretsch, 1988). The selectivity of barriers to market entry can be accounted for primarily in terms of the superior financial power of large firms. The central importance of a firm's equity capitalization and its ability to acquire outside capital has been emphasized particularly by Kalecki (1969, p. 92): "The variety in the size of enterprises in the same industry of a given time can be easily explained in terms of differences in entrepreneurial capital. A firm with a large entrepreneurial capital could obtain funds for a large investment whereas a firm with small entrepreneurial capital could not. Differences in the position of firms arising out of differences in their entrepreneurial capital are further enhanced by the fact that firms below a certain size have no access whatever to the capital market." Also, the existence of venture capital funds does not alter the fact that small firms are of little significance in industries with high barriers to market entry, such as, for example, the automobile, aviation, computer or steel industries (Acs and Audretsch, 1988).

Whereas in industries with high barriers to market entry small firms only rarely appear on the market as autonomous product suppliers, they play an important role as suppliers and project partners of large firms. On account of complementary skill profiles, for large companies cooperation with small firms often proves more beneficial than production based exclusively on internal resources. Complementarities related to size emerge particularly in the course of innovation processes, when both the material advantages of large firms (financial strength) and the behavioral advantages of small firms (flexibility) are needed. To be sure, the form of small-firm flexibility needed in innovation processes is "active versatility", that is, the ability to exploit market niches and quickly respond to environmental changes, as opposed to "passive pliability" which simply means to pass on the flexibility requirements of the market to the workforce in a coercive manner (Semlinger, 1991).

On the basis of analyses of the interplay between small and large firms in the development of the semiconductor industry as well as the CAD industry, Rothwell (1989, p. 58) coined the term "dynamic complementarity", the central elements of which may be sketched as follows:

- The initial impetus originates in basic innovations by established large enterprises. In many cases, the initial innovation activity was intended for internal use or for a few "lead users" (Hippel, 1988).

- In the following phase, the development of applications is pushed ahead particularly by small firms, often spin-offs. The basis of these small firms is the know-how acquired in large enterprises. This phase, which is characterized by intense competition between different technological designs, fulfills primarily the function of a "discovery procedure" in Hayek's sense.

- Once the major fields of application and the direction of further technological development have become visible, the relationship between large and small firms tends to shift again in favor of the former. Large firms enter those increasingly lucrative markets and fields of technology developed by small firms that usually are not able to provide "cospecialized assets" for an efficient commercialization of the innovation, as specialized marketing, manufacturing, and after-sales support services (Teece, 1986).

However, and at this point we return to the networks, the increased importance of large firms should not be regarded solely as a result of acquisitions of small firms by large enterprises. As Doz (1988, p. 315) explains, there are a number of arguments against acquisitions and in favor of a loose coupling between large and small firms: "Acquisitions of smaller firms have seldom been a success, as the anticipated synergies most often did not materialize ... Large firms have become increasingly reluctant to acquire smaller firms, particularly as these usually command a high price. Investments through venture capital funds usually result in conflict of interests between the large investor interested in acquiring the venture's technologies, and the other investors' and the entrepreneurs' interest in capital gains, two often contradictory objectives." Acquisitions of small firms often lead to an organizational integration within the large companies. Tight integration of small firms, however, jeopardizes the organizational flexibility and "hot-house" atmosphere which made the small firms previously so attractive for the large companies (Olleros and MacDonald, 1988).

These theoretical considerations regarding the mode of cooperation on the one hand, and the size-related cooperation inputs on the other, furnish the conceptual framework for an analysis of current changes in the relations between large and small firms in the coal, iron, and steel complex of the Ruhr area.

3 From Hierarchies towards Networks: The Changing Relations between Large and Small Firms in the Ruhr Area

This analysis originates from the research project "Interfirm Networks and Innovation: Changes in the Division of Labour between Large and Small Firms in the Coal, Iron, and Steel Complex (Ruhr Area) and the Chemical Industry (Rhine–Main Area)" conducted by the author at the Science Center Berlin for Social Research, Research Area Labour Market and Employment. The empirical material presented is, if not indicated otherwise, based on interviews of the central management, and the heads of the R&D and the purchasing departments in the steel as well as the plant engineering divisions of the seven leading Ruhr firms.[1]

3.1 The "lock in" of the coal, iron, and steel complex

The Ruhr area, a polycentric urban agglomeration of more than five million inhabitants, was the motor of the "industrial take-off" of Germany. The development of the economic core of the Ruhr area, the coal, iron, and steel complex, in its crucial aspects was shaped by a hierarchical model of industrial development. The regional core firms were established in locations which allowed a profitable exploitation of natural resources, but which frequently lacked even the rudiments of a preindustrial handicraft infrastructure (Herrigel, 1989). The missing infrastructure forced industrial enterprises to provide to a large extent supplies and services of their own: "cathedrals in the desert" (Lipietz, 1980) evolved. Except for raw materials, the regionally dominant large companies were largely self-

---

[1]These interviews, conducted between May and June 1988 and between September and November 1989, were supplemented with interviews at the regional planning authority of the Kommunalverband Ruhr (KVR), the center of innovation and technology in North Rhine-Westphalia (ZENIT), the technology center Dortmund (TechnologieZentrum Dortmund), the regional trade association (Industrie- und Handelskammer), and the association of the machine building and plant engineering firms (Verein deutscher Maschinen- und Anlagenbauer, VDMA).

sufficient with respect to both the building and the maintenance of their production facilities and the marketing and distribution of their products.

There was little change in the parallel existence of self-sufficient, vertically integrated large enterprises during subsequent phases of development for two reasons: first, the regionally dominant large enterprises sought to secure their monopsony position on the regional labor market through wage and real-estate policies which made it more difficult for potential competitors on the regional labor market to establish themselves (Müller, 1989, p. 192). Second, on account of their high degree of internalization, the dominant large companies deprived the region of agglomeration economies, thus reducing the potential for establishing enterprises in the region. The existence of small firms, while in the process of establishing themselves, frequently depends on the regional market. The missing supply opportunities resulting from the high degree of internalization thus constituted an impediment for the establishment and growth of small firms, stopping the further differentiation of a regional sectoral structure (GEWOS *et al.*, 1988, p. 52).

The long shadows cast by the dominant large companies, particularly in periods of strong growth and relative labor scarcity, provided favorable conditions for development only for those firms which oriented their products and services towards the needs of the large companies. The sometimes feudal dependency relationships between the dominant large companies and the regional supplier firms resulted in serious shortcomings in the so-called boundary-spanning functions. The boundary-spanning functions are most important in scanning the economic environment and in making external information relevant for the firm. Moreover, they are concerned with identifying and mobilizing external resources (Aldrich, 1979, pp. 248–255).

First, knowledge of the long-term investment plans of the core firms made it possible for the suppliers largely to dispense with their own long-term R&D aimed at developing new products for a new clientele. The still strong orientation of development and innovation activities towards regional core firms has been borne out in a recent analysis of machine building firms supplying the coal industry of the Ruhr. Fifty-seven percent of the machine building firms supplying the coal industry developed new products in close cooperation with their main customers; 33 percent cooperated just with their single most important customer. This cooperation proved to be of crucial importance for the success of product innovations: just 9 percent of the machine building firms supplying the coal industry would have been able to realize innovations without their cooperating partners. Further on, 35 percent of these machine building firms draw innovation ideas from their main customers. By comparison, innovation ideas of machine building firms that do not supply the coal industry stem primarily from observing the competitive environment (43 percent) and from their own R&D department (20 percent). In realizing innovation ideas these firms draw resources from a wider network of cooperating partners including suppliers, universities, and professional associations (Lehner, Nordhause-Janz and Schubert, 1990, pp. 44–47).

Second, good personal connections with the middle management of core firms quite often took the place of the suppliers' own marketing. Personal ties to a few client firms were given preference to the development of own channels of distribution. Consequently, the distribution departments of supplier firms within the coal, iron, and steel complex are generally of little significance. The qualification levels of distribution personnel in machine building firms supplying the coal industry, for example, are considerably below the industrial average (Lehner, Nordhause-Janz and Schubert, 1990, p. 18).

These shortcomings in the boundary-spanning functions resulted from the hierarchical relations within the coal, iron, and steel complex. To be sure, these hierarchical relations proved to be highly efficient in terms of transaction costs. However, the transaction cost efficiency of the hierarchical relations also had its price. Tight coupling resulting from long-term mutual adaptations locked firms into specific exchange relations and undermined their ability to leave the technological trajectory of the coal, iron, and steel complex. For example, the machine building firms of the coal, iron, and steel complex adopted CNC, CAD, CAQ, and FMS technologies significantly earlier than the machine building firms outside the coal, iron, and steel complex, and are at present leaders in the field of computer integration of manufacturing (CIM). However, shortcomings in the boundary-spanning functions restrain these firms from leaving the technological trajectory of the coal, iron, and steel complex and from shifting to more promising markets (Lehner, Nordhause-Janz and Schubert, 1990, p. 34). This "lock in" inevitably resulted in the "sailing ship effect" (Rothwell and Zegveld, 1985, p. 41). The sailing ship effect refers to the fact that the most important improvements to the sailing ship occurred after the introduction of the steamship. As Rothwell and Zegveld (1985, p. 41) emphasize, "it illustrates how established companies can become locked into existing technological trajectories. Rather than capitalize on the possibilities offered by the emergence of a superior new substitute technology, they vigorously defend their position through the accelerated improvement of the old technology."

3.2   The emergence of networks: new cooperative arrangements between large and small firms in plant engineering and environmental technology

The "lock in" of the coal, iron, and steel complex prevented an appropriate and timely reorganization of the Ruhr. The dramatic aggravation of the crisis in the early 1980s, however, broke open this "lock in". Plant closures and a shift of economic activities to the prosperous south of western Germany were the most obvious signs of the start of a reorganization triggered by repeated sharp downturns in demand for steel. For example, the oldest firm of the coal, iron, and steel complex of the Ruhr, Gutehoffnungshütte (founded in 1758), removed its headquarters and R&D department from the Ruhr town Oberhausen to one of the major centers of Germany's electronic industry, Munich. In all, the old steel firms cut down by more than 60,000 jobs since 1980 (Heinze, Hilbert and Voelzkow, 1989, p. 33). However, leading Ruhr firms also made considerable progress in reorganizing their business and their interfirm relations. They began to reduce the "steel" divisions in favor of new fields of production with a significantly higher value-added component. The strategic reorientation of former steel companies towards new markets can be observed especially in the development of revenue shares accounted for by the "processing" divisions (Table 4.1).

Thus Thyssen alone, the largest of the former steel companies, increased the revenue share of its processing division between 1970 and 1986 from 4.2 percent to 23.7 percent. During the same period, the steel division was reduced from 60.3 percent to 35.9 percent. Mannesmann increased its processing division from 23.8 percent to 53.8 percent between 1970 and 1986. At the center of the strategic reorientation are the sectors plant engineering, environmental technology, mechanical engineering, and electronics. Plant engineering in particular was traditionally part of the production range of large steel enterprises, though initially it was limited to serving the internal needs of the enterprise within maintenance and repair departments. With the cutting down of steel capacity to a level which no longer allowed the full utilization of these maintenance and repair departments, the companies began marketing their plant engineering know-how externally (Geer, 1985, p. 86). This led to an organizational differentiation and decentralization which was oriented towards product markets rather than towards internal production processes.

With the retreat from steel and the move into plant engineering and environmental technology, the hierarchical interfirm relations within the coal, iron, and steel complex also came to be challenged. The conditions in the targeted markets favor network-type relationships between firms.

Table 4.1: Shares of central divisions in total sales of the five most important steel enterprises in West Germany (percentages)

		1970	1980	1986
Thyssen[1]	steel	60.3	37.8	35.9
	non-steel	39.7	62.2	64.1
	processing	4.2	22.5	23.7
Krupp[2]	steel	31.9	36.3	27.6
	non-steel	68.1	63.7	72.2
	processing	34.0	36.5	47.0
Mannesmann[3]	steel	43.9	30.4	25.1
	non-steel	56.1	69.4	74.9
	processing	23.8	43.9	53.8
Klöckner	steel	60.7	60.8	49.5
	non-steel	39.3	39.2	50.5
	processing	28.3	38.8	49.5
Hoesch[4]	steel		40.5	40.9
	non-steel		59.5	59.1
	processing		33.3	38.4

[1] Up to 30 September 1975 Thyssen-Gruppe, thereafter Thyssen-Welt.
[2] Steel, including about 50 percent high-grade steel.
[3] Only pipes to be subsumed under steel; 1970: domestic corporation, from 1975: global corporation.
[4] Until 1981 together with Estel.
Source: Grabher (1991a, p. 10).

With respect to cooperation inputs, networks are aimed at combining the financial power of large firms and the special problem-solving capacities of small firms. Large firms see their own strength in offering integrated system solutions, from the conception of plants and equipment to their maintenance and servicing, rather than – and this is the decisive difference to the old structure of coal, iron, and steel companies – producing all components themselves. Large firms now concentrate on playing the role of a general contractor assembling the work of specialists into a customized system. The strategic know-how of plant engineers, as a Krupp manager has put it, consists precisely in "knowing the right project partner for each problem". The general contractor, and therein lies the specific strength of large firms, is responsible for the enormous financial expenditures connected with the planning and management of large projects, which would pose an insuperable barrier to market entry for small firms. The specific strength of the latter consists in adding to

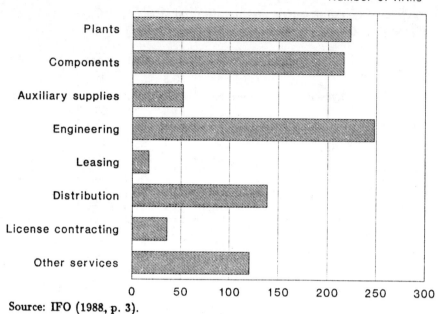

Source: IFO (1988, p. 3).

Figure 4.1: Profile of suppliers of environmental technology in North Rhine-Westphalia.

the project their specialized competence. In North Rhine-Westphalia, the federal state to which the Ruhr area belongs, approximately 220 firms of the environmental technology industry are suppliers of special components (Figure 4.1).

However, the economic importance of small firms goes far beyond their role as suppliers and cooperating partners of large firms. Especially in environmental technology, small firms play a crucial role in developing further the initial innovations of the large steel firms and in opening up new fields of application. The large steel companies in the main did not enter the field of environmental technology as the result of an explicit marketing strategy. Rather, the plant engineering divisions were confronted with the requirements of customers that had to adhere to new environmental regulations. These customers figured large as "lead users" (Hippel, 1988). Their experience stemming from the operation of pilot plants was applied directly in the research and development process of the producer. The exchange of ideas between user and producer contributed considerably to the final design of the plants. Although this "user–producer interaction" (Lundvall, 1988) triggered innovation, it reinforced a concentration of resources upon specific problems of the coal, iron, and steel complex. The cooperation with the traditional clientele resulted repeatedly in products based on "end-of-pipe technologies" that are aimed at mitigating already existing environmental problems. Cases in point are filtration plants and decontamination plants that have been designed by Ruhr firms to repair environmental damage caused by Ruhr firms. To give an impression, in North Rhine-Westphalia more than 8,500 areas are contaminated with noxious substances. These areas consist mainly of former mining and steel mill sites that are concentrated in the Ruhr area. More than 80 percent of all sites of the regional real-estate pool of the Ruhr area (Grundstücksfond Ruhr) are under suspicion of containing noxious substances (Der Minister für Wirtschaft, Mittelstand und Technologie des Landes Nordrhein-Westfalen, 1988, p. 7).

Beyond doubt, environmental regulations such as the new water and soil protecting regulations will transform these environmental problems into effective demand also for the end-of-pipe technologies supplied by the Ruhr firms. Investment in end-of-pipe technologies, however, is generally considered as a transition stage. In the long run, the costly *ex-post* reduction of pollution with end-of-pipe technologies will be replaced by production processes that *ex-ante* prevent environmental pollution. This bias of the diversification strategies of large companies towards end-of-pipe technologies is partially compensated by newly founded small firms: more than 50 percent of firms that have been founded during the last three years are mainly concerned with pollution-preventing technologies (IFO, 1988, p. 5). Thus, small firms contribute considerably to the development of new fields of environmental technology. As the first cooperative development projects between large companies and newly founded small firms in the technology center of the Ruhr town Dortmund indicate, large firms are increasingly stepping into these fields of technology, which have been pioneered by small firms (Förderverein Forschungszentrum Umwelttechnologie, 1989).

With respect to the mode of cooperation, the question arises as to what arguments support the superiority of network as opposed to hierarchical or market forms of exchange. Networks have been demarcated above from market relations by their stability resulting from mutual adaptations. The economic functionality of stability in networks can be understood in terms of the special characteristics of plant engineering and environmental technology. The length of time and the complexity of production and service in the framework of supplying customized solutions favor relations with firms that have already demonstrated their competence and reliability in previous cooperation. Moreover, the increasing technological interconnection of plant components through control systems requires more intensive processes of coordination and adaptation of the firms taking part in production. Such coordination is facilitated by a common technical jargon

Table 4.2: Structure of orders in plant engineering (shares in total volume of orders)

Plant infrastructure	30%
Steel engineering and machine components of low complexity	20%
Mechanical engineering of high complexity	20%
Control systems and system know-how	30%

Source: Expert interview at Krupp, 20 May 1988.

and common negotiating procedures as will evolve in cooperation over time. Knowledge of the competence and efficiency of cooperation partners as well as a common technical jargon are significant particularly with respect to mechanical engineering of high complexity and microelectronic control systems which account for about 50 percent of orders in plant engineering (Table 4.2). On account of the high demands made on the cooperation partners, there is great potential for reducing, through stable cooperative relations, transaction costs arising from frequent changes of cooperation partners.

The mutual adaptations of cooperating firms, however, do not end in hierarchical relations as characterized the coal, iron, and steel complex. Rather, firms are loosely coupled in cooperation networks. From the perspective of the general contractors there are several reasons against having very dependent project partners: First, strongly dependent project partners will be threatened in their existence as soon as cooperative relations are interrupted even for a short time. Interruptions, however, are characteristic for plant engineering since demand is rather discontinuous. Yet the loss of project partners entails high costs in searching for new partners for cooperation. Second, the general contractors offer their clients not only hardware, but also "cospecialized assets" permitting the greatest possible degree of utilization of the capital-intensive plants (Teece, 1986). Above all, these cospecialized assets include training of the plant operators, maintenance services and spare part guarantees. Since these cospecialized assets would also have to be provided by the project partners, the general contractor's interest in the stability of his cooperation partners becomes understandable. Finally, if project partners cooperate with several partners, it will allow them to realize economies of scale. Individual system components can be offered at a cheaper rate if utilized repeatedly.

As a consequence of loose coupling, and in contrast to the coal, iron, and steel complex, the cooperating firms of the general contractors have to be well equipped with their own boundary-spanning and strategic entrepreneurial functions, i.e. R&D and marketing. The role of cooperating firms consists not simply in supplying components produced according to the blueprints of the general contractors. Rather, they must be able to develop solutions for problems that are only roughly specified by the general contractors and that evolve in the course of the planning and production phase (GEWOS *et al.*, 1988, p. 123). Obviously, only firms with research and engineering capacities of their own are able to meet this high demand for flexibility. Loose coupling of these functionally relatively autonomous firms provides redundancy and encourages the openness and reflectivity of the entire network since information stemming from different sources and evaluated against different backgrounds flows together. It is this ability to generate new interpretations that is essential for the network's capacity for self-organization and learning to learn.

4 Conclusion: A Brief Plea for Inefficiency

The cathedrals in the desert are crumbling. The diversification of the vertically integrated, self-sufficient large companies of the coal, iron, and steel complex into new markets is accompanied by drastic changes in their internal organization and their relations to the environment. In the new markets of plant engineering and environmental technology the large firms, rather than producing all components themselves, concentrate on the role of a general contractor that assembles the work of specialized and small firms into a customized system. The emergence of networks between large general contractors and their smaller cooperating partners, however, must not lead to the hasty conclusion that large firms in general are losing influence on regional economic development. In the role of the general contractor the large firm, like the spider in the web, still has a central strategic function in creating and controlling the network. Although there is much less interdependence and much more redundancy within the plant engineering and environmental technology networks than within the coal, iron, and steel complex, the degree of interdependence and redundancy is controlled by the large firms.

In a period of reorganization and a dramatic increase of turbulence due to diversification, the economic functionality of redundancy is obvious. But will this also hold true after positions in the market have been consolidated and further technological development seems foreseeable? This is probably one of the major challenges for the large general contractors and, more generally, for the long-term future of the Ruhr area: to resist the economistic temptation to streamline the plant engineering and environmental technology industry in order to minimize transaction costs. As the decline of the coal, iron, and steel complex has demonstrated, stubbornly reducing transaction costs had a high price: it locked the region into its trajectory and undermined its ability to learn and self-organize. In other words, one of the major challenges for the Ruhr area is to allow for inefficiency in the form of redundancy. It will be crucial for the long-term adaptability of the region.

References

Acs, Z.J., D.B. Audretsch, 1988. Small Firm Entry in US Manufacturing. *Economica*, Vol. 56, pp. 255–265.

Aldrich, H.E., 1979. *Organizations and Environments*. Prentice-Hall, Englewood Cliffs, NJ.

Argyris, C., D.A. Schon, 1978. *Organizational Learning: A Theory of Action Perspective*. Addison-Wesley, Reading, Mass.

Bain, J., 1956. *Barriers to New Competition*. Harvard University Press, Cambridge, Mass.

Bateson, G., 1972. *Steps to an Ecology of Mind*. Ballantine Books, New York.

Birch, D., 1979. *The Job Generation Process*. M.I.T. Program on Neighbourhood and Regional Change, Mimeo, Cambridge, Mass.

Blau, P., 1968. The Hierarchy of Authority in Organization. *American Journal of Sociology*, Vol. 73, pp. 453–467.

Cyert, R.M., J.G. March, 1963. *A Behavioral Theory of the Firm*. Prentice-Hall, Englewood Cliffs, NJ.

Coase, ·., 1937. The Nature of the Firm. *Economica*, Vol. 4, pp. 386–405.

Der Minister für Wirtschaft, Mittelstand und Technologie, 1988. *Neues im Westen: Stellenwert der Umwelttechnologien in der NRW-Wirtschaftsstruktur*. Düsseldorf.

Doz, Y.L., 1988. Technology Partnership between Larger and Smaller Firms: Some Critical Issues, in F.J. Contractor, P. Lorange (eds.), *Cooperative Strategies in International Business*. Lexington Books, Lexington.

Förderverein Forschungszentrum Umwelttechnologie, 1989. *Umwelttechnik und Umweltindustrie*. Report No.1, Dortmund.

Geer, T., 1985. Internationaler Wettbewerb und regionale Entwicklung: preisunempfindliche Branchen, in *Nordrhein-Westfalen in der Krise – Krise in Nordrhein-Westfalen?* Duncker & Humblot, Berlin.

GEWOS, GfAH, WSI, 1988. *Strukturwandel und Beschäftigungsperspektiven der Metallindustrie an der Ruhr*. Final report. Hamburg.

Grabher, G., 1991a. Against De-Industrialization: A Strategy for Old Industrial Areas, in E. Matzner, W. Streeck (eds.), *Beyond Keynesianism: The Socio-Economics of Production and Full Employment*. Edward Elgar, Aldershot.

Grabher, G., 1991b. *The Embedded Firm. On the Socio-Economics of Industrial Networks* (forthcoming).

Granovetter, M., 1973. The Strength of Weak Ties. *American Journal of Sociology*, Vol. 78, pp. 1360–1380.

Granovetter, M., 1985. Economic Action and Social Structure: The Problem of Embeddedness. *American Journal of Sociology*, Vol. 91, pp. 481–510.

Heinze, R.G., J. Hilbert, H. Voelzkow, 1989. *Strukturwandel und Strukturpolitik in Nordrhein-Westfalen*. Unpublished report. Wissenschaftszentrum Nordrhein-Westfalen, Institut Arbeit und Technik, Gelsenkirchen.

Herrigel, G.B., 1989. Industrial Order and the Politics of Industrial Change: Mechanical Engineering in the Federal Republic of Germany, in P. Katzenstein (ed.), *Toward a Third Republic? Industry, Politics and Change in West Germany*. Cornell University Press, Cornell.

Hippel, E.v., 1988. *The Sources of Innovation*. New York, Oxford University Press, Oxford.

Hirschman, A.O., 1970. *Exit, Voice and Loyalty*. Harvard University Press, Cambridge, Mass.

Ikeda, M., 1988. Evolution of the Japanese Subcontracting System, in *Tradescope*, Vol. 4, pp. 2–16.

IFO-Institut für Wirtschaftsforschung, 1988. *Das Angebot der nordrhein-westfälischen Wirtschaft auf dem Umweltschutzmarkt. Ausgewählte Ergebnisse einer schriftlichen Erhebung vom Frühjahr 1988*. Munich.

Johanson, J., L.G. Mattson, 1987. Interorganizational Relations in Industrial Systems: A Network Approach Compared with the Transaction Cost Approach. *International Studies of Management & Organization*, Vol. 17, pp. 34–48.

Kern, H., M. Schumann, 1985. *Das Ende der Arbeitsteilung? Rationalisierung in der industriellen Produktion*. Beck, Munich.

Kalecki, M., 1969. *Theory of Economic Dynamics*. August M. Kelley, New York.

Kaneko, I., K. Imai, 1987. A Network View of the Firm. Paper presented at the first Hitotsubashi–Stanford Conference.

Lehner, F., J. Nordhause-Janz, K. Schubert, 1990. *Probleme und Perspektiven des Strukturwandels der Bergbau-Zulieferindustrie*. Final report. Wissenschaftszentrum Nordrhein-Westfalen, Institut Arbeit und Technik, Gelsenkirchen.

Lipietz, A., 1980. The Structuration of Space, the Problem of Land, and Spatial Policy, in J. Carney, R. Hudson, J. Lewis (eds.), *Regions in Crisis*. Croom Helm, London.

Lundvall, B.A., 1988. Innovation as an Interactive Process: From User–Producer Interaction to the National System of Innovation, in G. Dosi, C. Freeman, R. Nelson, G. Silverberg, L. Soete (eds.), *Technical Change and Economic Theory*. Pinter Publishers, London.

Lundvall, B.A., 1991. Explaining Interfirm Cooperation and Innovation: The Limits of the Transaction Cost Approach, in G. Grabher (ed.), *The Embedded Firm. On the Socio-Economics of Industrial Networks* (forthcoming).

Morgan, G., 1986. *Images of Organization*. Sage, Beverly Hills.

Müller, G., 1989. Strukturwandel und Beschäftigungsperspektiven an der Ruhr.

WSI-Mitteilungen, No. 4, pp. 188–197.

Olleros, F.J., R.J. MacDonald, 1988. Strategic Alliances: Managing Complementarity to Capitalize on Emerging Technologies. *Technovation*, Vol. 7, pp. 155–176.

Piore, M.J., C.F. Sabel, 1984. *The Second Industrial Divide.* Basic Books, New York.

Powell, W.W., 1990. Neither Market nor Hierarchy: Network Forms of Organization. *Research in Organizational Behavior*, Vol. 12, pp. 295–336.

Richardson, G.B., 1972. The Organization of Industry. *Economic Journal*, Vol. 28, pp. 883–889.

Rothwell, R., W. Zegveld, 1985. *Reindustrialization and Technology.* Longman, Harlow.

Rothwell, R., 1989. Small Firms, Innovation and Industrial Change. *Small Business Economics*, Vol. 1, pp. 51–64.

Semlinger, K., 1991. Small Firms and Out-Sourcing as Flexibility Reservoirs of Large Companies, in G. Grabher (ed.), *The Embedded Firm: On the Socio-Economics of Industrial Networks* (forthcoming).

Teece, D., 1986. Firm Boundaries, Technological Innovation, and Strategic Management, in L.G. Thomas (ed.), *The Economics of Strategic Planning.* Lexington Books, Lexington.

Weick, K.E., 1976. Educational Organizations as Loosely Coupled Systems. *Administrative Science Quarterly*, Vol. 21, pp. 1–26.

Williamson, O.E., 1975. *Markets and Hierarchies: Analysis and Antitrust Implications.* Free Press, New York.

Williamson, O.E., 1985. *The Economic Institutions of Capitalism.* Free Press, New York.

5

A Network Approach to the Small Enterprise

Poul Ove Pedersen[*]

1 The Argument

Since the ILO published its study on the informal sector in Kenya in 1972, there has been increasing interest in the role of the small-scale or informal sector in development. However, governments in most developing countries still look upon the small enterprises and the informal sector with great skepticism, as a backward part of the economy which will (and should) disappear in the course of development. On the other hand, it has been realized that large, formal enterprises, at least for some time, will not be able to solve the rapidly rising unemployment problems. Therefore, partly under pressure from the World Bank and the large aid donors, the small-enterprise sector has increasingly been taken seriously. There is, however, a great deal of uncertainty about how the small-enterprise or informal sector should be understood and which political steps could and should be taken.

During the 1970s and 1980s, a large number of empirical studies have been carried out on the informal or small-scale sector in both rural and urban areas in many different countries.[1] However, the results of these studies have often been conflicting, partly because the structure of the informal sector varies from area to area, but also because the studies have focused on different aspects and parts of the sector. As a result there is no general agreement on how the empirical results should be interpreted.

---

[*]Centre for Development Research, Copenhagen.
[1]See, e.g., Aboagye, 1986; Chuta and Sethuraman, 1984; ILO, 1985; Liedholm and Mead, 1987; Lopez-Castaño, 1987; Sethuraman, 1981; Freeman and Norcliffe, 1985.

Many different attempts have been made to understand and explain how the small, informal enterprises operate. However, though the explanations may differ in detail, they all seem to be based on either one or the other of the main theoretical frameworks, namely the neoclassically inspired modernization theories, which tend to take a positive view of the small enterprise, or the Marxist-inspired dependency theories, which tend to have a more negative view. The views of the small enterprise in these theories are presented in Section 2. The two theories lead to very different policy prescriptions so that it becomes necessary to clarify these conflicting views. The purpose of this paper is to contribute to that clarification by looking at some of the assumptions implicit in the theories.

Although the two theoretical frameworks differ in a number of ways they both rest on the same basic assumption that small enterprises are less efficient parts of the economy which will and ought to disappear in the course of successful development. This assumption originates from nineteenth-century Europe when the classical development theories were written. Since then it has been widely believed to be true although, as we want to show in Section 3, it is refuted by the empirical evidence. The small enterprise did not disappear as expected because many functions are performed more efficiently in small enterprises than in large ones.

The two theoretical frameworks are often presented as alternative political explanations of the small-scale, informal sector. This of course is partly true, but we want to show that they also tend to describe different parts of the very heterogeneous sector. In fact our main argument is that it is this very heterogeneity which is the key to the understanding of the enterprise. To develop such an understanding we shall look at the interaction between scale economies and specialization in Section 4.

The two theoretical frameworks make different but very limiting assumptions about the structure of the environment of the small enterprise. In Section 5 we want to show that a better understanding of the small enterprise must rest upon a new and more differentiated view of the small enterprise's interaction with its environment. This view partly allows us to bridge the gap between the two traditional theories, but of course does not resolve the political differences dividing them.

If heterogeneity is a key characteristic of the small-scale sector the many attempts in the literature to define a narrow homogeneous sector are bound to fail because they eliminate the very problem they should be investigating. Consequently, throughout the rest of the paper we shall talk about the small-scale sector and the small enterprise in a very broad sense of the words, and well knowing that this is not a homogeneous concept and that smallness is often a relative rather than an absolute term. In fact though we use the word "small", smallness is hardly interesting in itself. It is a convenient common denominator for a host of other characteristics of enterprises, e.g. informality, which tends to be highly correlated with size, but which is not identical with it.

2 Theoretical Conceptions of the Small Enterprise

2.1 Modernization theories

In the modernization theories, the basic assumption has been that the countries of the Third World will experience a process of industrialization and urbanization, not identical, but similar, to that which has taken place in the developed countries, only with a delay. Development in the developed countries is seen as a process where agriculture is gradually mechanized, where small, low-productivity artisan workshops are substituted by large-scale mechanized industrial enterprises with higher productivity, and where production is increasingly concentrated in the towns to exploit urban and agglomeration economies. This is the process which development policies should try to replicate in the Third World.

The unit of analysis in these theories is usually the enterprise, and the industrial enterprise is conceived of as a stable technical production machine which produces standardized commodities by means of a small number of specific inputs in the form of labor, raw materials, and possibly semi-products. Inputs (including labor) are bought and output sold on open homogeneous markets operating under perfect competition. Here price and amount are the only information necessary to determine the market conditions. Buying and marketing functions are thus of little importance, and consequently, trade and services are seen to play only a passive role in development.

The main task of the entrepreneur or manager is to decide how much of one or more commodities should be produced and how that production should take place so as to minimize costs and maximize productivity, basically by exploiting scale economies and by increasing the capital intensity and labor productivity. Since the large enterprise is assumed always to have greater productivity than the small, owing to scale economies, it will only be a matter of time before the small enterprises will be driven out of the market and disappear. The persistence of small enterprises in the Third World today tends to be seen as a sign of backwardness. However, the view of the small enterprise may also be positive, because the small enterprise is seen as a carrier of innovations and, therefore, considered to play an important role in innovation and renewal of the production system. Those which are successful will in time grow large and efficient, the less successful will stagnate or close. Thus, although the individual small enterprise is seen as temporary, as a group they may survive. Investigations based on this viewpoint normally focus on the entrepreneur (which can be a collective) and his enterprise, its production process, production conditions, and development strategies.

Policies to support the small enterprise/informal sector tend to be policies which help already established individual enterprises grow larger either by providing them with credit, inputs, services, advice, education, etc. or by improving their general environment by investing in infrastructure or education and training of the labor force and by economic policies to increase demand (see, for example, Sethuraman, 1981; Chuta and Sethuraman, 1984; Little, 1987; Hansen, 1987). The problem with such policies is that it will primarily be the more resourceful parts of the small-scale sector which will be able to obtain direct support. At the same time, the general economic policies will usually benefit enterprises according to their turnover, and thus especially favor the largest. Another serious problem is that even though such policies may support development of a more differentiated and efficient production system, they are only to a limited extent likely to solve employment problems.

2.2   The dependency theories

In the dependency theories, the present conditions for development in the Third World are considered to be so different from the conditions during the past development in the developed countries that a direct comparison does not make sense. Rather, their development is seen as a sort of negative picture of that in the developed countries. The world economy is seen as dominated by large national and multinational corporations. These corporations have headquarters in the capital cities and especially in the large capitals of the developed countries, while large mass producing and relatively footloose production plants are spread over regions and countries where the production conditions, especially labor, are cheapest. They often operate in monopolistic or semi-monopolistic markets. They exploit both scale economies and cheap labor. Since peripheral regions and countries often compete for them, they may even be able to obtain public support. They are assumed to be much more profitable than the small local enterprises. Still, small local enterprises may survive, not because they are technically competitive, but by accepting self-exploitation, very low wages and bad working conditions. The small-scale activity may survive either by direct dependency on the large enterprises as subcontractors or individuals doing outwork, or as petty producers or traders operating in extremely competitive markets and with no possibilities for earning a profit sufficient to accumulate and grow.

As in the modernization theories, the small-scale activities are seen to have low productivity. However, the mushrooming of small, informal enterprises in the Third World is seen not as a sign of backwardness, but rather as a sign of underdevelopment resulting from unequal conditions. In fact the swelling of the informal sector is often said to be much larger in the Third World than it was in the industrialized countries and seen as the main symptom of underdevelopment.

While in the modernization theories the small-scale sector is considered a part of the production sphere, in the dependency theories it is considered to be a part of reproduction. Empirical investigations usually focus on the laborer/household and his/its survival strategies, on the labor market processes and policies, and on the interaction between the informal sector and the household organization. When the small entrepreneur is studied, it is in his role as self-employed laborer rather than as entrepreneur. When the small enterprise is studied, it is as a part of the system of household reproduction rather than as a part of the production system. Focus is on the wage level and working conditions rather than on the product and production processes. The small-scale sector is seen as consisting of activities which people do as a last resort when all other possibilities to earn a living are gone. Such studies tend to emphasize the role of the social network of the entrepreneurs/laborers. The sector is recognized as having a redistributive function, but it is often seen as having little real importance for the production system (see, for example, Mkandawire, 1986, and the discussion in Kongstad, 1986).

Thus, from a policy point of view, the informal sector is usually looked upon with rather negative eyes. Often, it is considered neither possible nor desirable to promote the informal sector by supporting individual small enterprises, because such support would only lead to more profits for the large enterprises owing to the strong competition. Only by changing the structure through national policies in favor of small enterprises could the informal sector be developed (see, for example, Portes, 1983). Instead, it is often proposed to attack employment problems directly by establishing large, labor-intensive employment projects or so-called income-generating activities. The disadvantage of such projects, which usually focus more on their employment- or income-generating abilities than on the function in the economy of the products or services they produce, is that they seldom become economically self-supporting and, therefore, are difficult to maintain permanently by poor governments.

The two theoretical frameworks presented above are often considered as politically alternative descriptions and explanations of the small-enterprise sector. Since they tend to describe the development strategies of the entrepreneur/enterprise and the labor force respectively, this is of course true. At the same time, however, it is also evident, both from the theories themselves and from the parts of the small-enterprise sector which are normally investigated, that the two sets of theories emphasize different parts of the sector (see, for example, Nattras, 1987; Peattie, 1987).

Studies based on the modernization theories prefer to investigate the most independent, productive, and resourceful parts of the small-scale sector. It is often such enterprises which are emphasized in the empirical work, and it is of course these which are easiest to reach with the enterprise-specific policies which are proposed. On the other hand, studies based on the dependency theories typically choose to investigate the least resourceful or the most dependent parts of the small-scale sector, which are typically also the worst off. Which theoretical framework is relevant, therefore, depends not only on the political point of departure (economic growth or employment), but also on the characteristics of the small-scale sector in the area and at the time of investigation. Thus there is good reason to consider the two theoretical frameworks not only as political alternatives, but also as thematically complementary, because they tend to focus on different parts of a very heterogeneous small-scale sector. This is caused by the heterogeneity of the small-scale/informal sector.

3   Empirical Evidence: The Role of Small Enterprises in Danish Industrialization

One of the difficulties in formulating policies for the small-enterprise sector has been that both of the two traditional theoretical frameworks explicitly or implicitly consider the sector to be a less productive part of the economy which in the course of development will and ought to disappear. This assumption, which has been widespread in the economic literature since the last century, has led to the belief that the small-scale sector is much larger in the Third World than it ever was in the developed countries, where it is thought to have declined rapidly as a result of industrialization (see, for example, Bairoch, 1969, 1975).

Both of these views, however, rest on very weak grounds because data on the early development of the small-scale sector in developed countries is obviously scarce.[2] Most studies investigating the development of the developed countries during their early industrialization tend to:

- be based on data for the large-scale sector alone rather than on data for production as a whole (including the small-scale sector)
- be based on ownership rather than on functional geographical dimensions, which would lead to a smaller average size of production units

---

[2]Though in many cases better than in the developing countries today.

- be based on data for production alone, though a large part of the small-scale sector has always been found in commerce and other services
- be based on data from the heyday of industrialization rather than the earlier phases which may in many cases be a more realistic basis for comparison with the developing world
- be based on data from the large colonial powers, where large enterprises have probably played a larger role than in the smaller industrial countries.

All these points have tended to lead to an underestimation of the role of small enterprises in the development process. In order to illustrate this, we shall present some data on the development of the small-scale sector in Denmark since the beginning of industrialization.

Figure 5.1 (based on Hansen, 1983, Table 2) shows estimations of the development of the sectoral distribution of GNP in Denmark in the period 1818–1975. Production is here divided into three parts: an industrial sector comprising production enterprises with more than 5 employees, a small-enterprise sector comprising production enterprises with less than 6 employees, and a rural production sector comprising rural artisans, beer brewing and other mostly part-time activities which gradually disappeared by the end of the nineteenth century. The figure shows that during the first period of rapid industrialization from 1850 to 1910 large industry increased its contribution to GNP from 4% to 10–12% while the small-scale sector (incl. the rural artisans) decreased from 16% to 9%. Thus production as a whole throughout this period of early industrialization contributed about 20% of GNP, and although the contribution of the small-scale sector was decreasing, it was still responsible for about 40% of total commodity production in 1910.

After 1910 large industry increased its contribution to GNP to over 20% by 1960, when it topped. This increase, however, did not take place at the cost of the small-scale production sector, which remained almost stable at 8–10% of GNP throughout the period 1910–75. In addition a large part of the small-scale sector is found, not in production, but in trade, transport, and other services, which since the end of the last century have accounted for more than 40% of GNP. However, detailed historical data on the size of enterprises in those sectors is not available. Data for employment in large and small production enterprises, though scarce for last century, shows similar trends but with even less dominance of the large-scale sector (for more details see Pedersen, 1989).

By the middle of the 1980s 15% of the total workforce in Denmark still was either self-employed or employed in enterprises with less than 6 employees (see Table 5.1). A third of the workforce worked in enterprises

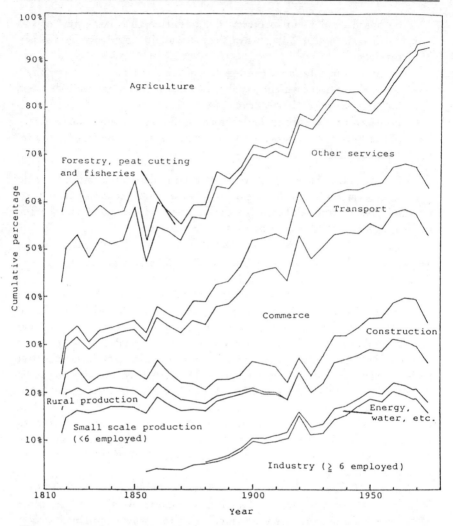

Figure 5.1: The distribution of GNP in real prices by sector: Denmark 1818–1975.

with less than 20 people employed. For the manufacturing sector alone the small enterprises meant relatively less. But even here 45% of all enterprises had less than 6 employees and employed 7% of the workforce. More than 20% of the manufacturing workforce worked in enterprises with less than 20 people employed.

Consequently one can hardly claim that large-scale industry displaced the small production enterprises as anticipated by the classical theories. Rather, small- and large-scale production seem to have grown hand in

Table 5.1: Employment in small enterprises, Denmark 1983

	All sectors		All sectors except agriculture		Manufacturing	
Total workforce	2,798,000					
Number of people in work	2,540,000	100%	2,353,100	100%	489,000	100%
Self-employed (incl. helping wives) without paid employee	180,000		106,600*		12,300*	
Persons working in enterprises with 1–5 persons employed+	255,000		220,800		23,300	
Total workforce in enterprises with 1–5 persons employed	435,000	17%	327,400	14%	35,600	7%
Persons working in enterprises with 1–9 persons employed*	171,000		164,100		22,800	
Total workforce in enterprises with 1–9 persons employed	606,000	24%	491,500	21%	58,400	12%
Persons working in enterprises with 10–19 persons employed*	290,000		282,400		46,600	
Total workforce in enterprises with 1–19 persons employed	896,000	35%	773,900	33%	105,000	21%

+   Incl. self-employed and helping wives.
*   Estimated on the basis of data for all self-employed and helping wives.

Sources: Based on the register-based work place statistic and the labor market statistic. Here the term enterprise refers to a work address. A table based on ownership would show a higher degree of concentration.

hand during the process of industrialization. Our conclusion, therefore, is that a theory of the small enterprise must explicitly accept the small enterprise as an important part of the economy in both developed and developing countries. The small-enterprise sector may change over time, but it is there to stay.

4   Scale Economies and Specialization in Economic Development

In our search for a new understanding of the small-enterprise sector, which at the same time accepts the small enterprise as a permanent and valuable part of the economy, and allows for the heterogeneous nature of the sector, we shall reconsider the concepts of scale economies and specialization.

Since Adam Smith it has been generally recognized that the process of industrialization and economic development has proceeded through a process of specialization and increasing scale of production. However, though increasing scale and specialization are two sides of the same process, most development theories and policies have explicitly or implicitly focused on scale economies rather than on specialization. One result of this strong focus on scale economies has been that scale economies very often have been associated with large-scale production. However, scale economies may be obtained by all sizes of enterprises; a production increase from 1 to 10 units at a time may in some cases lead to relatively larger-scale economies than an increase from 1,000 to 10,000.

It is often forgotten that the exploitation of "scale economies" also requires a sufficiently large market in which the large production might be sold. In the liberal economic theories, this is implicitly taken care of by assuming that there exists a homogeneous market (which actually implies that there exist a large number of small or medium-sized competing commercial enterprises). In the Marxist-inspired theories, this is taken care of by assuming the existence of a basically monopolistic market organized either by private capital or by the state. However, in both types of theories, the assumption about the necessary market is often given relatively little attention, because the commercial activities are considered to be derived activities of secondary importance. Many studies of both large- and small-scale production focus on the production activities alone, and do not see them in relation to the way the marketing is organized.

This lack of attention to the market organization is critical when one considers that the first industrialization, in for example the textile industry, both in mercantilist Europe and in the present Third World countries, in many cases has been based on an efficient market organization rather than on scale economies in production itself (Heierli, 1986). This is also strange because during early industrialization commercial and transport activities have actually grown more rapidly than production (see Figure 5.1). To understand the role of small and medium-sized enterprises in the economy, we must understand the process of specialization and market creation. Large-scale markets are created through:

- improved transport and communication networks which permit a spatial integration of increasingly larger markets,
- standardization of products which increases their possible applications, and
- creation of efficient market systems or organizations.

However, at the same time as transport improvements, standardization and efficient market organization promote large-scale production, they also in themselves tend to create a need for small enterprises. Specialization and product standardization tend to leave "small tasks" (with an insufficient market) undone and small niches in the market (where the standardized product cannot be applied satisfactorily or which are too expensive to supply) unserved, if small and medium-sized enterprises are not able or willing to fill the gaps. These small and medium-sized enterprises will of course often be technically less efficient than the large enterprise in the sense that the unit costs for the specialized products and services will be larger than the unit costs for standardized products produced by the large enterprise. However, if the large enterprises were forced to supply the small market niches actually supplied by the small enterprises, the costs would probably be even larger, because the large enterprise would not be able to utilize its large production system efficiently and would often have larger distribution costs. Thus, one cannot *a priori* say that the small are less efficient than the large, because they are not doing the same work.

Transportation improvements in themselves tend to be subject to scale economies and thus favor large-scale production and large concentrated markets that can be served by cheap large-scale transportation. However, at the same time, this means that products and services with a small demand will often have relatively protected local markets because cheap, large scale transportation cannot be used.

One of the reasons why small-scale production seems to survive even in highly industrialized countries is that an increasing part of the production tends to be capital equipment, which in large, mass-producing industries tends to require non-standardized, custom-made equipment that is often produced by relatively small enterprises. Another reason is that with growing incomes an increasing part of the income will be used on luxury goods and services which are not mass-produced.

To be able to exploit large-scale "scale economies" not only requires a sufficiently large market; it also requires that intermediate products, capital and labor are available in sufficiently large quantities of the right quality and at the right time. On the other hand, by using different technologies small and medium-sized formal or informal enterprises may be able to exploit small amounts of resources, e.g. waste products, which would not be attractive to the large enterprise, small individual savings, which would not be available to the large enterprise, and laborers, who are not able or willing to offer their labor on the conditions offered or who have the wrong qualifications. Small enterprises, therefore, may also be able to survive by exploiting such small input markets which otherwise would lay idle.

Thus, there is no reason why enterprises of different sizes should not coexist when they do different things, use different resources, and serve different markets. In fact, product standardization and mass production technologies have not only led to large-scale production. They have also created their own need for small-scale production to fill niches in the demand which are not satisfied by the standardized products. As a consequence, the spatial market niches which were dominating in the early stages of industrialization have increasingly been substituted by technical and product niches. In the present-day developing countries, one of the problems is that we often attempt to provide them with highly standardized products which require both a spatially integrated market and the availability of niche production for situations where the standardized product does not work.

Recent experiences from both capitalist and socialist industrialized countries show that even here regions with production systems based on large-scale technologies alone are extremely vulnerable to changes in the economic system. In western Europe, some of the older industrial areas dominated by large-scale production (e.g. northern England, and some shipbuilding towns in Denmark) have run into serious trouble because they have not been able concurrently to renew their production systems when structural changes in the world economy made them obsolete. And in eastern Europe, where the small-scale sector has purposely been held back, it has increasingly been realized that high and increasing productivity cannot be achieved if the large-scale production is not supported by a differentiated small-scale sector.

The different specializations of the small and large enterprises mean that studies of scale economies based on the average productivity of small and large enterprises within broad sectors miss the point because they implicitly assume that small and large enterprises in a sector do the same things. Neither do the classical economic development theories take such specializations into account. Both the homogeneous product markets of liberal economic theory and the semi-monopolistic markets of Marxist theory basically describe markets for mass-produced standardized goods, and do not take into account the possibility of differentiated products and markets. A theory of the small/informal enterprise must specifically take these specializations, both between small and large enterprises and within the small-scale sector, into account, because it is these specializations which are the *raison d'être* of the small enterprise, rather than scale or informality.

5 A Network Approach to the Small Enterprise and its Environment

In a theory based on specialization between enterprises, the environment obviously has to play a larger role than in the classical theories that focus on large-scale production of standardized products. Where the classical theories describe the small enterprise as operating either in an environment of homogeneous commodity and labor markets or as part of (and completely dependent on) a large hierarchical monopolistic enterprise, more recent modifications to the theories often specify part of the environment, i.e. the innovative information network of the entrepreneur or the social network of him and his family. Thus new theories of the small enterprise increasingly describe the environment in terms of a much more specific, differentiated, and dynamic network, through which specialized commodities, labor, services, and information often flow; price is only one of many different determinants of the flow and through which learning processes are transmitted and enterprises adapt to each other.

On this common ground, a number of different but similar approaches to the understanding of the enterprise and its development have been emerging during the last 10–15 years (such as economic restructuring (Massey, 1984) and flexible production (also known as "the Italian model": Scott and Storper, 1988; Nielsen, 1988)). But the broadest approach and the one best suited to describe the role of small enterprise in the production system is what in Scandinavian literature is often called the network approach (Hägg and Johanson, 1982; Johanson and Mattson, 1986; Nord-ReFo, 1987).

The network theory sees the production system as a system of specialized enterprises linked to other enterprises (as customers or as producers of inputs, investment goods or services), consumers and workers by a network of commodity, person, and information flows. The specialized enterprises operate in different markets and use different technologies, resources, and labor qualifications. In so doing, the small enterprises rely not only on the economic network of enterprises, but also on the family and social network of the entrepreneur, and sometimes also of his employees. In fact, the small enterprise may be seen as suspended between the economic network of enterprises and the social network of the entrepreneur and his household.

5.1   The small enterprise as one of the reproductive activities of the household

The small enterprise and the household of the entrepreneur will often be highly integrated and thus difficult or impossible to distinguish empirically. To be able to understand the interaction between the enterprise and the household, however, we shall make this distinction. It is important because the enterprise has to be competitive on the market in order to survive, while the household need not survive on the market, but must command sufficient resources to reproduce itself.

The competitiveness of the enterprise, however, need not be based on technical efficiency; it may be due to resource transfers from the household or from government institutions. Also, the rules of the market need not be purely economic, but in general neither the enterprise nor the household will be able to change them, though they may evade them.

Usually, the entrepreneur and his household will provide the enterprise with capital, working time, and management and receive a profit in return. However, at times the household may have to subsidize the enterprise. The purpose of the enterprise will usually be to contribute to the reproduction of the household and to the accumulation of capital. The reproduction of the household may be secured by a combination of agricultural activities, wage labor in either the formal or the informal sector, government transfers (or taxation) or the family enterprise. The decision of a person or household to try to develop some "private or cooperative enterprise" depends partly on the possible alternatives and partly on the prospects for the new enterprise. For the urban household in the Third World, self-employment often will be the only alternative to wage labor in the formal sector. The small-enterprise sector, therefore, will tend to grow during depressions, when the large-scale sector contracts, even though the economic prospects of the small-scale sector also tend to be low. This is especially the case because many of the new entrepreneurs are likely to have very few qualifications and command few resources. Even in the developed countries, the small-scale sector tends to grow during depressions, though less rapidly than in the developing countries, because unemployment relief is a possible, though not attractive, alternative.

The resources that a person (or a household) commands not only depend on her (or its) own resources, but also on the access she (or it) has to resources of other households and to public resources in the form of, for example, resource allocations and contracts. Such access to other than one's own resources will often depend either on family and other social networks or on wage labor and the contacts which follow with it. Therefore, the structure of the small-enterprise sector will depend both on family structure and social organization and on the experience and incomes earned in the large-scale sector.

The family structure also influences the ability to accumulate. Where the successful entrepreneur in parts of Africa is met by customary obligations to support widespread family members, it may be very difficult to save enough to invest, even though in periods of crises the entrepreneur may expect to receive help from his family. However, in other parts of the world, the family organization rather operates as a mutual investment circle and thus tends to support the ability to accumulate. To a large extent this seems to be the case in China, and among the Indians in East Africa.

5.2 The strategies of large enterprises and their influence on the small

The conditions of the small enterprise will be set not only by the reproductive strategies of the entrepreneur's household, but also by the conditions and strategies of the larger, more capital-intensive enterprises with large fixed costs. These enterprises will have to attempt to secure for themselves large, stable markets and stable production conditions. To secure such stable conditions and to save capital, they often will externalize especially the simpler, less capital-intensive and more unstable production to smaller subcontractors and niche enterprises. Thus, the small enterprises are often burdened with relatively unstable markets and production conditions, and this is decisive for the structure and organization of small enterprises and for their demand for capital, technology and labor.

In many developing countries where the markets are limited, the large-scale enterprises are often not able to secure themselves a sufficiently large market. Therefore, they are often owned by state or parastatal companies, and in order to secure their markets, they are often granted almost monopoly status and favored with allocations of foreign currency and other scarce resources. Still, they are often operated with a very low capital utilization and have to be heavily subsidized. At the same time, such policies tend to aggravate the instability of the environment of the small enterprises because they will have much less access to the services and favors of the governmental bodies than the large enterprises and corporations. This especially holds true for peripheral regions.

During the very early industrialization of mercantilist Europe, a similar pattern was often found. Before 1850 many of the large-scale industries in Denmark were either state-owned or granted monopoly powers. Only gradually, as the level of industrialization increased and the market developed, did a more differentiated and integrated industrial structure develop, and then the process was supported by increasingly liberal economic policies.

5.3 The linkages between small and large enterprises

Many studies of the small-scale sector in developing countries now recognize the linkages between the small- and large-scale sectors (e.g. Freeman and Norcliffe, 1985). But most studies concentrate on the simple input–output linkages, and often see the small enterprises as subcontractors used by the larger enterprises and corporations to exploit cheap labor (see, for example, Portes, 1983; Acharya, 1983). However, studies from the developed countries (see, for example, Grøn, 1985; Pedersen, 1983) indicate that there are several other mechanisms of direct and indirect interaction between small and large enterprises. Although the cheap labor argument may be very important under certain conditions, it is always through the specific choices of products, markets, technology and labor qualifications that the exploitation of cheap labor becomes possible (see, for example, Storper, 1988).

The small enterprises usually will not operate in direct price competition with the large. Rather, the process of externalization will lead to market segregation and dependencies among the enterprises. In the case of subcontracting, this will be a direct dependency characterized by more or less regular flows of commodities or services between the enterprises. Who will dominate the relationship between the enterprises depends on the technology and qualifications necessary to fulfill the subcontract. Enterprises delivering commodities with many potential suppliers will be in a bad bargaining position and become dependent. On the other hand, enterprises delivering high-technology products with few potential suppliers tend to be in a strong bargaining position and may be dominating even though they are small. Large enterprises dependent on small, high-technology subcontractors will often attempt to buy them in order to control them.

In the case of niche enterprises, the dependency between large and small enterprises is rather an indirect one, operating through a process of market segregation, but not resulting in any commodity flow between the enterprises. Since dependency operates through the enterprises' choice of products, production technology and markets, the large enterprises will usually choose a combination of product, technology and market which secures them the largest, most stable part of the market. They will leave the smaller, less accessible and less stable niches in the market to other enterprises. Such niches may consist of small markets for highly specialized, high-quality products. This is the way niche industries are usually understood in the developed countries. On the other hand, they may also consist of low-income/peripheral markets with very low buying power and high distribution costs, which are too costly for the large enterprises to exploit. For small enterprises operating in such niches the risk is that if they become "too" successful in developing their market niche, it may become profitable for the large enterprise to change its product quality or marketing and attempt to invade the niche.

5.4   The strategies of the small enterprises

To survive in an uncertain market, small enterprises must choose a combination of technology and labor which makes them flexible. They can try to obtain this flexibility through two strategies:

- By using little fixed capital and an unskilled labor force which is easy to hire and fire. Flexibility is here obtained by reducing the cost of decreasing (closing) or increasing (reopening) production. This will be the case in most cottage industries and small household businesses based on family labor. Even rather large subcontracting enterprises with a simple production technique, e.g. in the textile industry, may also choose this strategy. They will often be operating in the informal sector and on the edge of the labor legislation. In small family enterprises, capital costs are often further reduced through self-financing and by treating investments as sunk costs which need not earn interest.

- By using a general-purpose technology and a skilled, more flexible labor force which can be used in more than one line of production. The more stable, and often more modern, small enterprises will typically attempt to follow such a strategy.

Thus, in general the small enterprises tend to be less capital-intensive than the large enterprises in their sector (e.g. Little, 1987). The uncertain production conditions in the small-scale sector tend to increase the risk to capital, and this is one of the reasons for the generally high interest rate paid to capital in the small enterprises. This further reduces their use of borrowed capital, and means that most of the capital in the small enterprises comes from personal savings (see, for example, Aboagye, 1986).

Small enterprises typically operate under strong competition, and even though they use relatively little capital, they must be able to compete. This competitiveness, however, might be obtained by paying lower wages, or by avoiding taxation and labor legislation rather than by being technically efficient. On the other hand, many investigations from the developing countries seem to indicate that the average income levels of small-scale entrepreneurs in general are not lower than the wages in the large-scale sector (see, for example, Lopez-Castaño, 1987; Aboagye, 1986; Fink, 1988, for similar results for Denmark at the beginning of the twentieth century). However, there are wide variations in income levels in the small-scale sector. Also, employment tends to be less stable, and thus annual income may be smaller even if the hourly wage is the same.

6   Conclusions

The picture which the network theories paint of the production system attempts to combine elements of the neoclassical market with elements of the Marxist dominance hierarchy. At the same time, it allows for an interaction between the enterprises, the social/family system, and the administrative/governmental system. It leads to a much more differentiated enterprise structure than the differentiation according to scale usually resorted to in the neoclassical theories, and the differentiation between petty commodity production and capitalist production which is used in most neo-Marxist theories.

The small enterprises are not seen as backward parts of the economy, but as specialized enterprises which in general have greater productivity than the large enterprise would have were it to supply the same small specialized market, or utilize the same resources. This of course does not mean that all small enterprises have high productivity, but the same is obviously true for large enterprises. Also, the small enterprises are not seen as passive victims to monopolistic practices of the large, but as more or less independent enterprises with strategies of their own to counteract the uncertainties enforced on them by their environment.

The interaction among the enterprises and between the enterprises and the state is seen to be much more differentiated and complex than in the classical theories, where the small enterprises are looked upon either as completely independent enterprises operating in free markets, or as completely dependent on the large enterprises or trusts and on state policy. Dependency between enterprises is determined not only by ownership and size, but by many other often qualitative factors such as technology, market, and financial relations. The small enterprises are considered as complementary to the large rather than alternative, and will often depend on one or more of the large enterprises. At the same time, the productivity of the large will often depend on the existence, not of a specific small enterprise, but of a network of small service and production enterprises. The small enterprise is operating in interaction with other small and large enterprises and public authorities in an interplay which in some situations may lead to dependency, but in others may lead to considerable autonomy (NordReFo, 1987; Johanson and Mattson, 1986).

The small enterprise also is part of the reproductive strategy of the entrepreneur and his household. The structure of the small enterprise, therefore, on the one hand depends on the alternative reproductive activities (e.g. wage labor, agricultural incomes, income transfers) available to them, and on the other hand on the resources they are able to command either directly or through their social and family network.

Policies based on modernization theory often attempt to make small enterprises grow big. Such policies of course may succeed in some cases, but in general they are likely to go wrong because the strength of the small enterprises is that they operate in small markets or utilize small resources which the large enterprises are not able to exploit economically. Therefore, policies to support small enterprises should attempt to increase their efficiency, and not necessarily make them grow. On the other hand policies based on dependency theory, which tend to focus on the reproductive functions of the small enterprises and often conceive of them as all having the same simple structure, go wrong because the small enterprises are highly specialized, though the specialization is often market or input specialization rather than a product specialization.

Only policies which recognize that the small enterprises are highly specialized and suspended in a complex network linking them both to the production hierarchy of large and small enterprises, and to the social and family networks of the entrepreneurs, are likely to succeed, because it is exactly by exploiting this complex network that the small enterprise succeeds at the individual level and at the same time becomes socially useful. Such a network theory of the small enterprise also explains why the small enterprise in some respects seems to follow a local development pattern linked to local practices and the expansion of the local market, and in others a national or international development trend linked to the economic, technological and political development of the world economy. Thus it may be the key to understanding the interaction between local and national/international development processes.

References

Aboagye, A.A., 1986. *Informal Sector Employment in Kenya: A Survey of Informal Sector Activities in Nairobi, Kisumu and Mombassa*, Jobs and Skills Programme for Africa, ILO, Addis Ababa.

Acharya, S., 1983. The Informal Sector in Developing Countries – A Macro Viewpoint. *Journal of Contemporary Asia*, Vol. 13, No. 4, pp. 432–445.

Bairoch, P., 1969. *Diagnostic de l'évolution économique du Tiers-Monde 1900–1968*, Gauthier-Villars, Paris.

Bairoch, P., 1975. *The Economic Development of the Third World since 1900*, University of California Press, Berkeley, Los Angeles.

Chuta, E., S.V. Sethuraman (eds.), 1984. *Rural Small-scale Industries and Employment in Africa and Asia*, ILO, Geneva.

Fink, J., 1988. Middelstand i klemme?, *Skrifter udgivet af Jysk Selskab for Historie*, No. 46, Århus.

Freeman, D.B., G.B. Norcliffe, 1985. Rural Enterprise in Kenya. Development and Spatial Organization of the Non-farm Sector. Research Paper No. 214, University of Chicago, Dept. of Geography, Chicago.

Grøn, J.H., 1985. *Arbejde-virksomhed-regioner – en analyse af arbejdsdelingen i industrien*, Sydjysk Universitetsforlag, Esbjerg.

Hansen, J.D., 1987. *Små og mellemstore virksomheder i Østasien*, CUF Notat, Centre for Development Research, Copenhagen.

Hansen, S.Å., 1983. *Økonomisk vækst i Danmark*, Vol. 2, 1914–1983, 3rd edn., Akademisk Forlag, Copenhagen.

Heierli, V., 1986. Division of Labour and Appropriate Technology from Adam Smith to E.F. Schumacher, in M. Bassand *et al.* (eds.), *Self-reliant Development in Europe*, Gower, Aldershot.

Hägg, I., J. Johanson (eds.), 1982. *Företag i nätverk*, SNS, Stockholm.

ILO, 1972. *Employment, Incomes and Equality – A Strategy for Increasing Production Employment in Kenya*, ILO, Geneva.

ILO, 1985. *Informal Sector in Africa*, ILO, Jobs and Skills Programme for Africa, Addis Ababa.

Johanson, J., L.-G. Mattson, 1986. Interorganizational Relations in Industrial Systems – A Network Approach Compared with the Transaction Cost Approach, *International Studies of Management and Organization*, Vol. 40, No. 2.

Kongstad, P., 1986. Work and Reproduction. How to Survive in Third World Countries, Working Paper No. 50, Institute of Geography, Socioeconomic Analysis and Computer Science, Roskilde University Centre, Roskilde.

Liedholm, C., D. Mead, 1987. Small Scale Industries in Developing Countries: Empirical Evidence and Policy Implications, MSU International Development Paper No. 9, Michigan State University, East Lansing.

Little, I.M.D., 1987. Small Manufacturing Enterprises in Developing Countries, *World Bank Economic Review*, Vol. 1, No. 2, pp. 203–235.

Lopez-Castaño, H., 1987. Secteur informel et société moderne: l'expérience colombienne, *Revue Tiers Monde*, Vol. 28, No. 110, pp. 369–394.

Massey, D., 1984. *Spatial Divisions of Labour, Social Structures and the Geography of Production*, Macmillan, London.

Mkandawire, T., 1986. The Informal Sector in the Labour Reserve Economics of Southern Africa with Special Reference to Zimbabwe, *African Development*, Vol. 11, No. 1, pp. 61–86.

Nattras, N., 1987. Street Trading in Transkei – A Struggle against Poverty, Persecution and Prosecution, *World Development*, Vol. 15, No. 7, pp. 861–875.

Nielsen, L.D., 1988. Flexibility – Between Economy and Local Labour Markets, *International Journal of Regional Science*, forthcoming.

NordReFo, 1987. *Regionalpolitik i en nätværksekonomi – en seminarierapport*, NordReFo, No. 4.

Peattie, L., 1987. An Idea in Good Currency and How It Grew: The Informal Sector, *World Development*, Vol. 15, No. 7, pp. 851–860.

Pedersen, P.O., 1983. *Vandringerne og den regionale udvikling – i et langsigtet perspektiv*, Sydjysk Universitetsforlag, Esbjerg.

Pedersen, P.O., 1989. The Role of Small Enterprises and Small Towns in the Developing Countries – and in the Developed?, CDR Project Paper 89.1, Centre for Development Research, Copenhagen.

Portes, A., 1983. The Informal Sector: Definition Controversy and Relation to National Development, *Review*, Vol. 7, No. 1, pp. 151–174.

Scott, A.J., M. Storper, 1988. The Geographical Foundations and Social Regulations of Flexible Production Complexes, in M. Dear, J. Wolch (eds.), *The*

Power of Geography, Winchester, Massachusetts.

Sethuraman, S.V., 1981. *The Urban Informal Sector in Developing Countries*, ILO, Geneva.

Storper, M., 1988. Industrialization and Regional Development in the Third World: Prospects of Post-Fordism, Paper presented at the conference of the International Sociological Association, Research Committee on Sociology of Urban and Regional Development, 26–30 Sept., Rio de Janeiro.

Part II

Innovative Local Districts and Milieus

6

The Innovation Process and the Role of the Milieu

Denis Maillat*

1 Introduction

For some time now the discussion of the mechanisms and origin of regional development has been evolving considerably. The usual models (polarization, spatial division of labor, endogenous development, etc.) have lost part of their ability to explain phenomena. The trend is increasingly towards a theory of milieu-initiated dynamism which combines internal regional impulses and external impulses.

This development is of course due to the modification of the predominant paradigms and the role small and medium-size enterprises (SMEs) have regained. Indeed, today the Fordian paradigm is opposed by the flexible production paradigm (Sabel, 1988; Freeman, 1987). The 1960s saw the development of research work stressing the predominant role of the large company and the multinational groups in the functioning of the industrial countries' economies. The emphasis was placed on the Fordian organization of labor, the spatial division of functions and the opposition between central and peripheral regions. Since the end of the 1970s, the increase in the number of small businesses and their substantial contribution to job creation have led to a revival of the discussion of new forms of production organization and regional development mechanisms.

Aydalot had sensed this trend when he addressed the problem from the angle of "reversal". He wrote: "Although the indicators have, since the nineteen seventies, been showing a continuation of the convergence of income levels between the regions, this process is no longer due, as it was

---

*Institut de Recherches Economiques et Regionales (IRER), University of Neuchâtel, Switzerland.

in the sixties, to the extension of effects originating from rich regions to the whole territory, but to the specific dynamism of peripheral regions" (Aydalot, 1985).

The functional logic of the large company, which led to the spatial fragmentation of production and to the spatial division of labor, has today declined in importance. The territorial logic is better able to account for the development certain regions are undergoing thanks to the innovation and dynamism generated by the milieu, since territorial structures have been remodelled not from outside but from within.

Thus there exists a development logic which starts from the milieus. They are regarded as the source of innovation. According to this approach, the innovating company does not pre-date the local milieus, it is secreted by them (Aydalot, 1986; Matteaccioli and Peyrache, 1989).

The various GREMI[1] teams wished to re-examine this problem and to try to test it. The main objective of their research work was as follows: to what extent does a technological break, evaluated by the launch of a new product by SMEs, constitute an opportunity for the region under consideration to restructure, strengthen the local fabric, accentuate complementarities, create new local networks, or, on the contrary, to what extent does it involve fragmentation, a loss of substance or autonomy to the benefit of multispatial integration (Maillat and Perrin, 1991)?

The idea was thus to pinpoint the factors which, in the innovative process, strengthen or restructure the local fabric or, as appropriate, cause it to fragment. In the course of this process enterprises may be required to set up local networks and to strengthen their proximity-based links or, on the contrary, to break the logic of existing local networks and to provoke (accentuate) their openness to non-local areas.

In order to answer these questions, the GREMI teams conducted surveys on the basis of a joint questionnaire in various regions. In each case the surveys were carried out on about twenty small or medium-sized enterprises (firms with a single establishment or a main establishment with local general management) employing less than 200–250 workers. The firms were selected in such a way that about two-thirds were derived from the sectoral tradition dominant in the area, while the others might have been the result of a transplant, that is, an enterprise implanted in the

---

[1]The European Research Group on Innovating Areas (GREMI) is composed of about twenty European and North American research units which have come together to study the processes of technological innovation in a regional context. The group's broad approach can be summarized as: the innovative firm is not a predetermined entity within a local milieu, but is generated by the latter, with innovative behavior dependent upon variables determined at a local or regional level.

region, might have been created recently and did not originate from the local specialization.

It was logical that the firms surveyed should be SMEs, because in the light of the initial hypotheses, one could assume that on account of their size these firms rely more on their milieu than large enterprises.

The various regions

The surveys were not, *a priori*, carried out in milieus regarded as innovative but in a variety of regions (nine in Europe, one in the United States). The regions surveyed belong to three main groups: slightly industrialized (Nice, Ticino, Poitou-Charente); industrialized (Bergamo, the Jura Arc, Wallonia) and metropolitan (southern Ile-de-France, Aix-en-Provence in the Marseilles metropolitan area, Silicon Valley and the north of the Milan area). In some cases the region studied is relatively autonomous (the Jura Arc, Ticino, Wallonia, Silicon Valley); in others, it is part of a more integrated territorial complex (in the case of the metropolitan areas). These different geographical situations influence the behavior of the milieus studied and that of the enterprises located there. Thus what constitutes internal (external) links in the case of "autonomous" regions does not necessarily do so in the "metropolitan" regions. This diversity of the zones studied has highlighted the multiple and varied relations between innovative companies and their milieus.

The results are sometimes ambiguous. This is due not only to the nature of the regions and/or of the enterprises, but also to the way the surveys' results are interpreted. However, it has been possible to shed light on innovative processes, to give an operational definition of the milieu and to propose a methodological approach to analyzing the links between the enterprise and the milieu.

2 The Innovation Process

2.1 Types of innovation

In order to facilitate selection of the enterprises, only those which have developed new products were selected (about twenty in each region). It is quite obvious that product innovation generally does not take place without process innovation or even without innovation affecting a firm's overall organization. The various surveys reveal this quite clearly. However, the key selection proved to be relevant, as it is certain that product innovation does not take place in isolation: it presupposes impulses that are external to the firm.

The innovations which have been identified are only rarely concerned with a perfectly new product (radical innovation). In most cases they are "adaptive" innovations (a substantial improvement on an existing product such as the introduction of an electronic function to a mechanical machine-tool) or "incremental" innovations (a small improvement to a product by the firm itself).

Generally speaking, the introduction of a new product is part of a strategy designed to ensure the growth or revival of the firm. It also originates from the determination to exploit the firm's technological potential or from the perception of new market requirements. The introduction of a new product therefore appears as a continuous (formal or informal) learning process designed to ensure the continuity and renewal of the firm. It is a state of mind which obliges the company to be constantly on the alert, i.e. constantly seeking information (evaluation of competitors, markets, new technologies, etc.) if it wants to maintain its competitive advantage. It should be noted that in many cases the sampled firms' strategy does not consist of ensuring their competitiveness by cutting the price of their product but rather of personalizing it, upgrading quality and maintaining their technological lead. This is one of the reasons which urges them to maintain numerous formal and informal contacts with their customers and environment.

2.2   The innovative process

Innovation is a complex process comprising several stages. It presupposes collaboration and successful linkage of complementary functions: fundamental research, applied research, development, preparation of prototypes, industrial investments, putting into production, marketing and adaptation of production to the market (Planque and Py, 1986). It is not a matter of claiming that this upstream–downstream process is linear, but of showing that it encompasses several aspects, several stages and thus multiple entry points. The factor triggering innovation is thus not necessarily upstream or downstream, it can appear at any stage (Maillat *et al.*, 1988). For methodological reasons it is this upstream–downstream scheme which was selected for designing the interview guidelines. The object of the survey was to highlight the relative importance of the internal and external sources which help to trigger the decision to innovate in the four main stages of the innovative process: the stages of product design, product development, manufacturing and marketing.

Whichever stage is selected, the motivation which leads to innovation incorporates elements which derive from within (internal component) and from outside the firm (external component). The enterprise is in fact an organization which is open to its environment. In general, innovation pushes it to open up to the outside world both upstream and downstream, which exposes the nature of the links it maintains with the latter.

The internal component corresponds to a supply logic sometimes neglecting the market. It aims to enhance the value of knowledge specific to the enterprise, its know-how and R&D capacities, or corresponds to the desire to keep pace with technology. The external component comprises elements which help to trigger innovation from outside the firm (customers, suppliers, consultants, newspapers, specialized journals, research laboratories, etc.). It relates to a demand logic.

In reality, innovation results from the combination and interaction of these two components. The relative importance of one rather than the other illustrates the different strategies pursued by companies. The external component in particular allows the firm to link up to its environment and to understand the latter's influence on the innovative process. In the particular case it was indispensable to draw a distinction between the internal and external components of the firm, since it was necessary to determine the role of the milieu in innovation.

Role of the internal component

The internal component appears to be fundamental for most of the firms surveyed. Thus it is primarily within its own walls that the enterprise finds the ferments of innovation. The know-how acquired by the enterprise or entrepreneur in the course of time plays a crucial role in this respect. Although representing a break with the past, innovation is integrated into the firm's activities, as it originates from exploitation of the know-how it has acquired. This fact stresses once again that the transfer of technological knowledge is not easy and that it implies a receptive element within the company (Foray, 1988). Moreover, the surveys confirm that product innovation cannot be improvised and that if it is to thrive it needs to find elements of continuity within the company.

The importance of the internal component naturally varies according to the different stages of the innovative process. It may be said that its role is more important in the upstream stages than in the downstream stages. This is particularly the case during the stages of product design, development, and preparation of the prototype. These results confirm – should this be necessary – that the epicenter of the innovation process lies within the company (technological knowledge, know-how, etc.) although it is pointless to deny the existence of external incentives or contributions (Camagni and Rabelotti, 1988).

Role of the external component

The external contributions are generally to be found in the stages down-stream of the innovation process: customers, suppliers and competitors play a decisive role. It is certain, for example, that perception of market potential is just as important as the desire to exploit a firm's technological abilities.

Thus we should avoid getting caught up in a dichotomous interpretation of innovation according to which the latter would originate either from the firm's technical abilities (supply logic) or from market signals (demand logic). In reality, situations are less clearcut. In particular, the idea elaborated and managed technically by the firm or by its research structure is nourished by more or less direct and informal stimuli from the market (Camagni and Rabelotti, 1988). Quevit and Bodson (1988) place great emphasis on this aspect of a company's relations with the environment. In their view, the triad of company–customer–supplier seems to be one of the main vectors of the corporate innovation process. It is the area of strategic interaction whence emerges not only the perception of a new need and/or of a new market opportunity, but also the innovation process itself.

For Senn and Bramanti (1988), although it is possible to distinguish two main groups of companies – those which derive ideas and suggestions from their market relations, and those which find design and production elements within their firm – it is nevertheless true that in most cases innovation is the result of a dynamic which is both internal and external, as a firm adapts its own resources and know-how to external requirements, in conjunction with its market.

Therefore, the enterprise cannot dominate all the elements of the innovative process. A strong internal component assures its control of its specific know-how. But in view of the speed of development it has to rely, at all stages of the innovative process, on outside skills. It therefore needs to identify these outside links, and to specify their importance and nature. It is possible to divide these links into two main categories: market-related links and non-market-related links. Through the networks they form, both of them are evolving towards a new form of interdependence between companies and between companies and their environment.

3   Types of Links and Spatial Proximity of External Contributions

3.1   Market links and non-market links

Market-related links (and the commercial transactions they imply) do not necessarily result in a balance of power between the company, customers and suppliers. Owing to the instability of technologies, market competition, the shorter life cycle of products, etc. firms are compelled to cooperate in the various stages of the innovative process. These forms of cooperation and exchanges of the partnership or co-production type are an expression of new forms of relations and interdependence which firms are setting up among themselves during the innovative process.

Although in the surveys the firms give clear replies on their market-related links, they are vaguer on non-market-related links (Maillat and Perrin, 1991). Since ambience phenomena are involved here, it is naturally more difficult to evaluate their importance and situate them in relation to the various stages of the innovative process.

Thus the various elements of the scientific and technical environment (research centers, universities, engineering schools, etc.) do not seem to have any obvious direct effects. In any case they are not emphasized by the firms which took part in the surveys, even in the product design stage.

However, the scientific and technical environment should not be neglected. As a center of knowledge and training, the university has a synergetic effect on engineering, technical and managerial staff through informal-type relations. In addition, the know-how and vocational experience contained in a region's technical culture through its labor market are determining factors in innovation patterns (Matteaccioli and Peyrache, 1989).

In sum, an analysis of innovative processes reveals new forms of interdependence which are expressed through market-related links and, to a lesser extent, non-market-related links. The question now is to determine the degree of proximity between the company and the various elements of the external component.

3.2   The degree of spatial proximity of external contributions

In most of the surveys the degree of spatial proximity of external contributions was determined in relation to the following areas: local, regional, national and international. "Outside" can thus be near or distant.

Innovative companies do not seem to find the information they need to define the characteristics of their new products in their immediate (local) environment (Quevit and Bodson, 1988; Senn and Bramanti, 1988; Camagni and Rabelotti, 1988). It follows that in several cases the local environment as a vector of innovation appears to be weak. For example, in the Milan area 72% of technical studies or market research surveys are carried out within the company, Italy and the Milan metropolitan area contribute 20%, while 8% of firms resort to local firms of consultants. The results are more or less similar in the Poitiers area (Guesnier and Strawczyski, 1988).

Moreover, enterprises often have the impression that their innovative activity has not helped to modify their integration into the local environment (Senn, 1988). One even has the feeling that the SMEs are not aware of the richness of their milieu and/or that they do not seek to take advantage of it (Tabaries and Peyrache, 1988). However, although an initiative taken within a firm has, initially, little effect on the local milieus, one must be wary of making a final judgment, as the technological break created by product innovation leads the head of the firm to get in touch with the local networks even if they are relatively discrete and, consequently, to stimulate their development (Guesnier and Strawczyski, 1988). One thing is certain, however: a firm's market area is rarely local, except in the metropolitan areas, where it is of significant importance. The results of the GREMI surveys confirm the tendency of innovative firms to broaden their market, not only to the national area but also to the international arena.

3.3 Spatial proximity of external contributions depending on innovation types

It is important to underline that the role of the local environment and consequently that of the external contributions of proximity depend upon the types and strategies of innovation.

Senn and Bramanti (1988), for example, note that links with the local environment correlate with the degree of innovation characterizing new products. The least innovative companies (those which come up with incremental-type product innovations) have few connections with the local environment, whereas the other categories have more. This amounts to saying that the less a firm is capable of generating internal skills, the more it depends on the distant environment to initiate an innovative process.

The results are also interesting when one assesses relations with the environment as a function of innovation strategies: exploitation of a technological trajectory and technology creation (Perrin, 1988; Tabaries and Peyrache, 1988).

In the first case, innovation is to be seen "as the process of adapting and disseminating a pre-existing technology". In the second case, innovation is to be conceived of as "the process of creating some new way of producing and consuming, where this process was not known *a priori* but emerges en route".

These strategies imply two types of relations with the territorial environment: the strategies of exploiting a technological trajectory which prevailed during the decades of growth amounted to regarding the territorial milieu as an external datum whence the firm derived its inputs. On the other hand, the technological upheaval we are witnessing today obliges enterprises to reconsider their relationship with the territory, at least for those which innovate on a large scale. Indeed, the creation of technologies presupposes that the environment becomes an essential component of innovation, that these various resources be used and combined to generate a new form of localized production organization. The enterprise is then no longer isolated in a territory which represents to it only an external component, it helps to create its environment by setting up a network of partnership-style relations, both with other firms (subcontractors, customers, suppliers) and with public or private training and research centers, technology transfer centers and local authorities (Gaffard, 1987; Perrin, 1988). According to Tabaries and Peyrache (1988), it would appear that enterprises having a technology creation strategy are more willing to resort to local partners and ones in the rest of the country to design their innovations than those which exploit a trajectory. At the same time, they resort less often to foreign partners than the others. For development, the two types of enterprise have the same behavior. As regards their information channels, firms engaged in technology creation are more willing to use external channels than the others: "on the one hand, these SMEs are more open to the outside world with regard to the various sources of information needed to innovate and on the other they use partners from the milieu more often than the others to design innovation" (Tabaries and Peyrache, 1988, p. 12).

Again it should be noted that innovation has more often enabled these firms to create new local networks and to feel supported by their environment. Therefore they are in general better integrated into their milieu or are in the process of becoming integrated, although their market is more frequently international than that of firms exploiting a technological trajectory. Thus firms which follow a technology creation strategy seem to have more links with their local environment, but the difference only becomes clear at the innovation design stage. These same enterprises contribute more to creating local networks than the others.

These results are partly corroborated by the example of Ticino. Ratti and d'Ambroglio (1988) note that the firms in the "trajectory development" category are all characterized by a low number of local links. On the other hand, firms classified in the "technology creation" category have more local links. The results relating to the Poitou-Charente region are slightly more qualified (Guesnier and Strawczyski, 1988). Although in that region innovative firms are characterized by a relatively low degree of integration into the local milieu, it may be noted that those which exploit a technological trajectory seem to utilize the area's marketing research and services. On the other hand, firms which follow a technology creation strategy resort to external service companies to the extent that they must prospect distant markets. The results are inverted when one considers the geographical origin of suppliers of new equipment. Whereas firms exploiting a technological trajectory turn to suppliers outside of the area for new equipment, it is the opposite for firms which have implemented a technology creation process.

This classification on the basis of two opposing concepts does not always produce very clear results, since both Perrin's and Ratti's work reveals an intermediate category between the creation strategy and the trajectory strategy. The reference to the territorial milieu is often significant for this intermediate category (Ratti and d'Ambroglio, 1988).

In fact, the surveys do not formally demonstrate that technology creation is accompanied by greater integration of firms into local networks and/or that trajectory development makes this integration less necessary (Tabaries and Peyrache, 1988).

The problems identified by Ratti and d'Ambroglio also allow us to gauge the degree of spatial proximity of external contributions. They distinguish between the market area, the production area, and the support area. As we have already noted, the market area is broadly non-local. On the other hand, that is not the case for the other two areas. The production area is defined by all the firm's relations with external establishments – whether or not they are integrated into the firm – in which certain production segments or suppliers of raw materials or components are located.

Two-thirds of the firms have production relations at the local level and in the border zone. The proportion of this subcontracting work varies between 2.5 percent and 25 percent of sales. Furthermore, Ratti and d'Ambroglio believe that this strategy helps to create local networks. This trend is confirmed when one considers the support area. This is made up of all the material or non-material resources liable to support the firm in its task of organizing a complex process of producing and selling goods and services. The results of the analysis are interesting: of 452 links identified, 90 concern the internal component, 142 concern the local level (Ticino and border regions), 114 concern the rest of Switzerland and 106 are located abroad.

Ratti's analysis demonstrates that the links which the innovative enterprise maintains with its immediate environment are more important than is generally supposed. Moreover, these firms seek to put in place high-performance local networks. However, the analysis does not indicate whether or not these links are crucial for the innovative process. All these attempts increase our knowledge of the role of external links in the corporate innovation process. Nevertheless the results of the analyses leave a certain ambiguity about the role of the environment in general and the close environment in particular.

4   The Role of the Milieu in the Innovation Process

Most of the surveys mention the importance of factors of spatial proximity such as external factors, the fertility of the environment, local synergies, etc. But, paradoxically, in trying to pinpoint the innovation-promoting factors in the milieu, results have been obtained which in many respects minimize the proximity-based links. In fact, it turns out that it does not suffice to take the firm as the starting point to understand what factors in its close environment contribute to innovation. With the problem posed in such terms, the firm appears as an "isolated" element which draws on its close or distant environment in accordance with its needs. Now in reality the enterprise belongs to a territorial system; it is but one of the links in that system (Maillat and Perrin, 1991).

4.1   The milieu as a constituted complex

If we wish to shape a theory of local dynamism, we must specify the role of the milieu. It is the milieu, not the enterprise, on which the analysis must focus. From there we should determine the extent to which the milieu generates and maintains an innovation process.

The milieu must be envisaged in such a manner that it has a significant action on the manner of giving life to the innovation process. The milieu is not a warehouse from which one obtains supplies, it is a complex which is capable of initiating a synergetic process. From this point of view the milieu cannot be defined merely as a geographical area, it must be envisaged as an organization, a complex system made up of economic and technological interdependencies. In our view, the concept of milieu refers to a coherent whole in which a territorial production system, a technical culture and protagonists are linked. The coherence between the different protagonists lies in a common mode of apprehending situations, problems and opportunities. The spirit of enterprise, organizational practices, corporate behavior patterns, ways of using technology, apprehending the market and know-how are both an integral and constituent part of the milieu (Maillat, 1988).

The milieu is characterized not only by the nature of the interdependencies but also by their quality (partnership, subcontracting) and through their complex forms of structuring (retroactive and reciprocity effects). The time frame is essential when considering the duration of the processes of building up and decomposing the milieus, but also to take into account the technical culture, know-how, the labor market, and all the non-material characteristics which are determining elements of local dynamism in the long term (Matteaccioli and Peyrache, 1989; Maillat *et al.*, 1988).

4.2 Innovation and milieu

Innovation originates from putting information into contact with resources (capital, skills, spirit of enterprise, creativity). Now, the milieu is a complex made up of resources (Stöhr, 1986). The latter may be generated by the milieu itself or come from the outside. The notion of milieu does not, *a priori*, refer to a geographical unit, rather it corresponds to the notion of an analytical framework having an inside and an outside, where priority is given to what is going on inside. From this perspective, the role of the company's internal component is not denied, but it is assumed that the behavior patterns, strategies and ways of pooling resources are a function of the milieu. The degree of integration of companies in the milieu depends on the way it is organized and the resources it offers to trigger or maintain the process of innovation.

This reversal of perspective which consists of focusing the analysis on the milieu as a constituted complex implies identifying the external links which have a determining influence on the innovative process and which help to structure the local sphere. In this case, a link will be regarded as determining if partnership-type relations are involved (requiring a certain degree of collaboration) and as trivial in the case of subcontracting that does not entail any form of cooperation. Market-related links or non-market-related links may be involved.

On the basis of this methodology the survey in the Jura Arc was carried out (Maillat *et al.*, 1988). Depending on whether or not the resources utilized by the firms during their innovation process belong to the regional milieu, it is possible to place them in categories ranging from non-integrated into the milieu to very strongly integrated.

There are of course several forms of integration into the milieu, and firms may very well innovate without using the resources of the regional milieu. However, it should be pointed out that more than three-quarters of the innovative firms surveyed in the sample have strong regional integration and that the latter is accompanied by significant links with the outside world (Maillat *et al.*, 1988). These are the firms which help to make a milieu dynamic. They belong to two different categories.

The first one is constituted by large companies operating primarily in electronics-related fields. For them, innovation consists above all of incorporating new technical performances into their products in line with technological development. In this sense they do not produce new technologies but remain in the vanguard in their application sector. The links they develop with the milieu are primarily based on scientific and technological relations. They may be describe as "science-based" and said to form, so to speak, the technical core in the milieu. Outside the milieu the relations maintained are mainly with their customers in that their production requires this type of collaboration, but also with specialized research institutes with which they collaborate.

The second category contains essentially local SMEs. The nature of their relations with the milieu differs in that they do not maintain any scientific or technical links with the milieu. Rather they are attached to it by traditional know-how and by the origin of the firm's head. In addition, they "consume" the services offered to companies by the milieu. Their capital structure is often of the family type and in some cases one can observe the presence of private capital and local venture capital.

5   Conclusions

Our analysis has shown that firms require resources from the milieu in order to innovate. But the milieu is not a simple warehouse. It is its organization that gives rise to the opportunities for innovation. It means that to stimulate innovation the milieu combines two characteristics: the interdependence of the elements located in it and the degree of extroversion (Maillat *et al.*, 1988; Senn and Bramanti, 1988).

Integration of the elements of the milieu favors the formation of a coherent whole. These characteristics retroact on the integration process and reinforce it. This integration process also increases the intensity of the relations and complementarities between the economic functions and the various local protagonists. Thus formal networks and informal relations take shape, emanating synergetic effects which enable firms to come up with innovative processes.

The integration between the firms within the milieu does not exclude integration of the firms in extra-territorial groups. Technological progress necessarily involves relations between the milieu and the other spheres. The milieu is at one and the same time open to "circulating information" and closed to "structural information". The milieu is open to "circulating" information on, in particular, scientific and technical knowledge, and on markets, which in today's world are often international. Without being open to the outside world from which the milieu and the firms integrated there draw new energy and information, the milieu and the firms cannot exist or at least they cannot develop. But at the same time the milieu is closed to "structural information" in the sense that it is a coherent sphere organized around its material and non-material structures (Matteaccioli and Peyrache, 1989).

When the milieu succeeds in reconciling openness (acceptance of new ideas which trigger innovation) and closure (coherence of the socio-economic fabric) it is able to stimulate and support the creativity of firms and, in return, to be enriched by the innovation they achieve.

References

Aydalot, P., 1985. *Economie régionale et urbaine*, Economica, Paris.

Aydalot, P. (ed.), 1986. *Milieux innovateurs en Europe*, GREMI, Paris.

Aydalot, P., D. Keeble (eds.), 1988. *High Technology Industry and Innovative Environments*, Routledge, London, New York.

Camagni, R., R. Rabellotti, 1988. *Knowledge Inputs and Information Channels in the Innovation Process: The Case of Milan*, Colloque GREMI II, Ascona.

Foray, D., 1988. *Industrial Dynamics and Technical Research: Toward a New Economic Representation. Theories and Policies of Technological Development at the Local Level*, Arco.

Freeman, C., 1987. Le défi des technologies nouvelles, in OCDE (ed.), *Interdépendance et coopération dans le monde de demain*, OCDE, Paris.

Gaffard, J.-L., 1987. *La création de technologie. Stratégies d'entreprises et politiques publiques*, Latapses-CNRS, Sophia-Antipolis.

Guesnier, B., S. Strawczyski, 1988. *L'intégration des PME innovatrices dans la région Poitou-Charente*, Colloque GREMI, Ascona.

Hansen, N., 1989. *Innovative Regional Milieux, Small Firms, and Regional Development: Evidence from Mediterranean France*, Department of Economics, University of Texas, Austin.

Maillat, D., 1984. Mobility Channels: An Instrument for Analysing and Regulating the Local Labor Market, *International Labor Review*, Vol. 123, No. 3, pp. 349–362.

Maillat, D., J.-C. Perrin (eds.), 1991. *Entreprises innovatrices et réseaux locaux*, ERESA-Economica, Paris (forthcoming).

Maillat, D., J.-Y. Vasserot, 1986. Les milieux innovateurs, le cas de l'Arc Jurassien suisse, in P. Aydalot (ed.), *Milieux innovateurs en Europe*, GREMI, Paris, pp. 217–246.

Maillat, D., J.-Y. Vasserot, 1988. Economic and Territorial Conditions for Indigenous Revival in Europe's Industrial Regions, in P. Aydalot, D. Keeble (eds.), _High Technology Industry and Innovative Environments_, Routledge, London, New York, pp. 163–183.

Maillat, D., O. Crevoisier, J.-Y. Vasserot, 1988. _L'apport du milieu dans le processus d'innovation: le cas de l'Arc Jurassien suisse_, Colloque GREMI II, Ascona.

Matteaccioli, A., V. Peyrache, 1989. Milieux et réseaux innovateurs: synthèse sous l'angle de la complexité, _Cahiers du C3E_ 78, Paris.

Perrin, J.-C., 1988. Nouvelles technologies et développement régional: l'analyse des milieux innovateurs, _Notes de recherche du CER_ 94, 95.

Planque, B., B. Py, 1986. La dynamique de l'insertion des PME innovatrices dans leur environnement, _Notes de recherche du CER_ 68.

Quevit, M., S. Bodson 1988. _L'entreprise innovatrice dans son environnement local, le cas de la Région de Liège_, Colloque GREMI II, Ascona.

Ratti, R., F. d'Ambroglio, 1988. _Processus d'innovation et intégration au milieu local: le cas du Tessin_, Colloque GREMI, Ascona.

Sabel, C., 1988. _The Reemergence of Regional Economics_, Centro d'Estudios de Planificación, Barcelona.

Senn, L., A. Bramanti, 1988. _Le cas de Bergame_, Colloque GREMI II, Suisse, Ascona.

Stöhr, W., 1986. Territorial Innovation Complexes, in P. Aydalot (ed.), _Milieux innovateurs en Europe_, GREMI, Paris, pp. 29–56.

Tabaries, M., V. Peyrache, 1988. _L'insertion locale des PMI innovatrices en Ils-de-France Sud_, Colloque GREMI, Ascona.

7

Local Networks, Innovation and Policy in Italian Industrial Districts

Gioacchino Garofoli*

1 Recent Patterns of Regional Development in Europe

During the last 10–15 years there has been a substantial reversal of the core–periphery relations in Europe. This trend inversion in location patterns of industries involves a shift from increasing spatial concentration of production (typical of development during the 1950s and 1960s) to a new territorial diffusion of the industrialization process. This phenomenon has neither produced a reduction in regional disequilibria in the European Community as a whole nor in the different countries, because depressed regions have meantime met new problems of transformation and development. Intermediate regions (almost everywhere in Europe) have experienced an improvement in industrial employment, compared with a reduction of employment in most developed regions. Almost everywhere this development has been accompanied by the crisis of big firms and a new role for small firms.

This phenomenon has been studied in various countries and different interpretations have been proposed. In any case, the change is very clear in Italy where some scholars have advanced a new interpretation of the core–periphery relation; their view stresses the degree of autonomy in the

*Università di Pavia, Dipartimento di Economia Politica e Metodi Quantitativi. A previous draft of the paper has been presented at the European Summer Institute of RSA on "Theories and Policies of Technological Development at the Local Level", Arco (Trento), Italy, 17–23 July 1988.

development in intermediate regions and the new organization of production, based mainly on interfirm relations. At the beginning, interpretations arising in other countries such as France or Great Britain were different. There it was considered the consequence of a decentralization of production and "branch-circuit" organization with a new form of "dependency" between the periphery and the central areas (cf. Lipietz, 1980; Damette, 1980).

On the basis of these changes, it is possible now to understand the real crisis of central and more developed regions, whose development was organized on the crucial role of big firms and of mass urbanization. At the same time it is possible to discover new forms of development in intermediate regions. New patterns of development are arising there that are different from those followed in advanced regions. In these cases, indeed, small firms and new entrepreneurship play a crucial role, yielding a process of "diffuse development" which is characterized by lack of strong urbanization, a co-presence of small firms and small towns, and a specific social structure, not so dichotomized as in the regions with big firms and a more ancient process of development.

The backward regions in various countries, especially in southern Europe, have not changed their position. They bore the problems of economic crisis without enjoying, at least until now, opportunities of new forms of development. These new patterns of regional development have arisen, on the one hand, by a specific combination of endogenous as well as exogenous factors linked to the relationship between the local and the international economic system. On the other hand, these phenomena led to dramatically changed interpretations of the spatial articulation of production. The new patterns of regional development have caused, for example, a "breakdown" of the dualistic paradigm, with the opposition of center and periphery. At the same time it has shown the explanatory inadequacy of the "filtering down theory" (Thompson, 1968; Berry, 1973). According to the latter theory, industrial relocation traces in space the path of a new product life cycle, with the progressive movement of standardized products toward the periphery. Both the dualistic paradigm and the filtering down theory consider territory as a passive framework in the process of development. The crucial factors of change are exogenous to the local and regional economic and social system. There is no opportunity for an autonomous process of development.

The new regional patterns of development have very often been considered strictly linked with a substantial change in the mode of organization of production which was realized during the 1970s with a progressive crisis of the Fordist pattern and the increasing role of flexible specialization (Piore and Sabel, 1984). Following the French school of regulation, the Fordist pattern of organization of production is determined by the combination of Taylorism and Keynesian state and is based on mass production, in which economies are obtained within the production process through fixed capital and increases in labor productivity. Standardized products (with long run production) are fabricated by use of monopurpose machinery and semi-skilled workers, performing fragmented and standardized tasks. The prevailing form of the market is oligopolistic and management of the economy is organized at the national level, especially with the goal to offset the immanent tendency to over-production. Finally, competition among firms is carried out through full capacity utilization and cost cutting.

The flexible specialization model instead is based on flexible automation: economies are obtained through working capital productivity increases. Differentiated products, with small batch production, are fabricated using, mainly, general or multi-purpose machinery and skilled workers, with close integration of mental and manual tasks. The products are very specialized for niche markets. Competition is combined with cooperative links among firms: the horizontal integration of production is based, in fact, on thick networks among firms and subcontracting relations, all of which leads to "just in time" organization. The forms of social regulations are mainly established at local level, with an important role for specific local institutions. Competition among firms is mainly carried out through innovation and the production of new products. The response of the organization system to falling markets is very flexible and is carried out through diversification of production, innovation, subcontracting, and lay-offs. Clearly with the second pattern of organization of production the role of local social forces is quite important and the opportunity arises for autonomous processes of development at local and regional level.

2   Territory and Local Patterns of Development

In Italy and in other European countries the new patterns of regional development have obliged economists and other social scientists to pay more attention to the relationship between economic development and territory, looking at the specific characteristics of local patterns of development.

This attention is not only the result of the differentiation of local economic situations or the emergence of new forms of industrialization and development, but above all it is a consequence of the crisis of the "functionalist paradigm" of development which considered space simply as coordinates that mark the place where the effects of the process of general development occurred. Or in other words, the place where "forces and economic functions occur, which as a consequence of their internal logic define the activities' location and hence the structure and hierarchy of economic regions" (Pecqueur, 1987, p. 85).

For some time territorially concentrated polarized development and the diffusion of development "from above" have been the dominant theoretical basis for development strategies and regional policies. Development was made possible by the continuous expansion of large-scale industry, prevalently localized in large urban centers since the type of technological innovation, economic policies and the development of infrastructure allowed the formation of large-scale economies and growing external economies (Garofoli, 1983d, 1984a, 1987). The development policy based on the model of "big business" (by implicitly relying on mechanisms of income multiplier and new economic linkages) characterized the greater part of government interventions for a number of decades, both in developed and developing countries.

In the last 10–15 years the growing inability of the functionalist model to explain a more complex redistribution of productive activities over territory and the emergence of autonomous patterns of development in intermediate regions have progressively attracted the attention of scholars to the territorial dimension of development and to the categories of environment (or "milieu") and territory. Territory is seen as the "sedimentation" of specific and interrelated historical, social, and cultural factors in local areas, which directly generate different processes of development.

These considerations lead us to a new paradigm for the research of economic development mainly based on territory, a paradigm which has also been called "development from below" (Stöhr, 1978, 1981, 1984). During the late 1970s and the early 1980s, the literature on endogenous and "self-centered" development,[1] on territorial and "agro-politan" development (Friedmann and Douglass, 1975; Friedmann and Weaver, 1979), and on the mobilization of "indigenous potential" (CCE, 1981), etc. began to increase notably at an international level.

The end result of these varied reformulations of the problem of development has been above all a different concept of space held by economists: space is not only the distance between different places, something which conditions the exchange of goods and is a source of cost for economic agents, as in the traditional theories of industrial location. In these new interpretations, territory is a strategic factor of development opportuni-

---

[1]The concepts of "self-centered" and "extraverted" development were first introduced by Amin (1973) and then adopted in regional analysis by Lipietz (1980) and Garofoli (1983d). Self-centered development represents a process of endogenous development in which the process of accumulation and the main decisions on the use of surplus are internally controlled in national or regional economy in opposition to a process of extraverted development that is exogenously controlled.

ties and their different characteristics. Territory represents a clustering of social relations. It is also the place where local culture and other non-transferable local features are superimposed, where individuals and business establish relationships, and where public and local institutions intervene to regulate society. To sum up, territory represents the meeting place of specific market relationships and social regulation forms, which determine different forms of production organization and different innovative capacities (regarding both products and processes). The relationship between business systems and environment is highlighted as the basis for the frequent existence of external economies to the firms, but internal to the area. These external economies make the adoption of different productive techniques possible, together with organization processes and strategies different even in areas where the same goods are produced. They are independent of and beyond the simple relationships between the prices of "factors" or those of the usable inputs (Garofoli, 1984c).

Territorial specificities are mainly based on localized networks among firms and also on the specific relationships between economic structure, the environment, and the local milieu. All this leads to different patterns of local development and gives local policies of development (cf., especially, local solidarities and the forms of social regulation at local level) a crucial role.

An analysis of the typology of local development immediately throws into relief the differences between patterns of "extraverted" or "exogenous" development (dependent on decisions mainly taken by economic agents outside the local area) and patterns of "self-centered" or "endogenous" development (based on variables mainly controlled by agents inside the local area) (Garofoli, 1983d, 1984a). The key variables which are the basis of the two groups of development models are obviously very different; the specific nature of the model, the interaction between the economic structure and the environment, the ability to "lead" the development process are clearly much higher in (or even exclusive to) the second group of patterns.

In reality, local development is characterized not only by endogenous factors but also by exogenous variables. There exist processes of development that are based mainly on exogenous rather than endogenous factors. Among the endogenous patterns of development there is also a wide differentiation according to the time scale of the industrialization process and to the organization of production.

The definition of local development used here is subsequently less restrictive than that proposed by Coffey and Polèse (1984), who have identified local development with endogenous development, with a determining and exclusive role of local agents. According to these authors, local development consists of a unique pattern based on a sequential set of the following four stages of development (Coffey and Polèse, 1984):

1. the emergence of local entrepreneurship;
2. the expansion of local firms beyond the region (both with exports and with direct investments in other regions);
3. the maintenance of local enterprises under local control;
4. the achievement of an economic structure with control functions and business services under local control.

Therefore, in their view there is a predetermined and obligatory path of development that acquires the status of a normative model. However, the continuous interaction in processes of regional development between endogenous and exogenous factors, combined with the regional effects of national economic policies, provokes wide changes in the socioeconomic structure at the local level. They cannot be interpreted simply as different stages of a unique development process.

Therefore, there is a plurality of local development paths such that predetermined development stages do not exist. Moreover, it is possible to identify at least some groups of models of local development which differ in the time scale of the development process, the structural characteristics, and in the position about the territorial division of labor.[2]

The literature on endogenous development has been extensive in the last years, particularly in southern European countries. This is necessary not only to understand the new patterns of regional development, the presence of growing local clusters of small firms, and the phenomenon of recent industrialization in rural areas[3], but also in an effort to reflect on development policies carried out at a local level that favor transformation and continuing innovation.

A model of endogenous development capable of guaranteeing the autonomy of local development must reflect certain characteristics and be based on the ability to control fundamental variables. In particular, it should be based on:

---

[2]For a discussion and the identification of different patterns of local development, cf. Garofoli (1988, 1990).

[3]The literature on the Italian case is extensive. A few examples are Bagnasco (1977), Bagnasco and Pini (1981), Becattini and Bianchi (1982), Brusco (1982, 1986), Fuà (1983), Garofoli (1981, 1983a, 1983d, 1984a, 1987). Also in Spain there has been much research during this decade; cf., for example, Vazquez-Barquero (1983, 1987, 1988), Granados (1984), Guinjoan and Santacana (1985), V.A. (1987). The last work identified 83 areas of endogenous development in Spain. France: cf. Houssel (1984), Courlet (1988), Courlet and Judet (1986). Portugal: cf. Lewis and Williams (1984), Silva (1987), Ferrao and Mendes Baptista (1988). Greece: cf. Kafkalas (1984), Hadjimichalis and Vaiou (1987).

1. use of local resources, work, historically accumulated capital, entrepreneurship, specific knowledge of production processes, and specific professional tasks,
2. the ability to control the accumulation process locally;
3. the capacity to innovate;
4. the existence of (and the ability to develop) productive interdependence at a local level, both intrasectoral and intersectoral.

Endogenous development does not mean "closed economy", even if some contributions underline the importance of the internal market.[4]

Endogenous development means in effect: (a) the capacity to transform the social-economic system; (b) the ability to react to external challenges; (c) the promotion of social learning; (d) the ability to introduce specific forms of social regulation at a local level which favor the aforementioned points. Endogenous development is, in other words, the ability to innovate at a local level.

3 The Structural Characteristics of the Small-Firms System

Among the endogenous patterns of local development we will now deal with the local systems of small firms; in our view they represent the most interesting cases, especially because they represent the "sublimation" of the model of flexible specialization. As already stated, the economic milieu and the relations between firms are determining elements of endogenous local development. If we limit the analysis to economic relations, it seems possible to identify the following structural characteristics in industrial districts[5] or local productive systems (Garofoli, 1981, 1983a):

1. A remarkable productive specialisation at the local level caused by the overpresence of one industry or a production system that links together various industries and sectors related to the productive cycle of the typical local product.

---

[4]This market should be covered by local production, solving the specific problems of the area and satisfying the basic needs of local communities (cf., for example, Friedmann and Weaver, 1979; Stöhr, 1984). Strategies of selective economic protection and "territorial closure" should be employed, which allow the continuous expansion of the use of local resources (especially labor) as opposed to the fetishism of economic growth and efficiency (Friedmann and Weaver, 1979, p. 195).

[5]For the reintroduction of the Marshallian category of industrial district into the debate cf. Beccatini (1979, 1987).

2. The production of the local system is quite important, covering a remarkable share of national, and sometimes international, production of the specific product or sector.

3. A high level of division of labor between the firms in the local productive system that gives rise to very close input–output relations, both intrasectoral and intersectoral. The high horizontal integration of production depends upon low costs of transaction among local firms.

4. The large number of local agents (the "plurality of the protagonists") and the lack of a leader or dominant firm. This prevents the formation of a monopsonistic market for subcontracting, avoiding an excessive bargaining power of "mother" firms and leads to diffuse adoption of "trial and error" behavior. This implies a greater likelihood of finding satisfactory solutions to economic problems by at least some actors, followed by immediate imitation by other actors.

5. A remarkable specialization of production at the level of the firm and plant which limits the field of activity, stimulates the accumulation of specialized knowledge, facilitates the introduction of new technologies, and, eventually, increases through the rise of labor productivity the economic autonomy of firms and subsystems in the area.

6. The existence of an efficient system of transmitting information at the local level that guarantees the rapid and efficient circulation of information about:

   (a) outlet markets;
   (b) alternative technologies;
   (c) new raw materials;
   (d) components and intermediate products which can be used in the production cycle;
   (e) new commercial and financial techniques.

   This helps transform the knowledge of each individual actor into the "common economic heritage" of the area.

7. The high level of skills of workers in the area, as a result of a historical sedimentation of knowledge of the applied technologies.

8. The increase in "face-to-face" relationships between economic actors (especially between suppliers and users of intermediate products and of business services). This facilitates the diffusion of technological and organizational improvements that increase the overall efficiency of the local system.[6]

---

[6]The effectiveness of this mutual support and cooperative links among local firms, particularly between innovators and users of innovation, reaches its highest level in local systems where the machinery for the typical local product is also manufactured.

When the local production system reaches a high level of development, a clear division of labor between firms arises, and production becomes more fully integrated, a definition of the local system based on sectoral specialization becomes more and more restrictive. The system gradually expands to different industries and sectors and creates the phenomenon which superficially could be considered as a process of "despecialization" and diversification. In reality, however, it must be interpreted as a strengthening and deepening of the original productive system. Local input–output relations between firms belonging to different product sectors are more frequent, and this gives rise to growing intersectoral integration within the local system (Garofoli, 1983c).

All this is, in fact, the consequence of the gradual growth and development of industries closely linked to the original sector of specialization and directly stimulated by it. Often these new industries are technologically and economically more evolved (there is a higher value-added content in production, higher labor productivity, and more intensive use of capital in relation to labor). In addition, they have a greater capacity for technical innovation and a greater control of the market. The combined operation of these processes improves the position of the local productive systems in the regional and international division of labor and progressively creates a distance between it and firms or areas that are purely imitative. Thus, a greater ability to defend the local system against outside competition (firms in other areas, both national and abroad) is assured.

3.1   A typology of local productive systems

A comparative analysis of the productive structure, of the characteristics of local social formations, and qualitative transformations of the small-firms system suggests the following classification (Garofoli, 1983c):

1. *Areas of specialized production:* This kind of area is characterized by a "horizontal structure" of the local system. There exist a large number of small and medium-sized firms producing the same product or productive component. There are few relationships among local firms, with the exception of some capacity decentralization for the less innovative and more labor-intensive phases of production, especially with home work and the putting-out system. This agglomeration of firms (cf. shoe industry in the province of Brescia, pottery industry in Civitacastellana, Lazio, and small-scale iron and steel industry near Brescia; Garofoli, 1983a, 1990) seems to depend upon

   • flows of information (about technologies and outlet markets),

- the formation of specific skills in the local labor market, and

- the sprouting of new firms with imitative strategies. Indeed new entrepreneurs have previous experience as workers in existing local firms.

Very often this kind of local pattern of development has been formed through the decentralization of production and/or relocation of external firms. The following are major features of this pattern of development:

- the prevalence of imitative strategies, at the level of the firm, mainly based on production cost cutting;

- cooperation among local firms does not exist because of the excessive burden of competition;

- usually, the perception of local identity does not exist;

- it is quite difficult to organize local economic policies.

2. *Local productive systems*: This kind of area is characterized by the presence of intrasectoral relations, which means the formation of a network among local firms that exchange complementary items at the local level. Other characteristics of this kind of pattern of development (cf. shoe industry in the Marche region, clothing industry in Urbania, Marche, and stocking industry in Castelgoffredo, Lombardy; Garofoli, 1981, 1983a, 1990) are:

- strong territorial integration;

- continuous formation of new subsectors, very specialized by product components and specific working phases;

- a high rate of new firm formation;

- transfer of technologies among subsectors (this implies an innovative fall out) and cooperative links among firms;

- continuous improvement of labor productivity both at a firm level and at local systems level;

- formation of specific tasks for the machinery care and repairs and for small adjustments to existing machinery.

Major features with reference to strategies and policies are:

- the perception of local identity;

- diffuse demand for local economic policies, both from local firms and from trade unions;

- the pattern of development is of an extensive type, which means there is a continuous increase both in the number of firms and in employment;
- there is great opportunity to organize local economic policies, because social bodies and local institutions have realized the existence of specific characteristics and problems to be protected and faced.

3. *System areas*: This is the most advanced kind of area among small-firms systems. The main characteristic is the presence of a very strict division of labor among local firms, which progressively diversifies the local systems and induces an increasing complexity. The interrelations among firms are very numerous and they operate at the intersectoral as well as the intrasectoral level. The complexity of the area is often so high as to include local production of machine tools for typical local products. This implies control over productive techniques and technological autonomy. Other characteristics of this kind of area (cf. especially, the wool industry in Prato and in Biella, the shoe industry in Vigevano, and the knitting industry in Carpi; Garofoli, 1981, 1983a, 1990) are:

- a continuous formation of new industries and subsectors, all of them integrated in a local productive system;
- the existence of "innovative fall-out" resulting from local firms' belonging to different industries and subsectors;
- the existence of local solidarities and local institutions, historically sedimented in the area;
- local economic policies have been and are usually introduced and implemented;
- business services have been usually introduced at local level (if often to an insufficient degree).

Furthermore in this kind of area there are:

- a capacity to control the technical frontier;
- an intensive pattern of development, which means that industrial employment does not increase any more;
- a "self-centered" pattern of development: the opportunity exists to control (from inside the area and from local agents) the transformation of the local production system and its position in the territorial division of labor, choosing the path of innovation and of introduction of high-quality and differentiated products.

4   Strategic Variables for the Strengthening of Local Productive Systems

As the productive system becomes more complex and makes external economies to firms more important[7] and as the productive system has made the most of specific local factors, the process of development has acquired all the characteristics of a "self-centered" pattern of development. The process of development becomes, in fact, completely endogenous when the best part of the resources used are local (local entrepreneurs, highly skilled workers with local training, financial resources accumulated locally, technological innovation introduced locally).[8] At this point, the local system[9] may be capable of controlling its own process of development and transformation, even if this obviously does not mean that the survival of the local system is assured.[10]

In fact, the conditions for survival change constantly. Industrial districts are characterized by continuous change, both in the relationships within the area (relationships among firms, with the economic milieu, and with the institutions) and those with the outside forces (markets, other competing areas, other territorial systems). All this has obvious consequences on the placing of the local system in the territorial division of labor. Change and innovation are therefore conditions for the survival of the local system. Consequently, a strategy of transformation of the local system is needed, which entails an ability to understand the relative position of the local system and to predict development scenarios in the medium to long term. It is difficult for individual small firms to have this ability, and so decisions need to be made at the consortia level[11] and suitable local economic policies will be called for.

---

[7]In these cases the economies of agglomeration often prevail even over the diseconomies of urbanization in such a way as to continue to favor localization in an area of growing clusters of firms (even if there are rising location costs and inadequate levels of territorial infrastructure and transport) (cf. Garofoli, 1983a, Chapter 4).

[8]Obviously this does not mean that the local system is closed to the outside world. One of the specific features of these systems is the great and growing openness to the international market. Indeed the efficiency of the local system is assured precisely by its presence on the international market. For a different definition of endogenous local development see Coffey and Polèse (1984).

[9]The local system, here, connotes the local social bodies and local institutions.

[10]Note, in this connection, the often irreversible crisis experienced by many industrial districts abroad (cf. Garofoli, 1983b).

[11]This means with extensive cooperation among competitors either directly or indirectly, through joint participation in the institutions regulating the local economy (cf. Sabel, 1987).

The fundamental condition for the strengthening of local productive systems is the achievement of a more and more "systemic" structure which reinforces the economic links between firms and relationships with the economic milieu, so that local specific characteristics become the most important factor in location and development. The crucial variables for the strengthening of the local system are both endogenous (completely controlled within the area) and exogenous. Among the variables which could be controlled within the local system are:

1. Technical-organizational innovation which more and more takes on (in small firm systems) the characteristics of a continuous process of a large number of incremental technological changes, all of them small, cumulative, and interdependent. Technological innovation in local systems is not only the result of the process of territorial diffusion but very often arises as the product of the local system, especially when associated with the original introduction of techniques and the machinery for the typical local product is produced locally. Shifting of the technological frontier is therefore crucial for the consolidation and survival of the local system.

2. A rapid and efficient information system assures timely circulation of information, an opportune knowledge of the markets, and the diffusion of information about technology and inputs, all of which are in fact the basis for correctly assessing the prospects of development for local enterprises.

3. The ability to control the product market is a feature of mature, endogenous local economies. Strengthening the commercial capacity of the system of local firms is one of the crucial factors for the autonomy of industrial districts. At the same time it is a continuous opportunity for the introduction of new products.

4. The forms of social regulation, which operate outside the market, depend upon a useful integration between the institutions and the local economy (cf. Sabel and Zeitlin, 1982; Zeitlin, 1985). A crucial role can be performed by: (a) quality control systems, technological centers, and business service centers established on the basis of agreements between local public bodies and consortia of firms; (b) centers for professional training and institutions that coordinate the worlds of school and work; (c) institutions that regulate competition between enterprises, favoring competition in new products and processes rather than brutal competition and price wars based on cost cutting and, indirectly, labor cost cutting.

5   Policy Implications

Local policies must be based on sound knowledge of local economic and social structure and their perspectives (diagnostic capability), on a coordination capacity between local agents (both public and private, including both social bodies and local institutions), and on the planning capability at the local level.

Three instruments of economic intervention at local level seem to be of strategic importance for endogenous local development:

- local development agencies;
- technological centers and technological diffusion agencies;
- business services centers.

5.1   The local development agency

A typical characteristic of many local patterns of development – and especially of small-firms systems – is represented by the wide "hiatus" between the production capacity of the local system and the strategic capability to reconvert the local economic structure: the typical advantages of local small firms (i.e. the productive flexibility) collide with the outlook capacity in the middle to long run.

For this, the role of corporate initiatives is important in dealing with common problems of the local firms. In this sense, some economic and social operators seem to be very important: those who could be defined as "pivots" of the local economy are able to catalyze the community's interests and identify innovative strategies for the entire local productive system.

This kind of experience is very well known in some European countries. It is sufficient to think of the Expansion Committees and Development Agencies in France,[12] the Industrial Development Officers and the Regional Development Agencies in Great Britain, and the Sagazde in the Basque country in Spain.[13]

Local development agencies are usually very flexible structures that function to promote and implement economic activities at a local level.

---

[12]The decentralization laws of 1982 and 1983 granted more autonomy to the local councils legitimizing some of their economic activities and with the formation of the so-called "Contrats de plan" and "Contrats de pays" (cf. Courlet *et al.*, 1987; Pecqueur, 1986, 1987; Mifsud, 1984).

[13]Cf., also, at local level the initiative of the Industrial Promotion Department in Lebrija, Andalusia, and of the "industrialde", a sort of industrial park, in Onate, Basque country, both studied by V.A. (1987b), and Vazquez-Barquero (1988).

They act as an interface between public and private actors and between the demand and the supply of business services, especially promoting the circulation of information. The principal aim is to stimulate the community's participation in local development projects through the creation of new associations, to push social and economic actors toward a global solution of the community's problems, to generate understanding and agreement capability among local actors and to develop new forms of solidarity.[14]

During the 1980s, the main objective of local development agencies was to take into account the local resources through the management and the improvement of the existing economic system rather than, as happened in the previous decades, by attracting external firms with a subsidized supply of infrastructure and industrial estates. The principal results of the initiatives of local development agencies in the various European countries have concerned the following spheres:

- the capability to diagnose the local economic situation and to evaluate its potentials;
- promoting the local industrial environment;
- reinforcing the links among local firms, developing relationships between them on the basis of mutual interests (for example facilitating the subcontracting linkages);
- promotion of the scientific and technological environment;
- establishing links with the outside world, with outward-oriented activities (seeking new outlet markets, developing exchange programs, cooperation and partnerships with firms in other regions and countries);
- mobilizing internal savings toward local industrial firms, which could then make use of extra local funds.

5.2 The technological centers

Local policies aimed to promote innovation must be very articulated and territorially differentiated according to the differences in both local economic structure and objectives. There are at least four kinds of local innovation policies:

1. technological parks in urban areas with a developed industrial fabric and with the presence of a techno-scientific infrastructure (research

---

[14]Cf., for example, the development of contacts between science laboratories and local entrepreneurs as in the Savoy Technolac operation and the creation of discussion groups with the main local economic actors, both public and private, in various Economic Expansion committees in France, studied by Courlet *et al.* (1987).

laboratories, universities, etc.), with the aim of facilitating the application of the research results into industrial production, allowing the introduction of new products and new processes, stimulating the creation of new firms in innovative sectors (cf., for example, the case of Cambridge Science Park;[15])

2. technological centers in industrial districts and system areas with the aim of horizontal transfer of new technologies to sectors that have not yet used them and, mainly, to facilitate the shift of the technological frontier in the areas in which machine tools for local typical products are already produced. The settlement of cooperative initiatives, technical centers, and consortia among firms is necessary to use an amount of technical and financial resources sufficient to obtain a technological advance that could not be pursued by an individual small firm alone producing machine tools. All this will increase the productivity of the final products sector and will improve the capability of exports of innovative technology;[16]

3. in areas of diffused industrialization and scarce networks among firms, the use of horizontal means of intervention would be convenient for promoting the diffusion of technological innovations and new processes already used in different industries or regions;

4. in the less industrialized areas, it is important mainly to promote both the formation of new firms (through policies of professional schemes and managerial capacity formation) and the strengthening of existing firms (through policies which could promote the demand of innovation and business services). Furthermore, it is important to promote the circulation of information concerning the experience of other areas and regions.

5.3   Business services centers

There are some common objectives for the diffusion of business services to different areas and typologies of local productive systems, namely:

- to make explicit the latent demand for business services of local small firms;
- use information about the effective demand for business services, particularly to understand the inadequacy and shortage of local supply, to promote the creation of new local firms in business services.

---

[15]Cf., for an analysis of Cambridge Science Park and other UK science parks, Monck *et al.* (1988).

[16]Cf., for an analysis of the technological centers in the small firms systems in Italy, Garofoli (1984b), Bianchi *et al.* (1986), Colnaghi (1987).

This is very important when we think about the significance of "cultural coherence" between seller and user of business services;

- promoting the capability of projecting business services agencies at local level.

The experiences of the business services centers are very varied: there are cases in which a direct production of business services is offered and others which sustain the services demanded (as in the case of RKW – Rationalisierungskuratorium der deutschen Wirtschaft – in Western Germany).

Business service centers organized as an interface between the demand of services and the supply seem to be a better approach. The main condition is the participation of local firms, both in financing and in management and control. This is, indeed, an effective way to stimulate the production of useful business services and to fulfill the goal of self-financing of the center (cf., in this respect, the case of Citer in the knitting area of Carpi in Italy).

The public support of this kind of initiatives and the support by the category associations are necessary, nevertheless, in the first stages of the organization of the center owing to the lack of the business services market at local level (cf. Brusco, 1984).

6   Summary

The historical importance of the forms of social regulation at the local level require local policies supporting innovation and the continuous process of transformation. Because of the wide variety of local patterns of development, it is necessary to take into account local specificities, problems and the perspectives of different areas so as to have territorially differentiated local economic policies. This means taking into account the relationships between economy, society, and local institutions that are at the basis of the forms of social regulation and represent the link between the state and the market, between the rules of competitiveness and economic efficiency, and the necessity of public intervention in the economy and in society.

Local development should take particularly into account local resources (material and human), the improvement of their productivity, and a process of consolidation and strengthening of the existing productive structure, especially activities that facilitate the access to innovation, information and strategic business services. The main objectives for policy intervention are:

- to improve the external economies of the local system, strengthening the networks among local firms (cf. cooperative links among local

firms vs. competitive relationships);
- to improve the productivity of local resources;
- to induce technological and organizational innovation and facilitate the transfer of techno-scientific knowledge into concrete adaptations of local production;
- to improve the relationship with the outlet market;
- to induce the diversification of the local economy, mainly the formation and development of business services (with the objective of improving the ratio between value added and gross production at local level);
- to improve economic and technical knowledge and social learning;
- to promote local solidarities and interfirm cooperation;
- to improve local capacity to solve local problems (i.e. reinforce the capability to introduce local planning projects; cf. Stöhr, 1984).

It has also been seen that the small-firms system – the most interesting and strongest cases of local development – shows some weak points in its structure and in its capability to face external challenges. According to this and following the historical success stories, it has been proposed to introduce social regulations and institutions continuously with the aim of reinforcing sound networks among firms and between the economy and society. All this should work as the engine of innovation and transformation in local economies. Networks and innovation become, then, the crucial factors for the strengthening of endogenous local development.

References

Amin, S., 1973. *Le devéloppement inégal*, Les Editions de Minuit, Paris.

Bagnasco, A., 1977. *Tre Italie – La problematica territoriale dello sviluppo economico italiano*, Il Mulino, Bologna.

Bagnasco, A., R. Pini, 1981. Sviluppo economico e trasformazioni socio-politiche dei sistemi territoriali a economia diffusa. *Economia e struttura sociale, Quaderni della Fondazione G. Feltrinelli*, No. 14, Milan.

Becattini, G., G. Bianchi, 1982. Sulla multiregionalità dello sviluppo economico italiano, *Note Economiche*, No. 5–6.

Berry, B.J.L., 1973. *Growth Centers in the American Urban System*, Ballinger, Cambridge (Mass.).

Bianchi P., N. Bellini, M. Giordani, F. Pasquini, 1986. Servizi reali e politica industriale a livello locale, *Stato e Mercato*, No. 16.

Brusco, S., 1982. The Emilian model: productive decentralization and social integration, *Cambridge Journal of Economics*, Vol. 6, No. 2, June.

Brusco, S., 1984. Quale politica industriale per i distretti industriali?, *Politica ed Economia*, Vol. XV, No. 6.

Brusco, S., 1986. Small Firms and Industrial Districts: The Experience of Italy, in D. Keeble, E. Weaver (eds.), *New Firms and Regional Development in Europe*, Croom Helm, London.

Coffey, W.J., M. Polèse, 1984. The Concept of Local Development: A Stages Model of Endogenous Regional Growth, *Papers of the Regional Science Association*, No. 54.

CCE, 1981. The mobilization of indigenous potential, *Internal documentation of regional policy in the Community*, Brussels, No. 10, Sept.

Colnaghi, A., 1987. Innovazione tecnologica e sistemi produttivi locali, *Economia Marche*, Vol. VI, No. 2, Dec.

Courlet, C., 1988. Nouveaux dynamismes spatiaux et politiques industrielle locales: l'example français, Paper presented at the workshop on "Depressed Regions in the Mediterranean European Countries and Endogenous Development", Scilla (Reggio Calabria), June.

Courlet, C., P. Judet, 1986. Nouveaux espaces de production en France et en Italie, *Les Annales de la recherche urbaine*, No. 29, Jan.

Courlet, C., B. Pecqueur, N. Rousier, 1987. Local Industrial Policies in Favour of Small and Medium-Sized Firms: The French Case, International Symposium "Nouveaux Regards sur l'Industrialisation", Tunis.

Damette, F., 1980. The Regional Framework of Monopoly Exploitation: New Problems and Trends, in J. Carney, R. Hudson, J. Lewis (eds.), *Regions in Crisis*, Croom Helm, London.

Ferrão, J., A. Mendes Baptista, 1988. Endogenous Development in Portugal: Problems and Perspectives, Paper presented at the workshop on "Depressed Regions in the Mediterranean European Countries and Endogenous Development", Scilla (Reggio Calabria), June.

Friedmann, J., M. Douglass, 1975. Agropolitan Development: Towards a New Strategy for Regional Development in Asia, in *United Nations Centre for Regional Development*, pp. 333–387.

Friedmann, J., C. Weaver, 1979. *Territory and Function: The Evolution of Regional Planning*, Edward Arnold, London.

Fuà, G., 1983. L'industrializzazione nel Nord-Est e nel Centro, in G. Fuà, C. Zacchia (eds.), *Industrializzazione senza fratture*, Il Mulino, Bologna.

Garofoli, G., 1981. Lo sviluppo delle aree periferiche nell'economia italiana degli anni settanta, *L'Industria*, No. 3, July–Sept.

Garofoli, G., 1983a. *Industrializzazione diffusa in Lombardia*, Franco Angeli, Milan.

Garofoli, G., 1983b. Aree di specializzazione produttiva e piccole imprese in Europa, *Economia Marche*, Vol. 2, No. 1.

Garofoli, G., 1983c. Le aree-sistema in Italia, *Politica ed Economia*, Vol. XIV, No. 11.

Garofoli, G., 1983d. Sviluppo regionale e ristrutturazione industriale: il modello italiano degli anni 70, *Rassegna Economica*, Vol. XLVII, No. 6, Nov.–Dec.

Garofoli, G., 1984a. Diffuse Industrialization and Small Firms: The Italian Pattern in the 70's, in R. Hudson (ed.), _Small Firms and Regional Development_, Institute for Transport, Tourism and Regional Economy, Copenhagen School of Economics and Business Administration, publication No. 39, Copenhagen.

Garofoli, G., 1984b. Barriere all'innovazione e politiche di intervento a livello regionale e sub-regionale, in R. Camagni, R. Cappellin, G. Garofoli (eds.), _Cambiamento tecnologico e diffusione territoriale_, Franco Angeli, Milan.

Garofoli, G., 1984c. Modelli locali di sviluppo, Paper presented at the 25th Scientific Meeting of the Società Italiana degli Economisti, Rome, Nov.

Garofoli, G., 1987 Il modello territoriale di sviluppo degli anni 70–80, _Note Economiche_, No. 1.

Garofoli, G., 1988. Modelli locali di sviluppo: tipologia di aree e politiche di intervento, CNR, Progetto Finalizzato "Economia Italiana", Sottoprogetto IV, Quaderno 7, Pavia, July.

Garofoli, G., 1990. _Modelli Locali di Sviluppo_, Franco Agnelli, Milan.

Granados, V., 1984. Small Firms and Rural Industrialization in Spain: Some Results from an OECD Project, in R. Hudson (ed.), _Small Firms and Regional Development_, Institute for Transport, Tourism and Regional Economy, Copenhagen.

Guinjoan, M., F. Santacana, 1985. PME y desarrollo endógeno. Las áreas de industrialización endógena en España, II encuentro de economistas italo-españoles, "Política económica y territorio", Girona, Oct.

Hadjimichalis, C., D. Vaiou, 1987. Changing Patterns of Uneven Regional Development and Forms of Social Reproduction in Greece, _Environment and Planning D: Society and Space_, Vol. 5, pp. 319–333.

Houssel, J.P., 1984. L'industrialisation spontanée face à la crise de 1973 en Europe Occidentale, _Revue Géographique de Lyon_, Vol. 59, No. 4.

Kafkalas, G., 1984. Small Firms and the Development of a Peripheral Region: The Case of Thraki, Greece, in R. Hudson (ed.), _Small Firms and Regional Development_, Institute of Transport, Tourism and Regional Economy, Copenhagen.

Lewis, J.R., A.M. Williams, 1984. The Formation and Role of Small and Medium-Size Industrial Enterprises in the Região Centro, Portugal, Paper presented to the 24th European Congress of Regional Science Association, Milan, Aug.

Lipietz, A., 1980. The Structuration of Space, the Problem of Land and Spatial Policy, in J. Carney, R. Hudson, J. Lewis (eds.), _Regions in Crisis_, Croom Helm, London.

Mifsud, P., 1984. National and Regional Planning in a Competitive International Environment: Comments on a Reform, _Papers of the Regional Science Association_, Vol. 55, pp. 13–24.

Momigliano, F., 1982. Determinanti ed effetti dell'attività innovativa: revisione di teorie e implicazioni di politiche per l'innovazione industriale, _Economia e Politica Industriale_, No. 35.

Momigliano, F., 1984. Revisione di modelli interpretativi delle determinanti ed effetti dell'attività innovativa, della aggregazione spaziale dei centri die R & S e della diffusione intraindustriale e territoriale delle innovazioni tecnologiche, in R. Camagni, R. Cappellin, G. Garofoli (eds.), *Cambiamento tecnologico e diffusione territoriale*, Franco Angeli, Milan.

Monck, C.S.P., R.B. Porter, P.R. Quintas, D.J. Storey, P. Wynarczyk, 1988. *Science Parks and the Growth of High Technology Firms*, Croom Helm, London.

Pecqueur, B., 1987. De l'espace fonctionnel à l'espace-territoire. Essai sur le développement local, Thèse de doctorat d'Etat des Sciences Economiques, Université des Sciences Sociales de Grenoble, Grenoble.

Piore, M., C. Sabel, 1984. *The Second Industrial Divide*, Basic Books, New York.

Sabel, C., 1987. The Reemergence of Regional Economies, Paper presented at the International Symposium "Nouveaux Regards sur l'Industrialisation", Tunis.

Sabel, C., J. Zeitlin, 1982. Alternative storiche alla produzione di massa, *Stato e mercato*, No. 5.

Silva, M.R., 1987. Développement industriel et éspaces productifs locaux: étude sur la Valée de l'Ave (Portugal), Paper presented at the International Symposium "Nouveaux Regards sur l'Industrialisation", Tunis.

Stöhr, W.B., 1978. *Center-Down-and-Outward Development versus Periphery-Up-and-Inward Development: A Comparison of Two Paradigms*, IIR-Disc. 4, University of Economics, Vienna.

Stöhr, W.B., 1981. Development from Below: The Bottom-up and Periphery-inward Development Paradigm, in W.B. Stöhr, D.R.F. Taylor (eds.), *Development from Above or Below? The Dialectics of Regional Planning in Developing Countries*, John Wiley, Chichester.

Stöhr, W.B., 1984. La crise économique demande-t-elle de nouvelles stratégies de développement régional?, in P. Aydalot (ed.), *Crise & espace*, Economica, Paris.

Thompson, W., 1968. Internal and External Factors in the Development of Urban Economies, in H.S. Perloff, L. Wingo (eds.), *Issues in Urban Economics*, Johns Hopkins Press, Washington.

V.A., 1987a. *Áreas rurales con capacidad de desarrollo endógeno*, MOPU (Ministerio de Obras Públicas y Urbanismo) – Instituto del Territorio y Urbanismo, Madrid.

V.A., 1987b. *Proceso de formulación de las políticas de desarrollo local – La experiencia española*, MOPU (Ministerio de Obras Públicas y Urbanismo)– Instituto del Territorio y Urbanismo, Madrid.

Vazquez-Barquero, A., 1983. Industrialization in Rural Areas: The Spanish Case, OECD, Intergovernmental meeting, Senigallia, June.

Vazquez-Barquero, A., 1987. Local Development and Regional State in Spain, *Papers of the Regional Science Association*, Vol. 61.

Vazquez-Barquero, A., 1988. Local Development Initiatives under Incipient Regional Autonomy: The Spanish Experience in the Eighties, Paper presented at the workshop "Depressed Regions in the Mediterranean European Countries and Endogenous Development", Scilla (Reggio Calabria), June.

Zeitlin, J., 1985. Distretti industriali e struttura industriale in prospettiva storica, in R. Innocenti (ed.), *Piccola città & piccola impresa*, Franco Angeli, Milan.

8

"Local" Development in Southern Europe: Myths and Realities

Costis Hadjimichalis, Nicos Papamichos*

1 Introduction

During the 1970s and 1980s, the changing role of southern European economies in the international division of labor (vis-à-vis northern Europe, the Middle East and North Africa) was affected among other ways by declining industrial growth in "old" growth centers and regions, reduced migration flows and the flourishing of new productive activities in certain semi-urban regions and away from large cities. This kind of productive decentralization – and the important role of small and medium enterprises (SMEs) in it – has been a major element in shaping a new geography of growth and/or marginalization and a new spatial organization of power.

A common interpretation of these characteristics until the 1970s was that of "backwardness" and "underdevelopment". More recent analyses based on changes in the international division of labor and on changes from Fordist to flexible production systems have interpreted these characteristics as "peripheral Fordism" (Lipietz, 1987), or as the rise of new innovative industrial spaces similar to those observed in northeast-central Italy, known as "Third Italy" (for Portugal see Cooke and Pires, 1985; for Spain see Costa Campi, 1988). And finally, since the mid-1980s, the

*Department of Urban and Regional Planning, University of Thessaloniki, Greece. An extended version of this paper has been published in *Antipode*, Vol. 22, No. 3, pp. 181–200. The authors thank Basil Blackwell for permission to use the paper.

combination of "development-from-below" theories with certain success
stories of local capitalist development has generated the widespread belief
that alternative policies promoting indigenous local development based
on SMEs would diffuse growth potentials like those in Third Italy all over
southern Europe, giving an end to long-standing social and spatial inequal-
ities (OECD, 1983; Piore and Sabel, 1983; Stöhr, 1986; Vasquez-Barquero,
1986).

"Local development" thus became the new catchphrase, a new kind
of development doctrine during a period of great financial difficulties on
the part of the central state. But, as has often happened in the past with
similar fashionable terms, they repeat old errors or create new confusions
in which everyone can read their own hopes and fears. Especially at the
policy level, while these interpretations avoid known mistakes of the past,
they are unable to take into account the particular local characteristics of
various success stories which cannot be transferred to other places. In this
respect a new mythology tends to be established with its optimistic and
celebratory visions of decentralized production, indigenous development
potentials and flexible specialization futures, based on an extremely simplistic and in our view wrong understanding of spatial and social change
(see also Amin and Robins, forthcoming).

The purpose of this paper is threefold. First, we address the significance of certain local characteristics for the development of southern European localities and discuss whether known successful examples of local
capitalist development can be used as a blueprint elsewhere. Second, we
describe an alternative interpretation of local development characteristics
based on six major restructuring issues. And third, we discuss the political implications of local development policies. Special attention will
be given to the "micro-foundations" of uneven development and the local
conditions of reproduction of exploitative work relations.

2   Current Changes in the Spatial Division of Labor and in Development Policies

Perhaps the most important change from the mid-1970s onwards was the
challenge of the traditional distinction between a prosperous industrial
core or cores and a stagnant agricultural periphery. For many years, commentators on uneven southern European development, influenced mainly
by the Italian pattern, repeated this explanation which in certain cases
acted as a model for Spain (Munoz *et al.*, 1979; Buruaga, 1983), for Portugal (Holland, 1979; de Oliveira, 1983) and to a lesser degree for Greece
(Evangelinides, 1979). These observations and ideas created a set of gen-

eral beliefs that people in rural southern Europe have a strong penchant for being idle and have low regard for thrift; that their lack of modernization does not permit a rational productive programme; that their low incomes are due largely to their inability to save and to adapt to new techniques and new demands of the market; and finally, that these inadequacies, especially the dualistic dichotomy between urban and rural areas, can be overcome only through deliberate and innovative planning policies (OECD, 1979).

In fact, regional policies introduced by different state agencies were founded in these hypotheses and in a relatively standard geographical picture of growth which was based on the north–south/urban–rural dichotomy in specific regions. So, "growth" in Italy was synonymous with northern regions (with the exception of Valle d'Aosta, Trentino and Friuli-Venezia). In Spain it was northern regions including Madrid though not Galicia, while in Portugal and Greece it was major cities along the coast with their hinterlands like Oporto, Greater Lisbon, Greater Athens, Thessaloniki, Patras and Volos. It was not by chance, therefore, that regional development policies until the 1970s were based on strong state intervention into "backward" rural areas via forced industrialization in large growth poles, agricultural modernization and mechanization, and large tourist projects (Hudson and Lewis, 1984).

Since the mid-1970s distinctions, like urban–rural, north–south, development–underdevelopment, and regional strategies, like growth poles, have become highly problematic, hazy and inefficient, both in describing uneven regional development and in guiding state invention in southern Europe. From a theoretical point of view, they tended to use dualistic and monocausal explanations for a very complex socio-spatial process. From an empirical point of view, they were unable to understand the signs of a new kind of rural and semi-urban dynamism that would have been considered unlikely even a decade ago (Bagnasco, 1977; Paci, 1982; Lewis and Williams, 1988). Capitalist development started to flourish not around the poles as a planned trickling-down effect, but spontaneously in other regions and localities, whose economic performance, social division of labor and degree of state intervention was at an intermediate level, between that of old industrial centers and traditional rural regions. The pattern has become clear in Italy since the early 1970s, in Spain since the mid-1970s and in Portugal and Greece since the late 1970s or early 1980s.

Numerous factors have been picked out as contributing to this process of rural transformation, and productive decentralization ranging from push factors such as shortage of space and traffic congestion in large urban centers to a combination of pull factors to explain the present urban–rural shift in the same way as described for Britain by Keeble (1980) and for central Europe by Keeble *et al.* (1983).

An alternative view has been promoted by those who analyze evidence on the current expansion of small-scale manufacturing activities in non-metropolitan areas (Bagnasco, 1977; Fuà, 1983; Hudson and Lewis, 1984);[1] on the current transformation of agriculture (Garcia-Ramon, 1985; Hadjimichalis, 1987; Mottura and Mingione, 1989), and on the role of services, particularly tourism (Garcia-Herrera, 1987; Williams and Shaw, 1988; Leondidou, 1988). The extent of economic expansion away from the traditional urban and manufacturing centers in the four countries should not be exaggerated. The bulk of activity is still to be found in the major cities, while multinational investments still prefer urban settings, such as Japanese manufacturing investment around Barcelona and Arab banks in Athens. However, the clear evidence from case studies is that during 1972–83 older industrial centers were losing their share of employment and productive dynamism to what have been called intermediate areas (see Arcangeli *et al.*, 1980; Garofoli, 1983; Ferrao, 1985).[2] The sectoral and geographical composition of their productive system is more flexible and diversified compared with old industrialized regions or marginal mountainous areas. In these areas the relative development of infrastructure and communications, certain regional incentives to capital, and the existence of good irrigated land, beaches, and monument sites – along with the lack of strict land use regulations – have permitted the coexistence of medium and small industrial firms, tourist facilities and intensive agricultural production. Through efficient use of local resources, certain local entrepreneurs have been able to weather the recession and the present economic crisis which hit old industrial regions particularly hard.

Since the mid-1980s, empirical research on local development processes in these regions combined with theories of development from below or autonomous and self-reliant development have resulted in strong proposals for regional action. According to these views, while in the past local development has taken place in a spontaneous manner, now it can be designed to implement a policy "from below" (OECD, 1983; Musto, 1985; Stöhr,

---

[1]In 1978, industrial firms employing less than 100 people accounted for 99.4% in Greece and 93.7% in Spain of all industrial units. In 1985 these figures remain almost the same with 98.3% in Greece and 92.5% in Spain, while similar trends are to be found in Italy and Portugal.

[2]For identifying "developed", "intermediate" and "marginalized" regions in Greece, we calculated for 1981–85 the sum of Z-scores for every nomos (prefecture) for the following variables: 1. index of gross regional product per capita, 2. index of per capita income, 3. annual rate of growth of gross regional product, 4. net population increase, 5. annual change of industrial employment 1973–84, 6. index of labor productivity in agriculture 1973–84, 7. tourist beds per 1,000 people 1984, and 8. women's activity rate 1983. See Hadjimichalis and Vaiou, 1987.

1986). The proposal has gained substantial support in Spain (Vasquez-Barquero, 1986; Instituto del Territorio y Urbanismo, 1987), Greece (EE-TAA, 1988) and Italy (Garofoli, 1988). It has also attracted substantial interest and support from various EC programmes such as the Social Fund (training programmes for advisors on local development planning) and the programme SPRINT (helping SMEs in local areas for technological improvements, as in Prató). While in official documents European Community (EC) policy still promotes regional development, much attention and money are channeled towards local small-business initiatives, without necessarily passing through national or regional committees for approval.

As in the past with other catchy ideas, "local development" has rapidly spread among technocrats, politicians, and local authorities as a new doctrine of development. The emphasis, however, has still been on industrialization, which will now take place via SMEs in rural areas or in small and medium towns. These "local areas" will take advantage of existing local skills and networks and, if properly helped and guided, will develop along a different path from known big-scale industrial projects in growth poles. In this growing euphoria, very few are interested in what "local" really means or how autonomous an industrial sector can be in an EC competitive framework. On the contrary, all seem to agree that "bad" exogenous forces (mainly mobile capital and the state) were unable to mobilize regional economies in the past, while "good" local endogenous forces will now successfully replace them.

A basic reference to these policies from below is the Third Italy, with its innovative SMEs and dense local networks of cooperation. To what extent evidence from success regions like the Third Italy is idealized and to what extent it can be used as a development alternative remains an open question, to which we turn in the next section.

3 "Third Italy" as a Model: False Hopes and Hard Realities

This wave of industrialization in the non-metropolitan areas of southern Europe has been studied in detail first in Italy, where Italian sociologists, geographers and labor historians have opened two major interrelated research paths.

The first is identified with the introduction of the "Third Italy" via Bagnasco's seminal book *Tre Italie* (1977), challenging the classical North–South distinction. It was in this rural area, from Trentino-Alto Adige in the North-East to Lazio and Marche in the Center, that industrial growth was occurring in the 1970s, rather than in the old northern industrial core or the heavily subsidized growth poles of the South (see also Paci, 1982; Fuà, 1983). Research in this area – known as the North-East-Central (NEC) model – stresses the essential continuity in rural economic and social relations with SMEs industrialization, not least because of the importance that is given to specific local politics including Christian Democrats (DC), and the Communist Party (PCI).

The second research path was the "fabrica diffusa" debate from the mid-1970s onwards (Magnaghi and Perelli, 1978; Garofoli, 1983). Diffused industrialization, as is well known, consists mainly of the "splitting-up" of production tasks and the "putting-out" to smaller subcontracting firms and/or to individual (female) homeworkers of parts of production previously organized under one roof. Today it is well documented that whole products from sectors like clothing, leather, toys, engineering and plastic – to mention only a few – are produced in this way in this part of Italy. Advanced mass-fashion design in firms like Benetton combines high-tech control with extremely labor-intensive production methods, producing high-quality products with low labor cost inputs (Nardin, 1987).

While Italian analysts are focusing on these multiple factors to explain the dynamism of the Third Italy, a growing literature outside Italy often reduces this multiplicity to one or a few categories focusing mainly on SMEs, technology and innovation. We can identify four major misunderstandings.

1. Third Italy cannot be used as the explanatory model of capitalist dynamism observed in other southern European regions as argued for example by Cooke and Pires (1985), Lewis and Williams (1988), Costa Campi (1988) and Leondidou (1989). The dynamism of Third Italy has particular historical, political and territorial components which are difficult to find elsewhere, even in other Italian regions (Mingione, 1985). Characteristics, such as multiple employment in different sectors, SME networks, diffused industrialization and part-time farming emphasized by the NEC model, exist in many regions such as north central Portugal, Valencia, Catalonia, Madrid, and the Basque Country, the Mezzogiorno, Macedonia, and Thraki, and the tourist islands. None of these areas, however, had either the industrial tradition and entrepreneurial skills, or the financial and political support for promoting markets, that Third Italy enjoys. They are simply "imitators", while Third Italy generates important innovations, not least because of the exploitation of specific conditions of work, taxation, and loan policies. Similar observations are applied within Third Italy itself. While many commentators draw their experience from the innovative structure of small engineering firms in Emilia-Romagna, or high-quality clothing in Toscana (Sabel, 1986),

they tend to overlook other cases of footwear, clothing and furniture SMEs in Veneto, Marche and Abruzzi, which simply survive on the basis of an artisanal capacity and self-exploitation of the family labor rather than through producing industrial innovations (see also Amin, 1989).

2. Third Italy's success cannot be analyzed only through its innovative industrial structure (using the Marshallian concept of "industrial district") without taking into account its rich agricultural heritage and the present importance of family farming and cooperatives. This important observation is often neglected by non-southern European commentators, who prefer to approach Third Italy only through its industrial flexibility. The dense network of rural SMEs, however, could never expand in these areas without the historical support of particular land tenure structures like *mezzandria* and share-cropping (both disappearing today), which provided land for investment, infrastructural networks, and skilled and semi-free labor (Paci, 1978). Furthermore, as Pugliese (1982) argues, various rural policies during Fascism to isolate the proletarian triangle of Milan–Turin–Genoa from lawful "rural central Italy" favored Third Italy regions.

Perhaps the most crucial, neglected factor characterizing Third Italy is its relatively stable local society since the 1950s. These areas have experienced low rates of in- and out-migration throughout the 1960s, 1970s and 1980s (compared to high in-migration and out-migration in the North and South respectively), which combined with local traditions and skills permitted a unique continuation of craftsmanship and social networks. This social stability has been followed by a remarkable political stability as well, organized by two distinctive political subcultures: the PCI in the central regions and the Catholic/DC in the North East. These have favored a localist regulation of SME economy, of family and cooperatives in agricultural production and of tourist facilities, through their influence on every aspect of local life, from industrial relations and land use to the activity of local government and public festivals (Trigilia, 1986; Bellini, 1989).

These observations are often neglected or devalued by those who see Third Italy only as a case of post-Fordist/flexible specialization similar to Silicon Valley, Orange County, the French technopoles or other "new industrial spaces" (Piore and Sabel, 1983; Scott and Storper, 1987; Stöhr, 1986; Scott, 1988) and by those who criticize them (Amin, 1989; Amin and Robins, forthcoming). We think that both are wrong in basing their analysis and their critique on industrial structure and industrial relations only, failing to take into account the complementarity of other sectors and the general social milieu. Bagnasco (1988) calls this "the social construction of the local market": exploring different paths of modernization where exchange, tradition, reciprocity, politics and organization have joined together in a unique socio-spatial ensemble.

3. Third Italy comprises not only innovative SMEs, but also men, women, children, and recently increasing numbers of foreign immigrants (coming mainly from North Africa) who work for them. This obvious statement is often neglected owing to a fetishization of small-capitalist success and a parallel blindness about its costs. Some have gone so far as to claim "limited class polarization" between employers and workers in SMEs, where both often change their work position and enjoy high incomes. These arguments see only the core section of the local labor force which, as expected, is male, skilled, adult, and with a party affiliation. Behind them, however, are many other workers – mainly women, young and elderly people, even children below 14 years, and now foreigners, whose work is not adequately remunerated, is regarded as peripheral or marginal, but is also essential to support the high incomes of the core group.

   The key factor remains therefore the structure and segmentation of local labor markets (Paci, 1982). Local labor works part-time but intensively in skilled and semi-skilled positions, often producing high-value products but accepting inferior conditions of work and payment. As research has shown, the family plays a key role in this through its involvement in: informal activities and "black" work; household work activities for family consumption; and housekeeping, child rearing and assistance to the ill, the old and the handicapped. Hard work and self-exploitation of family labor is strongly related to the rural context and the strong ties that the local population keeps with land. The land constitutes both a refuge for times of crises and a permanent source of family income (Vinay, 1985). The basis, however, for the reproduction of the whole social system has been the sexist division of labor (Bimbi, 1986). Women's inferior position in the labor market as semi-skilled or unpaid workers is crucial and ironically is in contradiction to tasks performed and the production of high-value products (Vinay, 1987). Women's 18-hour work days, of sewing T-shirts, doing housework and working in the fields, are remunerated less than men's low-productivity 8-hours' work in an office.

4. Finally, external and internal pressures confront the more successful parts of Third Italy. Since the end of the 1970s, as Camagni and Capello (1988) argue, there has been a reversal of the previ-

ous ten years' trends of fast manufacturing productivity growth in Third Italy. Furthermore, the regional wage/productivity gap which worked to the locational advantage of Third Italy had by 1985 begun to show signs of change in favor of the north-west regions, since wages were rising more slowly than productivity. Most important, however, were the internal changes in the social structure. As Vinay (1987) demonstrates, the very social and political conditions which fostered the flexible local economic system now constitute the main reason for its present problems.

The social compromise between capital and labor, established in these areas since the 1960s on the basis of high productivity and flexibility in the economy and acceptance of "black" work and semi-illegal working conditions, is slowly being abandoned. In the late 1980s and early 1990s there is a process of social disintegration, where the cultural values of a semi-rural society (so important for a decentralized economy) are disappearing. Young people's work is no longer seen by them as a value *per se*: they place more importance on the quality of life and do not accept hard work either in industry or in the fields (Ascoli, 1979). The important social institution which supported Third Italy for decades, the family, has recently been showing evidence of disintegration (Vinay, 1987). Marriage rates are declining, while women, tired of their secondary role on the labor market and of the sexist division of labor, claim equal work opportunities in the formal economy and equal rights within the family. Also, the local regulation of diffused industrialization seems now to be failing. The productive system is becoming more complex, while old party patronage systems are inadequate to compensate for unpredictable changes, such as the new wave of Mafia investment in Third Italy SMEs in engineering and arms production.

To sum up, Third Italy has been an important case of capitalist development during a period of crisis based on industrial SMEs, intensive agriculture, and tourism. It has succeeded in mobilizing local resources, but its many positive aspects cannot disguise its important social shortcomings, especially on the labor side. Today, Third Italy is pressured by economic, social and political conditions which the very capitalist industrial development has progressively weakened. Problems typical for industrial societies arise while international competition is pressing. In this situation, promises about the "end of centralization" and "top-down" planning, or the end of Fordism based on Third Italy's experience must be rejected, or at least re-evaluated.

4   Toward an Alternative Interpretation of Local Development Characteristics

We advocate here a more cautious approach which does not blend different realities into one, or use vague generalizations and exaggerated proposals for planning practice. In this context diversities between and within regions are not understood as simple outcomes of global processes of capitalist restructuring. Such processes are modified and reproduced as they are inscribed on particular productive structures, unique labor processes, class, gender and ethnic hierarchies, institutional and cultural domination, all of which define specific regions and localities but also form part of the explanation of uneven regional development (Hadjimichalis and Vaiou, 1990).

A useful concept for approaching regional development from this perspective is the local labor market, mediating between the specific and the general socio-spatial context (Bleitrach and Chenu, 1979; Offe, 1985). Furthermore, local labor market analysis is a more operational concept in the case of southern Europe, where the labor factor seems to play a key role in recent socio-spatial changes. Through an analysis of changes in the labor process we can identify not only local development potentials, but also the degree of integration or disintegration of each local economy within the European division of labor. Local areas are viewed in this sense as geographical entities where the development process produces and is in turn stimulated to reproduce spatially diverse divisions of labor (Massey, 1984). Well-paid, secure, prestigious jobs with substantial qualification requirements concentrate in some areas, while other areas display the inverse of these features (Cooke, 1983). Such differences can be understood by looking into the workings of local labor markets; the conditions and relationships under which the exchange of labor power occurs in particular places. The geographical specificity of local labor markets introduces in addition a multiplicity of relationships that are difficult to understand through functional models of labor market segmentation (Berger and Piore, 1980; Edwards *et al.*, 1975). Spatial differentiation of the labor market brings labor to the forefront at a time when the tendency towards ever greater flexibility requires a variety of labor markets to fit different, fractional operations of capital.

We confine ourselves to certain aspects combining the dominant tendencies in the European division of labor – the "exogenous" factors – and the main local characteristics – the "endogenous" factors – to be found in southern Europe. The limitations for a comparative analysis of such a perspective are obvious: southern Europe is not at all a homogeneous entity, while local labor markets cannot be easily grouped. By looking at recent developments, however, we can identify six major restructuring issues that have differentiated local labor markets and through them in turn, the development potential of each locality. In certain cases some or all of the following restructuring issues have contributed to the rise of dynamic intermediate areas. But this does not necessarily lead to the use of them as explanatory processes. The point is not to replace "dualism" with "tripartism", a legacy of the tradition from two to three Italies debate. We would like to propose instead a more skeptical approach, indicating the many different development paths that are now opened up in southern Europe, which each "local development plan" must seriously consider.

First, the present position of southern European economies in the international and particularly the European division of labor caused a progressive specialization of their productive structure towards certain industrial products (or activities) for which small firms are especially functional; their agricultural production combines traditional Mediterranean crops with new short-cycle, soft products for which small family farms can compete with large capitalist enterprises; and their monuments, history, and sunny beaches are attracting a mass tourism, moving away from large complexes to small-scale tourist resorts or preserved vernacular settlements.[3]

Up to 1988, this specialization particularly hit old industrialized urban areas depending on steel, shipyards and chemical products, like Piraeus, Barcelona, Brindisi-Taranto, Genoa, Cadiz, the Basque provinces and Lisbon/Setubal. In agriculture, certain regions like the Mesetas in Spain, Alentejo in Portugal, Thessaly and Epirus in Greece and large parts of the Mezzogiorno were not able to adjust to new market demands, owing to local operational difficulties, land tenure, crop specialization, and inadequate infrastructure. The opposite was true in certain minifundia regions having good accessibility, where high-value products in glass houses now predominate (e.g. in Crete, Marche, Málaga, Alicante, Valencia). This particular specialization in industry, agriculture and tourism is strongly linked to two factors: the uncertainty of demand, taste and consumption patterns; and the maturity of the existing technologies which move towards important labor-saving innovations and more diffused patterns of production. Changes in these two factors will cause considerable unevenness among and within southern European regions.

Second, the search for more flexible production systems in all sectors had social, technological and territorial consequences but should not be exaggerated or idealized as an alternative. The recently celebrated "flexible

---

[3]According to the Greek National Tourist Organization, large cities and "old" tourist resorts like Corfu and Rhodes lost 25–30% of their visitors, who now prefer smaller islands and villages. In the latter places tourist traffic increased by 85–105% during 1985–88.

specialization" model did occur in some places, but its generalized extension as a measure for successful capitalist development is debatable even within Italy. It is unquestionable, however, that new methods of labor control and new technologies have been used to allow the establishment of working processes of fairly high productivity and great flexibility even in regions lacking the economies of scale previously required (Mingione, 1987).

But this quest for flexibility has not been the only or the major reason why old industries declined and new ones arose (Sayer, 1989). Old industrial areas facing de-industrialization may decline simply because they are less efficient than competitors, while in the same areas and in some rural zones there have been rapid increases of industrial employment because they have higher output per unit of costs and more saleable products (e.g. Third Italy, central Macedonia, Valencia, Aveiro, Braga). Flexibility need not have anything to do with this, or if it does, this must be demonstrated rather than assumed.

In cases where flexibility has been documented, we distinguish several kinds which are highly diversified across southern Europe. There exist major differences in numerical flexibility in employment and output (the case of the majority of small firms), the ability to innovate, or the flexibility arising from networking within a vertically disintegrated industry. Thus, there are few similarities between "flexible" clothing SMEs in Terrasa and Sabadel (near Barcelona; Recio, 1988) and those in Abruzzi and Marche (Vinay, 1985), or those in Kilkis and Serres in northern Greece (Hadjimichalis and Vaiou, 1990). On the contrary, for specific local conditions – where historical tradition is a key factor – the leather industry in Ubrique (near Cadiz) has much in common with the leather industry around Naples (Sanchis, 1984). Similarly, subcontracting methods among engineering firms in Emilia Romagna are convergent but different from those in the Thessaloniki area. The latter are not generating the same innovation, and economies of scale and scope, that characterize among other things the industrial districts of Third Italy. What these cases and many others offer in common, though in different terms, is the concrete possibility of flexibility of specific working processes. This kind of flexibility intensifies existing differences among localities and permits some of them to play an active role in the wave of productive decentralization and relocation.

Thirdly, a specific characteristic which calls for attention in the present context is the importance of the quantity and quality of work in the informal sector. Although informal activities are an important and wide-spread phenomenon in southern Europe, or perhaps for this very reason, the situation has not attracted great attention until recently with the exception of Italy.

In particular, there are five areas where we would like to locate the present informal sector: the "traditional" and "modern" type of criminal activities, like drug traffic, prostitution, gambling, now in continuous expansion; the "traditional" type of "street-corner" economy in urban areas, now declining; the "traditional" type of rural informal activities for local consumption and self-reliance, now growing again; that informalization found in the processes of widespread rural industrialization and tourism, namely the type based on small and medium-sized specialized firms; and lastly, the innovative/creative and alternative informal type, in the "technological-service" sectors (see EEC, 1988). This new articulation is neither restricted to agriculture alone, nor can it be associated with conditions of backwardness. In fact, as many studies have shown, the development of small and very small industrial and tourist firms in rural regions is the flexible response to new demands and to direct needs for restructuring and surviving during a prolonged economic crisis. Thus, new forms of informal activities have spread, such as subcontracting, piece-work at home, room letting, operating bars and restaurants, in parallel to traditional agricultural work.

Activities in the informal sector, however, are not considered as marginal or outside the capitalist relations of production. On the contrary they are integral components of the new pattern of development, which provides fresh room for accumulation. In this context, it is not the lack of control of informal activities which calls for attention, but their specific integration/subordination through specific actions (including tolerance) of different social actors. Informal activities are determined to a great extent by the "formal" regulatory system. Moreover, the same activity or practice may be perfectly regular in a certain place at a particular time, but irregular or even illegal in another context. Thus, in order to avoid commonly invoked dualistic explanations, the historical and spatial origins of what we now call "informal activities" should be considered, along with various forms of struggle around the "institutional/formal" regulatory system (Mingione, 1985; Hadjimichalis and Vaiou, 1990).

Fourthly, segmentation in the local labor markets is an important component of the new development pattern. In many localities in which dynamic growth occurs – and with important variations from place to place – segmentation is combined effectively with formal and informal employment, with less unionization and, in certain cases, with a lack of syndicalist tradition. The labor hour *per se* is not cheaper than in old industrial centers, but part-time jobs in different sectors and firms are more widespread and acceptable to local workers (Ginatempo, 1985), allowing small firms to escape full-year payrolls and social security payment. The picture is completed by seasonal work (in agriculture and tourism), piece-work at home, and a variety of other irregular jobs. In many cases the industrial experience of returning migrants plays a key role as they act as mediators between large foreign firms and small local subcontracting firms (e.g. Macedonia, Thraki, Naples, Alicante, Braga and Vila Real).

A recent development which calls for attention is the influx of illegal migrants from Third World countries working in industry and agriculture with the lowest possible wages and no social security, and living in very poor conditions. ISTAT estimates for Italy (1984) that more than half a million non-declared foreigners work illegally. For Greece (1987) the figure is more than 150,000, not including foreign sailors (mainly Filipinos) working semi-illegally in the large Greek merchant fleet. Ironically, as in some Greek and Italian cases they are treated as non-humans by the same return migrants from West Germany who experienced similar treatment two decades ago. The social picture must be completed by mentioning the gender composition of the various groups of working people. The definition of unskilled, seasonal, and marginal labor is always related to the gender of its bearers. This has to do more with jobs being identified as "women's work" than with their technical characteristics (Vaiou, 1987).

This range of activities is not a single worker's operation. It is accommodated within the household, whose members (taken as a group) have formal, full-time employment, and are engaged in informal, home-based activities, in seasonal work, and even "black" work (Vinay, 1985). In this respect the uneven demographic and cultural characteristics of rural southern Europe provide preconditions for the spread of this development pattern. This new role of the household is one of the consequences of the current employment crisis in the context of which unemployment and non-employment increase without a parallel decrease in the cost of reproduction of the labor force. Thus, working commitments within the family unit not only tend to increase, taking up nearly all available leisure time, but also vary discriminatorily between genders and various age groups. In this respect, old patriarchal and authoritarian relations are reproduced within the family, with women at the bottom of the hierarchy (Bimbi, 1986).

Fifthly, the service industry (including tourism) has for many years been expanding on both the public and the private fronts. Initially, and for a long time, it was solidly anchored to the results of the increase of industrial productivity, giving rise to increasing demand for services on the part of the firm and the public. The technological process not only stimulates the growth of service industries but also influences the costs of their operation. These are generally highly labor-intensive working processes in which it is not possible to increase labor productivity directly (e.g. school and educational services, services to the public, such as restaurants, bars, retail trading). Since the mid-1970s, however, provision of services is related with "unskilled", "seasonal" work providing a large number of irregular and low-income jobs.

This development has had important territorial consequences in coastal areas and in the islands and it tends to be accentuated by the current phase of economic reorganization in combination with the persistent crisis of southern European states. The ways of putting pressure on income from services vary: the exploitation of family work, exploitation of female labor and that of ethnic minorities, and invasion of the sector by informal, clandestine, illegal, and casual labor. The difficulties of different state agencies, in a context of technological innovation which continues to increase industrial productivity and tends to polarize incomes, favor this modality. A vast informalized service sector is already typical of all urban areas in southern Europe. The pressures for new forms of informalization or of compression of the operators' incomes give rise to very problematic forms of labor selection. One of the most evident signs of the process is constituted by the current migratory flow of Third World migrants not only to rich regions but also to overpopulated areas in which the local labor supply does not accept excessively poor working conditions (e.g. Crete, Calabria, Andalusia).

Last but not least, the sixth issue concerns the state and certain local authorities, which play an important role through both their active policies and their passive tolerance of the situation. Among these policies we could point to regional incentives, the allocation of public investments, specific development projects, tax exemption of agricultural incomes up to a specific annual amount, and others that have different effects in each region. Active policies are accompanied by lack of land-use control, lack of effective control over employment conditions, acceptance of multiple employment and informal activities, limited power to control tax evasion, and so forth.

Under these circumstances, in many regions (e.g. Mezzogiorno, Crete, Andalusia, the Mesetas, Peleponnese, and south Portugal) many economic activities depend directly and indirectly on state choices. Thus, political affiliations have become more important than social or economic ones. Political clientelism and patronage find a very favorable environment in which, to develop (Mouzelis, 1986; Giner, 1985). Furthermore, historical contingencies have played their role in making the state the tool *par excellence* used by politically antagonistic strata against each other and, at the same time, the final objective to be won (Tsoulouvis, 1987).

Traditional political clientelism and patronage – that is, a system of stable social relations distributing resources through personal contacts and favors – was always present in southern European societies, though with great internal variations from country to country and from region to region. The key to understanding the new form of processes of patronage, however, lies in the fact that the direction of policies and welfare service provision and the criteria for their distribution are now dependent on the political parties' structure. The structure of mass parties, whether of the Right, Center, or Left, has been created since the mid-1970s in parallel with the system of social control, with the result that the state and party apparatuses grew together and were structured by patronage relations.

The main lines of consolidation of the party-patronage system as a system of social control are not difficult to trace. It is difficult, on the other hand, to understand fully its thus far irreversible consequences. The expansion of the central and local state bureaucracy and welfare service apparatuses has made available an increasing quantity of resources which the party-patronage system has used to strengthen its position as a central element in local politics. Some examples are illustrative. In Greece when PASOK came to power in 1981, district councils – an important new institution – instead of being elected, were appointed by PASOK and chosen on the basis of party membership. Thus, the rural population is still largely excluded from direct participation in local decision-making, but through the new patronage system can enter politics in a dependent manner. In Sabadel and Terrasa (near Barcelona) local authorities (communist and socialist) are in favor of industrial homeworking in textiles and clothing, since the operations of putting-out firms contribute 30–40% of those cities' wealth (Recio, 1988). And in the fur processing industrial district of Kastoria in northern Greece local authorities, local deputies, and businessmen mounted a common protest against the state when it tried to impose social security payments on subcontracting firms for mainly female homeworkers.

Similar observations can be made for southern Portugal and the Mezzogiorno. In both cases a new "mediator" class appears on stage: the state petty bourgeoisie (Pinnaro and Pugliese, 1985; Ferrao, 1987). Its new role is to keep social tensions in rural areas at least partly under control and to replace direct class conflicts by other, more mediated ones. It is not "bosses and workers" as such any more, but "local authorities and the marginal population" (Ginatempo, 1985). The farm-worker's position develops into what Pugliese (1982) calls a "worker on state benefits, a precarious client of the welfare state". He points out that in southern Italy a large number of people survive by making a living through employment in public works. This type of employment and its allocation process (through personal favors and exclusions) lead to new forms of social control and reproduced ties of clientelism to different parties and local authorities.[4]

---

[4]In Portugal's interior local authorities in the conselhos are the main direct employer from administrative tasks to building and road repairs. A conselho with 5,000 people (about 2,000 active) can have more than 100 people working directly

These six restructuring issues emphasize the multiplicity of factors influencing spontaneous and uneven development in southern European regions. There are many similarities as well as differences among places, while "successful" regions have always combined endogenous and exogenous forces. So, instead of comparing selectively some localities and then turning the results into planning proposals, we will try to formulate a typology of areas (a kind of alternative regionalization), based on these restructuring issues, and on local market characteristics described previously. We would like to point out again that these six restructuring issues are not processes common to all localities, neither can they be used as homogeneous categories in explaining causes of growth at particular places. The typology's modest attempt is to depict changes and differences among localities which local development plans (if any) must take into account. In this respect it is a "meso"-analytical approach which needs further "micro"-analysis before any development strategy can be applied. Thus, we consider the following seven-area typology which, we believe, describes changes in the division of labor among southern European regions up to the late 1980s:

1. *"Old" urban-industrial centers*, where relatively high levels of unemployment coincide with wage employment in mass industrial production and mass service sectors. Less successful productive specialization in basic industries is combined with flexible local production systems in consumer products. Taylorism predominates together with high levels of unionization. These areas enjoyed strong state intervention and produced economies of scale in the 1960s and 1970s. Urban informal activities are widely diffused and the same is true for "precarious" workers.

2. *"Old" latifundia regions*, where agricultural workers and unskilled part-time industrial workers predominate. Mass production in agriculture and in sporadic branch plants. "Old" productive specialization is characterized by strong ties to clientelism and by limited flexibility in labor relations.

3. *"Old" tourist coastal areas* and certain islands are characterized by intensive temporary employment in services following Taylorist practices. Large hotels and similar facilities for mass tourism predominate under less flexible labor relations, while informal activities depending on irregular demand are rapidly expanding. These areas also experienced strong state assistance in the 1960–70s and party patronage control.

---

for the local authority. We thank J. Ferrao for pointing this out to us.

4. *Industrial districts* and *"new" rural-industrial growth centers*, where
   the new productive specialization is dependent on highly skilled labor and extensive use of flexible working processes. They are characterized by innovations and localized economies of scale and scope.
   Feminized out-working is widely diffused in modern industries and
   revitalized craft industries. Multiple employment in agriculture and
   tourism coincides with historical tradition. Communal networks of
   cooperation are reproduced based on stable local society. To these
   should be added highly exploitative conditions of work in traditional
   and modernized informal activities.

5. *"New" intermediate regions*, where a conjunctural productive dynamism depends on policies of "adaption" using cheap labor, working part time in capitalist family farms, industrial SMEs and small-
   scale tourist facilities. These areas have recently enjoyed some type
   of regional assistance and are characterized by in-migration and low
   unionization. Flexible but not innovative local production systems
   based on extensive use of unpaid family labor. Limited but important appearance of branch plants.

6. *Marginal rural areas* depending on old productive specialization in
   remote mountainous regions or islands. High levels of unemployment
   and underemployment in backward non-irrigated farming, with high
   out-migration rates and traditional informal activities in decline.
   Political clientelism is important in the distribution of state benefits
   and coincides with ethnic discrimination and cultural domination.

7. *Marginal medium-size urban centers*, which were unable to adjust
   to new productive specialization and are characterized by rigidity in
   working relations. High levels of male unemployment coincide with
   the appearance of feminized branch plants and traditional urban
   informal activities.

5   Local Politics and Social Control: Some Concluding Comments

From the discussion so far three points should be emphasized: the shortcomings of this "new" development pattern, the rise of new social actors
in non-metropolitan areas and the appearance of a new mode of social
control.

From the mid-1970s onwards, southern European regions experienced
deep transformations associated with the wider international economic crisis and capital restructuring. We saw how these transformations changed
the relationship between economic sectors, the state, local authorities and

party systems. The spatial component of those changes was very important. Rural and urban space acquired new political importance owing to the emergence of new contradictions associated with restructuring within agriculture, productive decentralization, and flexible and irregular forms of employment in industry, tourism, and the service sector. These new contradictions provided opportunities to quite a large number of small peasant producers, part-time workers, and middle strata in the service sector to avoid so far the family disintegration and social marginalization and pauperization which have struck poor peasants in mountainous regions and certain sections of the working class in large cities.

But this pattern of decentralized development is neither stable nor able to provide solutions to regional and local needs in a direct and concrete way. As for the old centralized model, it is based on the rules of capitalist competition and exploitation of specific work processes which in turn reproduce conditions of unevenness and degradation. In the past, regional policies in southern European countries, inspired by the Italian distinction between North and South, aimed to provide "backward-southern" regions with modern industrial growth poles. Today local development policies from below are replacing regional ones, inspired again by another Italian prototype. Third Italy's supposed local development, however, based in part on post-modern flexibility, must not be idealized and cannot be duplicated elsewhere. Nor is it a "leftist alternative" solution for other localities on the grounds that the PCI was responsible for local administration of some parts of it. This does not mean a total rejection of Third Italy's experience, but a more careful evaluation, especially by those who see it from the outside.

Thus, despite logical improvements and the use of some radical rhetoric, local development approaches based on rationalization of existing cases suffer both in theory and practice from the same inherent limitations of two decades ago. The "new" development pattern is like the old one, i.e. uneven capitalist development, since the mode of conceptualizing the relationship between local society and social change remains unaltered, leaving the emphasis on procedure empty of content.

Despite inherent limitations and ineffectiveness on the development side, local strategies in southern Europe are in good currency today because they serve the interest of new rising middle strata in semi-urban areas, the owners of dynamic SMEs in agriculture, industry and tourism. These "nouveaux riches" in non-metropolitan regions have changed the structure of local hegemonic blocs, that is, a local system of exploitation, a specific mode of social regulation and a local form of alliance between dominant social classes and other social actors (Hadjimichalis, 1987). These new social strata, while they operate under conditions of free competition, are dependent on central state and local authorities in many ways,

not least for continuation of many illegal or semi-illegal practices. This
is why local hegemonic blocs are taking defensive or demanding positions
vis-à-vis the national state, the EC or other hegemonic blocs competing for
investments and public resources, labor legislation, and markets for their
products. Furthermore, these new middle strata have been the political
basis for mass-populist socialist parties like PSOE in Spain and PASOK
in Greece and to some extent in Portugal, while in Italy they form an
important pressure group within the PCI, DC and PSI.

Above all, local development seems to be of high priority among neoliberals in the EC inspired by Thatcherite policies in southern England, the
"paradise" of small, individual success. Neoliberals argue against statist
regional policies and against Jacques Delors' advocated "integrated social
space", a minimal check on the undermining of labor conditions and national levels of social provision by the single market in 1992. Instead, they
prefer "local areas" to compete freely among themselves for resources, investment, jobs and prosperity, as individual firms do in the "free" market.
It seems, therefore, that European integration will strengthen such views
among rightist governments, and what today appears as a trivial development alternative could be developed to an offensive rightist strategy in a
few years.

Uneven development in the 1980s has thus contributed to both geographical and social differentiation, taking advantage of old polarizations
to promote new ones. Anyone who stays in some southern European region for more than a short period of time learns to "appreciate" – with
great variations among regions – just how important these differentiations
are, how extensive the inadequacies of the state are and to understand the
party-patronage system trying to cope with the demands and objections
of the new middle strata. The subsequent legitimation of needs has today
turned "old regional assistance" into an obligation which the state, local
authorities, and political parties have to meet. Virtually all spatial issues
have thus become open political questions.

The latter has two effects. Either state obligations mediated through
the party-patronage system generate a popular apathy, with the majority of people "waiting for solutions from above" from the state and the
parties, as in the Greek case. Or, when political conflicts at the local
and regional levels do take place, they are substantially convoluted and
shunted aside by the inability of the mass-integrative apparatuses to react to concrete and goal-directed regional interests which are not related
to the centralized process of bargaining and compromise as in the case of
Spain and Italy. In both cases a new mode of social control develops based
on the political characteristics of the present socio-spatial differentiation
in southern Europe and mediated in the most dynamic regions through
local development plans. It is urgent therefore to see the conditions under

which this new mode of social control is in the making. Further research is required to identify local business interests, clientelistic relations, political parties' involvement and planning policies introduced either by national states or by the European Community.

In this respect "local" is not an alternative development scale to unsuccessful national and regional policies, but an arena for struggle, where "non-capital" – all those whose labor is appropriated by capital under many work relations and conditions – can organize and oppose, or simply cope with, pressures deriving from global restructuring strategies.

References

Amin, A., 1989. Flexible Specialization and Small Firms in Italy: Myths and Realities, *Antipode*, Vol. 21, pp. 13–34.

Amin, A., K. Robins, forthcoming. Industrial Districts and Regional Development: Limits and Possibilities, *Society and Space*.

Arcangeli, F., C. Bozzaga, S. Grogli, 1980. Patterns of peripheral development in Italian regions 1964–77, Paper presented to the 19th European Congress of the RSA, London.

Ascoli, U., 1979. Ecomia periferica e società periferica, *Inchiesta*, Vol. 37, pp. 85–99.

Bagnasco, A., 1977. *Tre Italie*, Il Mulino, Bologna.

Bagnasco, A., 1988. *La Construzione Sociale del Mercato*, Il Mulino, Bologna.

Bellini, N., 1989. Il socialismo in una regione sola: il PCI e il governo del' industria in Emilia-Romagna, *Il Mulino*, Vol. 38, pp. 707–732.

Berger, S., M. Piore, 1980. *Dualism and Discontinuity in Industrial Societies*, Cambridge University Press, Cambridge.

Bimbi, F., 1986. Lavoro domestico, economia informale, communità, *Inchiesta*, Vol. 74, pp. 25–31.

Bleltrach, D., A. Chenu, 1070. *L'Usine et la ville: luttes régionales Marseille et Fós*. Maspero, Paris.

Buruaga, G., 1983. Towards a New Regional Policy in Spain, in D. Seers, K. Öström (eds.), *The Crisis of the European Regions*, Macmillan, London, pp. 68–83.

Camagni, R., R. Capello, 1988. Italian success stories of local development: theoretical conditions and practical experiences, Università Luigi Bocconi, Milan, mimeo.

Cooke, P., 1983. Labour Market Discontinuity and Spatial Development, *Progress in Human Geography*, Vol. 7, pp. 543–565.

Cooke, P., A.R. Pires, 1985. Productive Decentralization in Three European Regions, *Environment and Planning A*, Vol. 17, pp. 527–554.

Costa Campi, M.T., 1988. Descentramiento productivo y difusión industrial: el modelo de especialización flexible, *Papeles de Economía Española*, Vol. 35, pp. 251–276.

de Oliveira, L.F.V., 1983. Regional Development of Portugal, in D. Seers, K. Öström (eds.) *The Crisis of European Regions*, Macmillan, London, pp. 68–82.

Edwards, R., M. Reich, D. Gordon, 1975. *Labour Market Segmentation*, D.C. Heath, Lexington.

EEC, 1988. *Programme de Recherche sur l'Evolution du Marché du Travail Noir*, Final Report, 8 Vols. (for all EEC countries), Brussels.

EETAA (Agency for Local Development), 1988. Local Development Projects in Greece, Athens, mimeo (in Greek).

Evangelinides, M., 1979. Core–Peripheral Problems in the Greek case, *Greek Review of Social Research*, Vol. 5, pp. 125–150.

Ferrao, J., 1985. Regional Variations in the Rate of Profit in Portuguese Industry, in R. Hudson, J. Lewis (eds.), *Uneven Development in Southern Europe*, Methuen, London, pp. 211–245.

Ferrao, J., 1987. Social Structures, Labour Markets and Spatial Configurations in Modern Portugal, *Antipode*, Vol. 19, pp. 99–118.

Fuà, G., 1983. Main Features of the NEC Model, in *Italy: Analytical Report*, OECD, Paris.

Garcia-Herrera, L.M., 1987. Economic Development and Spatial Configuration in the Canary Islands, *Antipode*, Vol. 19, pp. 25–39.

Garcia-Ramon, M.D., 1985. Agricultural Change in an Industrialized Area: The Case of the Tarragona Area, in R. Hudson, J. Lewis (eds.), *Uneven Development in Southern Europe*, Methuen, London, pp. 140–154.

Garofoli, G, 1983. *Industrializzazione Diffuse in Lombardia*, F. Angeli, Milano.

Garofoli, G., 1988. Industrial Districts: Structure and Transformation, Workshop: Depressed Regions in the Mediterranean Countries and Endogenous Devlopment, Reggio Calabria, mimeo.

Ginatempo, N., 1985. Social Reproduction and the Structure of Marginal Areas in Southern Italy: Some Remarks on the Role of the Family in the Present Crisis, *International Journal of Urban and Regional Research*, Vol. 9, pp. 99–110.

Giner, S., 1985. Political Economy, Legitimation and the State in Southern Europe, in R. Hudson, J. Lewis (eds.), *Uneven Development in Southern Europe*, Methuen, London, pp. 309–350.

Hadjimichalis, C., 1987. *Uneven Development and Regionalism: State, Territory and Class in Southern Europe*, Croom Helm, London.

Hadjimichalis, C., D. Vaiou, 1987. Changing Patterns of Uneven Regional Development and Forms of Social Reproduction in Greece, *Society and Space*, Vol. 5, pp. 319–333.

Hadjimichalis, C., D. Vaiou, 1990. Flexible Labour Markets and Regional Development in Northern Greece, *International Journal of Urban and Regional Research*, Vol. 14, pp. 1–24.

Holland, S., 1979. Dependent Development: Portugal as Periphery, in D. Seers, B. Schaffer, M.L. Kiljunen (eds), *Underdeveloped Europe*, Harvester, London, pp. 139–160.

Hudson, R., J. Lewis, 1984. Capital Accumulation: The Industrialization of Southern Europe?, in A. Williams (ed.), *Southern Europe Transformed*, Harper & Row, New York, pp. 179–202.

Instituto del Territorio y Urbanismo, 1987. *Areas Rurales con Capacidad de Desarrollo Endógeno*, MOPU, Madrid, mimeo.

Keeble, D., 1980. Industrial Decline, Regional Policy and the Urban–Rural Manufacturing Shift in the United Kingdom, *Environment and Planning A*, Vol. 12, pp. 945–962.

Keeble, D., P. Owen, C. Thompson, 1983. The Urban–Rural Manufacturing Shift in the European Community, *Urban Studies*, Vol. 20, pp. 405–418.

Leondidou, L., 1989. *Geographical Space and Social Transformation*, National Technical University of Athens, Athens (in Greek).

Lewis, J., A. Williams, 1988. Factories in the Fields: Small Manufacturing in Rural Southern Europe, in G. Linge (ed.), *Peripheralisation and Industrial Change*, Croom Helm, London, pp. 113–130.

Lipietz, A., 1987. *Mirages and Miracles*, Verso, London.

Magnaghi, A., B. Perelli, 1978. *Ristrutturazione e diffusione territoriale del ciclo produttivo: formazione della "fabrica diffusa" in Italia*, ATTI-10 Seminario Inter. del Area Mediterranea, Milan.

Massey, D., 1984. *Spatial Divisions of Labour*, Macmillan, London.

Mingione, E., 1985. Social Reproduction of the Surplus Labour Force: The Case of Southern Italy, in N. Redclift and E. Mingione (eds.), *Beyond Employment*, Basil Blackwell, Oxford, pp. 14–54.

Mingione, E., 1987. *Class Transformations in Southern Italy since World War II*, International Conference on Inequality and Development, Utah.

Mottura, G., E. Mingione, 1989. Agriculture and Society: Remarks on Transformations and New Social Profiles in the Case of Italy, *Agriculture and Human Values*, Vol. 21, pp. 47–58.

Mouzelis, N., 1986. *Politics in the Semi-Periphery*, Macmillan, London.

Munoz, J., S. Roldan, A. Serrano, 1979. The Growing Dependence of Spanish Industrialization, in D. Seers, B. Schaffer, M.L. Kiljunen (eds.), *Underdeveloped Europe*, Harvester, London, pp. 161–176.

Musto, S., 1985. In Search of a New Paradigm, in S. Musto (ed.), *Endogenous Development: A Myth or Path?*, EADI-Book Series 5, Berlin.

Nardin, G., 1987. *La Benetton: strategia e struttura di un impresa di successo*, Edizioni Lavoro, Roma.

OECD, 1979. *Re-appraisal of Regional Policies in OECD Countries*, Paris.

OECD, 1983. *Small Firms and Industrial Development*, Paris.

Offe, C., 1985. *Disorganized Capitalism*, MIT Press, Cambridge, Mass.

Paci, M., 1978. Il mercato del lavoro dall'unità d'Italia oggi, in N. Tranfaglia (ed.), *Il mondo contemporaneo*, Einaudi, Florence, pp. 31–60.

Paci, M., 1982. *La Struttura Sociale Italiana*, Il Mulino, Bologna.

Pinnaro, G., E. Pugliese, 1985. Information and Social Resistance: The Case of Naples, in N. Redclift, E. Mingione (eds.), *Beyond Employment*, Macmillan,

London, pp. 228–247.

Piore, M., C. Sabel, 1983. Italian Small Business Development: Lessons for U.S. Industrial Policy, in J. Zysman (ed.), *American Industry in International Competition*, Cornell University Press, Ithaca, pp. 120–136.

Pugliese, E., 1982. Farm Workers in Italy: Agricultural Working Class, Landless Peasants, or Clients of the Welfare State, Paper presented in the Conference on National and Regional Development in the Mediterranean, University of Durham.

Recio, A., 1988. *El trabajo precario en Catalanya: la industria textilanera des valles occidental*, Comissión Obrerra Nacional de Catalanya, Barcelona.

Sabel, C., 1986. Flexible Specialization and the Re-emergence of Regional Economies, in P. Hirst, J. Zeitlin (eds.), *Reversing Industrial Decline? Industrial Structure and Policy in Britain*, Berg, Oxford.

Sanchis, E., 1984. *El trabajo domicilio en Pais Valenciano*, Instituto de la Mujer, Ministerio de la Cultura, Madrid.

Sayer, A., 1989. Post-Fordism in Question, *International Journal of Urban and Regional Research*, Vol. 13, pp. 666–693.

Scott, A., 1988. *New Industrial Spaces*, Pion, London.

Scott, A., M. Stoper, 1987. High Technology Industry and Regional Development: A Theoretical Critique and Reconstruction, *International Social Science Journal*, Vol. 112, pp. 215–232.

Stöhr, W., 1986. Regional Innovation Complexes, *Papers of the Regional Science Association*, Vol. 59, pp. 29–44.

Trigilia, C., 1986. Small Firm Developments and Political Subcultures in Italy, *European Sociological Review*, Vol. 213, pp. 161–175.

Tsoulouvis, L., 1987. Aspects of Statism and Planning in Greece, *International Journal of Urban and Regional Research*, Vol. 11, pp. 500–522.

Vaiou, D., 1987. Invisible Forms of Work, *TO KAPA*, Vol. 18, pp. 22–26 (in Greek).

Vasquez-Barquero, A., 1986. Local Development Initiatives under Incipient Regional Autonomy: The Spanish Experience in the 1980s, Universidad Autónomas de Madrid, mimeo.

Vinay, P., 1985. Family Life Cycle and the Informal Economy in Central Italy, *International Journal of Urban and Regional Research*, Vol. 9, pp. 82–97.

Vinay, P., 1987. Women, Family and Work: Symptoms of Crisis in the Informal Economy of Central Italy, *Samos International Seminar Proceedings*, University of Thessaloniki, Thessaloniki.

Williams, A., G. Shaw (eds.), 1988. *Tourism and Economic Development*, Belhaven, London.

Part III

Sectoral Dynamics of Regional Restructuring

9

The Industrial Transition: A Comprehensive Approach to Regional Development

John Friedmann*

It has become commonplace to speak of the present era as one of general restructuring. Waves of technological innovation sweep through the economy, and when they converge, which is experienced as a time of turbulence, a broad restructuring of familiar patterns is the result. New forms of production, new modes of organizing production, and new spatial patterns are the more visible facets (Storper and Walker, 1989). But no aspect of life is left untouched.

Restructuring poses enormous challenges for regional planners. The new forms of economy, culture, and society seek incubators away from the older industrial regions which are left to deteriorate. Planners' tasks are therefore twofold: to cope with the consequences and solidify the new urban forms that are emerging – some have called them silicon landscapes, others suburban cities – and to halt the downward spiral of decline in former growth poles that have seemingly exhausted their economic potential. Sometimes the two phenomena occur within the same space, as in Los Angeles, where, as Edward Soja tells us, "it all comes together," growth and decline rubbing against each other, cheek by cheek (Soja, 1989).

Walter Stöhr was one of the first to raise the question of regional policy in an era of restructuring (Stöhr, 1987). I shall follow his footsteps, "revisiting" the question of what especially older industrial regions – those which have been abandoned by the new forms of production and control

*University of California, Los Angeles. This paper was initially presented at the Conference on Regional Development Policy in Declining Industrial Areas at San Sebastian, Pais Vasco, September 21-23, 1987. It has been substantially revised for publication in the present volume.

and, like beached whales, are slowly decomposing – should do to avert
disaster. I have no recipes to offer; each region will have to find its own
path of recovery. What I can do is to point out the general directions that
must be taken at a time when halfway measures may be worse than none
at all.

My approach will be to describe the tasks facing planners and, more
broadly, regional leadership in five overlapping regional "environments":
cultural, political, physical, economic, and institutional. Only by dealing
with all of these in their multiple interrelations can we mount a successful
response to the challenge of regional decline, as we transit at hyper-rapid
speed from the second to the third industrial revolution.[1] The challenge
is not only to replace old infrastructure with new, adapting it to the requirements of the global competition in which the new economic relations
lie embedded. It is also to deal successfully with the human and social
costs which the transition engenders. In this context a progressive regional
policy must aim at creating opportunities that will lead to a wide sharing
of prosperity.

1 The Cultural Environment

In discussing the transition, I am thinking primarily of regions that have
acquired a historical identity and a capacity to act for themselves. Not
all regions are like that: some are the result of administrative fiat, others
reflect purely economic relationships. Here I am interested in cultural
and/or political regions, such as New England, Scotland, the Ruhr Valley,

---

[1]The concept of a third industrial revolution raises fundamental questions
about the nature of productive work. It used to be that primacy was given to
manufacturing. And so long as industrial processes were labor-intensive, it made
sense to speak of the productivity of labor. But manufacturing is a rapidly shrinking source of employment, though it continues to make an important contribution
to regional and national product. New economic activities, such as the design
of software, do not fit neatly into a traditional category such as manufacturing;
neither are they a service. They are best regarded as information-generating
activities.

Productivity measures, too, are becoming outdated. A robotized factory, maintained by a handful of specialists, does not permit one to base salaries or wages
on a calculated "product" of labor. The relation between human effort (labor)
and final product is becoming more tenuous. As a result, income payments are
increasingly calculated on grounds other than productivity. This is important for
an information society which has a tendency to create a polarization of incomes
between a relatively small professionalized labor force on the one hand and a mass
of semi- and unskilled labor on the other, engaged in low-level services (Sassen,
1988).

or the Basque Country. Only regions that have a cultural identity also
have a capacity to develop "from within". And their presence in the world
can make a difference (Friedmann and Forest, 1988).

But identity and a desire for greater political autonomy have to be as-
serted against the hegemonic system and, just because of that, the asser-
tion of cultural difference is frequently backward-oriented, inward-looking,
and parochial, seeking the essence of regional culture in the old ways,
traces of which are perhaps still preserved in remote mountain valleys. In
this context, the large regional cities which are the centers of economic and
political life – Boston, Glasgow, Duisburg-Dortmund, Bilbao – present an
anomaly. Of necessity, they are linked to the outside world; a significant
part of their population may be from outside the region; they participate
in global economic relations. They are cosmopolitan centers.

One consequence of the transition is the creation and consolidation of
a global system of markets and production which has been made possible
by the new information technologies. A successful transition, therefore,
requires that a region peripheralized by changes in economic relations regain its place among the concert of regions by becoming more closely
integrated with the emerging world system. The challenge is this: can
integration be accomplished without losing what is specific and unique
about the region, without losing its historical identity? In other words,
can the contradictory forces of cosmopolitanism and cultural regionalism
be joined? Regionalists often denigrate cosmopolitan culture: they call
it rootless. A more positive way is to understand it as a culture that is
open to the world and to continuous, irreversible change. A rooted cosmopolitanism is one in which the particular and the universal are brought
together. It derives from a regional culture that is unafraid to engage the
world in open discourse, that can envision a future worth struggling for
precisely because it has a long historical lineage.

2   The Political Environment

Planning the transition to an information-based society involves restructuring a number of different but overlapping environments. Such planning
calls for more than technical judgement. Enlightened political leadership
and a broad social consensus are essential to it. Should they fail to obtain
widespread agreement on the ends to be achieved and on a sharing of the
costs (and benefits) of the transition, planners will be unable to deal with
anything other than marginally important issues; their main tasks will
have been removed from the agenda.

Social consensus in this context means not only an aggregation of views
across individuals (as in voting) but a conjoining of wills across the major

social sectors. The suspension of political conflict which social consensus implies is a rare event in the history of any region. To bring it about, an immense educational effort is needed that clarifies for all social strata and organized interests the choices facing the regional community. Such an effort must be an exercise in mutual learning, however, something more than a one-way communication from political elites to the subordinate classes. It must become a truly participatory process. For if it is to sustain the project of the transition, the suspension of conflict must be based on intelligent insight by all concerned.

Some people have suggested that a broad social consensus implies a shift from a democratic polity to more corporate arrangements in which organized capital, organized labor, and the state work in harmony under the latter's tutelage. But corporatism is not what I have in mind. Rather than proposing political principles, I wish to describe the conditions that would allow the project of the transition to proceed apace. By definition, this project is limited in time. It is "for the duration" that the consensus must prevail, much as a national consensus is necessary for successfully combating, say, hyper-inflation. Moreover, the suspension of political conflict concerns only the transition project itself, not its detailing. Specific restructuring proposals will call forth strong political arguments on all sides. And this is as it should be. For planners do not possess exclusive wisdom and, in the absence of certainty about the future, open argument about specific courses of action is the only reasonable way for arriving at decisions.

3   The Physical Environment

Within the last two decades, the older industrial areas of the American Northeast, once the industrial heartland of the nation, have come to be known as the nation's "rust-belt". The name stands for a region that is past its prime, deteriorating, and heavily polluted. It is a region abandoned by capital, and from which many younger people are leaving for opportunities elsewhere.

But the physical environment does not merely reflect economic conditions, it also helps to bring them about. No one wants to move into a "rust-belt", and further deterioration in physical conditions accelerates the process of abandonment.

How does one reverse this process? Although reconstructing the physical environment will not, by itself, rescue a region from economic decline, neglecting it will make the tasks of economic revitalization much more difficult. In the course of the transition, planners must address four tasks: creating a pollution-free environment, preserving landscape and recreational resources, recycling old industrial buildings, and improving transport and communication linkages with the rest of the world.

The time is long past when people were tolerant of high pollution levels. Belching smokestacks are no longer regarded as a symbol of modernity. The romance has gone out of dense London smog (which, anyway, has long been a thing of the past) or the notorious photochemical smog of Los Angeles that is still with us. People are also becoming increasingly alerted to the hazards posed by toxic chemical wastes and the destruction of fisheries and beaches from raw sewage and oil spills. Higher levels of education are leading to lower tolerance thresholds for noise (as in the vicinity of airports) and for the thoughtless destruction of aesthetic values. In short, the second industrial revolution was purchased at a cost which was partly extracted from the regional environment. It has left regions with a legacy that is dangerous to physical and mental health. Although a pollution-free environment is probably an unattainable goal, the substantial reduction of pollution has become technically, financially, and politically feasible. Closely related to the reduction of pollution levels is the preservation (and enhancement) of the landscape and recreational resources of a region. If the second industrial revolution was accompanied by high rates of urban growth and metropolitanization, the next phase will take place in an already urbanized environment. Thus, the danger is posed of the wanton destruction of landscape values and natural sites for the recreation of an increasingly affluent, motorized, and thoroughly urbanized population. Different population sectors have distinctive recreational preferences. Blue collar workers may be less drawn into the out-of-doors than, for example, professionals. But overall, people living in the information age will make much more intensive use of natural environments in the vicinity of large urban concentrations than earlier generations.

A closely related problem is the empty hulls of factories and warehouses that are scattered throughout the region and have closed their gates forever. Some of these buildings may be over a hundred years old, a reminder of the time when the second industrial revolution was still young. Some of them are significant examples of an industrial architecture that may be worth preserving as cultural monuments. Others can perhaps be converted to contemporary uses, to serve, for example, as incubators of small high-tech firms, artists' lofts, shopping centers, restaurants, schools, community centers. Buildings that cannot be converted (or saved) will eventually have to give way to other projects. But the very sturdiness of factory walls is a reminder of a less ephemeral technology and of an often turbulent labor history. They help compose the image of the region and should be treated more as a cultural asset than a liability.

Finally, there is the matter of physical infrastructure in transport and communication. Their adequacy relative to both national and international markets must be carefully assessed in the light of contemporary requirements. In comparison to the way global cities are linked into the world economy, most regional cities will be found wanting. Upgrading facilities – airports, harbors, and major access routes by land – does not by itself ensure a successful transition but is surely one of its essential conditions.

4   The Economic Environment

The economic restructuring of the region, which relates to questions of production, capital accumulation, labor markets, and labor-management relations, faces at least four challenging tasks: the phasing out or restructuring of non-competitive industries, the channeling of regional capital into new ventures, the rethinking of educational policies in the light of information-age requirements, and progress towards new forms of labor–management relations. None of these tasks will come easy, and their accomplishment will be a slow process. A beginning must nevertheless be made.

One reason for requiring a broad political consensus is that the transition is going to be costly. An important criterion of a successful transition ought to be the alleviation of the burden of change for the individuals and households most affected by the phasing out or modernizing of non-competitive industries. The question is much debated of the extent to which older industries (and the jobs dependent on them) should be protected against lower-cost producers elsewhere in the world. It involves the important political question of a worker's right to a job. But, in the face of beckoning change, obstinately to hold on to the past will ultimately lead to even greater costs than the opposite course. The real issue is the desirable pace of change and the protection of individuals (and households) against a too-sudden disruption of their lives. While the transition obviously holds risks, so does an overly protective attitude toward entitlements. The social capital used up in protecting already existing jobs (usually through some form of capital subsidy) can be more productively invested in efforts to create conditions favorable for the transition or new employments directly. In some situations, older industries may be able to regain their world-competitive position through the introduction of new technologies, such as robotization, a process that will involve large redundancies in the workforce. And so, unless ways can be found for dealing with the human side of the equation, the move into the information-age is almost certain to be resisted. When all is said and done, however, technological updating is to be preferred over a strategy that will leave the industrial sector of a region further behind in the competitive stakes.

The second task is the redirection of regional capital into new business ventures. The traditional strategy for the re-industrialization of declining regions involved generous subsidies to extra-regional capital. Tax holidays and the assumption of a large part of the needed infrastructure costs by local government, such as industrial estates or enterprise zones, were used to lure potential employers from central locations. This policy was graced with moderate success, though when subsidies ended, industries often pulled out from the lagging region, returning to more profitable locations.

The new model is distinguished by two characteristics: on the one hand, it is much more broadly conceived as the restructuring of a series of overlapping "environments" (which is the subject of the present chapter); on the other hand, it relies more on regional resources than on those provided by the central state. Among them are the intellectual (scientific-technical) capabilities found in the region's universities and other institutions of higher learning, a commitment to R&D work in fields where the region may have a competitive edge (e.g. in biotechnology), the provision of venture capital through local financial institutions, technical assistance to young management groups, the conversion of old industrial buildings into locations for fledgling firms trying to establish themselves in the market, and the financing and construction of modern industrial parks (Stöhr, 1986).

The creation and support of these resources for information-age industrialization requires intelligent and flexible guidance, and the kind of knowledge that may be available only to already successful regional firms. One of the characteristics of the new age is that monopoly power based on particular inventions (and markets) has become less significant as a source of profits than the ability to keep on innovating (and successfully marketing the innovations). This opens up heretofore unknown possibilities of cooperation among firms which benefit from the proximate location of even their competitors, because their presence in the region creates external economies (e.g. a more complete range of business services, or the joint funding of basic research).[2] It is this phenomenon which has given rise to so-called Silicon Landscapes, as in California's Orange County, which are characterized by the concentration of large numbers of related industries based on micro-electronics (Hall and Markusen, 1985).

The rethinking of educational policy in relation to the variable needs of the emerging information society is the third major task facing planners of the economic environment. Our understanding of what these needs might be is not yet very profound, but the following suggestions may be plausible

---

[2]An excellent example of such cooperation will be found in the special issue on public–private partnerships in southwestern Pennsylvania (Weaver, 1987).

(Handy, 1985).

- The composition of the labor force is shifting rapidly from blue-collar or manual, to professional and semi-professional occupations.
- Careers of individual workers are being redefined, as more workers seek interesting and varied jobs that offer greater autonomy over the carrying-out of defined tasks. Lateral mobility – workers shifting from one kind of work (and employer) to another – is becoming more common. As a result, job security becomes less valued.
- More workers, and especially women, say that they prefer part-time work and flexible work schedules. The average age of first entering the labor market is likely to rise and work careers may be interrupted, from time to time, by longer periods of worklessness (i.e. dedication to tasks other than earning money, such as raising children).
- The collective participation of workers in decision-making by the firm is likely to become a more widespread practice.
- Workers need to develop a capacity for keeping up with and adapting to continuous and rapid technological and social change. Polyvalent workers will be increasingly in demand.

Since a good part of the state's effort in shaping education is to "reproduce" the labor force, that is, to shoulder the burden of preparing young people for a working life and at the same time to instill in them the "correct" disciplines and attitudes, a deep review of educational policy needs to accompany the transition into an information-based economy. What implications for educational policy can we draw from our list of labor force "needs"? This is not the place to be overly specific, and certainly the job of researching educational policy needs to be undertaken. But a few hints of how educational policy may need to change will illustrate what I have in mind.

- Education should be seen as a life-long process and not be confined to, say, the twelve years from six to eighteen. Education for life would mean expanding adult, post-secondary education and creating conditions at work that will allow employees to take advantage of them. Diligent workers should be rewarded for this effort. A variety of channels of post-secondary education could be opened up with the help of cooperatives, unions, employers, and local government, including night schools, summer schools, short-term institutes, and site visits to innovating centers.
- Although the acquisition of specific skills will continue to be an important part of worker education, especially in on-the-job training,

there will increasingly be a need to stress the principles and theories that underlie the new information-based technologies. It is this general knowledge that will enable workers to adapt to an ever-changing working environment.

- Workers should learn to think critically about the transition in the context of their own region. They should come to grips with such concepts as a rooted cosmopolitanism, the politics of the transition, the problems of physical regional planning, the restructuring of the economic environment, and the need for new institutional arrangements. This would involve a different kind of "civic education" that would prepare workers for the new tasks of political and economic citizenship.

- Critical thinking should extend beyond the region into the sphere of the international economy, the role of international capital, the dilemmas of Third World development, and the social (and spatial) implications of the new technologies. All this must be brought into relation with one's own life space and actions, rather than taught abstractly as "subject matter". And like critical thinking about the regional transition, relevant material should be introduced at all educational levels, including the primary grades.

We come now to the final task of economic restructuring, the recasting of labor–management relations. Organized labor has traditionally resisted technical innovation, particularly when jobs were at stake, and bitter struggles have been waged over the introduction of new technologies, for example, in the printing trades (Cockburn, 1983). This has put organized labor in an anomalous, essentially conservative position: it is fighting rearguard actions. But in an age where all the advantages lie with adapting to change, blanket resistance leads to no-win situations. Proposed changes should be carefully evaluated: how will jobs be affected? the physical environment? the future competitive position of the regional economy? These and related questions need to be asked (and answered), but they need to be addressed in the context of the general consensus about the necessity of the transition itself. Organized labor must thus become interested in a wider range of issues than those related to wages, job security, and the quality of the working environment. A region-based unionism that links community and workplace issues is called for. Such a unionism would become less confrontational and more reliant on the politics of negotiation, conflict resolution, and mediation based on a recognition of mutual interest between community, employer, and self.

All of this brings me to the question of new institutional arrangements for the transition, which is my final topic.

5   The Institutional Environment

Within a single country, the process of transition to an information society is likely to require for its completion between one and two generations. There are neither short-cuts nor quick fixes to this end, and the final outcome is not predictable. All we can do is to keep the goal clearly in view while adopting a flexible and adaptive approach capable of responding to new information as it becomes available. And because planning for the transition must be both transformative and adaptive to continuous change, it is the process of intervention itself that assumes primary importance, rather than the outlining of an ideal future or plan.

Central, hierarchical planning is inappropriate to this task. What is needed is a form of concerted planning that brings together major regional actors in a set of loosely linked networks: organized civil society, cooperatives, labor unions, private enterprise, universities, political parties, and the local state. This form of planning is designed to make proposed solutions isomorphic with the complexity of the problem itself. (Central planning operates on the contrary assumption: the problem is simplified to fit the state's capacity for solutions.)

Concerted planning accomplishes a number of other things as well. It makes planning for the transition endogenous to the region. It is both conducive to and a result of a growing popular consensus. And it allows for different co-participants to assume the lead in planning where they have a special interest or competence: now universities, now private enterprise, now the provincial government, now cooperatives, and so forth. None of the participants in these networks can exercise complete control over the process, and they become dependent on the continued goodwill and cooperation of the remaining actors. A genuine politics based on conflict, negotiation, and compromise thus ensues. It would be presumptuous to suppose that this process, described here in barest outline, could be implemented in any given region without specific adaptations to local political culture. Different countries have their own ways of doing things. The US is pluralist and tends to prefer pragmatic solutions based on contending group interests. It favors a highly decentralized system of decision-making and control. French political culture (to take a European example) assigns a far greater role to the state: it is more centralist and technocratic. But even accepting the variety of political cultures as given, at least in the medium term, the proposed logic of the institutional approach to regional restructuring remains valid.

6 Conclusions

I have tried to outline a general approach to the problem of restructuring old industrial regions as they transit from the second to the third industrial revolution. The problem was shown to be far more complex than attracting a number of high-tech industries producing for export through a program of linked state and local subsidies. Five "environments" were identified, including culture, politics, the physical environment, the economic environment, and the institutions necessary for planning and implementation.

My argument was premised on reasonable assumptions about the character of an information-based economy, especially its capital and labor markets. Rapid innovation not only in technology but also in industrial organization, the organization of work, and the spatial organization of the global economy was found to be at the core of the emerging system, requiring the cultivation of a refined adaptability. Since regions are relatively powerless to affect the behavior of the systems to which they are linked, they must discover ways of successfully adapting to exogenous change. This is possible only if they evolve a rooted cosmopolitan culture that is ready to engage in vigorous social and political experiment. And such experimentation requires not only a broad popular consensus but an orchestrated effort by all of the relevant actors. A creative response to crisis is to see in it new opportunities for acting decisively in unprecedented ways. My intention in this paper has been to point in the direction of these opportunities.

References

Cockburn, C., 1983. *Brothers: Male Dominance and Technological Change.* Pluto Press, London.

Friedmann, J., Y. Forest, 1988. The Politics of Place: Towards a Political Economy of Territorial Planning, in B. Higgins and D.T. Savoie (eds.), *Regional Economic Development: Essays in Honour of François Perroux.* Unwin Hyman, Boston.

Hall, P., A. Markusen (eds.), 1985. *Silicon Landscapes.* Allen & Unwin, Boston.

Handy, C., 1985. *The Future of Work.* Basil Blackwell, London.

Sassen, S., 1988. *The Mobility of Labor and Capital: A Study in International Investment and Labor Flow.* Cambridge University Press, New York.

Soja, E.W., 1989. *Postmodern Geographies: The Reassertion of Space in Critical Social Theory.* Verso, London.

Storper, M., R. Walker, 1989. *The Capitalist Imperative: Territory, Technology and Industrial Growth.* Basil Blackwell, New York.

Stöhr, W.B., 1986. Territorial Innovation Complexes, in P. Aydalot (ed.), *Milieux Innovateurs en Europe*, Paris.

Stöhr, W.B., 1987. Industrial Structural Change and Regional Development Strategies, in H. Muegge and W. Stöhr (eds.), *International Economic Restructuring and the Regional Community*, Avebury, Aldershot.

Weaver, C. (ed.), 1987. Public-Private Partnerships in Southern Pennsylvania. *Journal of the American Planning Association*, Special Issue, Vol. 53, No. 1 (Fall).

10

Manufacturing and Labor Market Recovery in Victoria, Australia

Kevin O'Connor*

1 Introduction

Victoria, located in the south-east corner of Australia, is the most densely settled part of the continent, and has long been one of the main locations of commercial activity in the country. From about the mid-1960s population growth in Australia tended to favor northern and western areas of the country, and that, in association with industrial structural change, disadvantaged Victoria. In the early 1980s these trends were turned around as national forces of structural change moved in Victoria's favor (O'Connor, 1987). This paper explores the recent recovery of the Victorian economy within the overall context of Australian development, and outlines the important role played by manufacturing in that recovery. In particular the paper highlights the role that the location of research and development activity has played in the manufacturing growth in Victoria.

2 Manufacturing and Services in Regional Growth

Analysis of the changing role of manufacturing in regional and metropolitan growth has foundations in two sources of ideas. The first queries the emphasis placed upon services in the long-term growth of metropoli-

---

*Department of Geography and Environmental Science, Monash University, Melbourne, Australia.

tan economies, and the lack of attention to manufacturing. The second
recognizes a new and different form of manufacturing that has emerged
owing to structural and financial changes. Related to these ideas is the
geography of research and development, though it is not altogether clear
whether manufacturing location and research and development need to be
coincident. These two aspects will be reviewed in turn.

In recent years much attention has been given to the role of tertiary
industry, not only in the structure of the national economy but also in
the growth and change of metropolitan areas. At the national scale, Bell's
(1976) work showed that tertiary industry was where job development
was concentrated. For metropolitan areas, Stanback (1985) found the
share of employment in services was an accurate measure of the growth
and influence of metropolitan areas. At the scale of the individual city,
Gans (1985) used results for Boston to show how service growth accounted
for most expansion and development in recent years. Across this spectrum
there was little scope to suggest that manufacturing could be important
to metropolitan or regional growth. Indeed, the most common dimension
in work in this general area was on de-industrialization (Bluestone and
Harrison, 1982). At a city scale it was common to follow that broad
theme into the negative impacts of plant closure, as done for example by
Buss and Redburn (1983).

These approaches associated the much smaller employment in manufacturing with a less significant role in overall economic development. The
preoccupation with employment numbers may have masked some important new aspects that would put manufacturing in a new light, had the
emphasis been upon output or interindustry linkages. Harris (1987) has
studied the contribution to regional output by manufacturing and services
in the UK, and found the role of manufacturing to be paramount. This
provides a lead toward a different interpretation of manufacturing's role
in the economy.

Cohen and Zysman (1987) have moved in this direction. Querying the
post-industrial thesis, they stress the important part that manufacturing
plays in the US economy, and how that needs to be strengthened rather
than weakened. In particular, they emphasize the importance of close
geographic linkages between product development and daily production
activity, and see in this proximity important opportunities to maintain
market leadership, quality control and innovation. They also recognize
that many activities that may not at present be counted in manufacturing
actually derive their vitality from the demands of manufacturers. The
strength of interindustry linkages, and the importance of manufacturing
to many activities that may be counted in other industrial groups such as
finance, wholesale and retail trade, and transport, lead them to the claim
that "manufacturing matters".

The most detailed regional scale analysis of changes in the role of manufacturing in a regional economy has been carried out by Harrison (1984). Following the development of the New England economy since World War II, he has been able to trace the shift in the mix of industries in that region. Significantly, after a long period of change, remnants of the old manufacturing base still survive. Although there was considerable change in numbers of people employed, the mill-based manufacturing industries (food, textiles, clothing, footwear) are still a part of the New England economy; these have generally undergone major technical and structural change, but remain competitive in specialized markets. The balance of the New England industry is in "so called high tech industries fabricating the newest generation of producers' goods (computers and peripheral equipment) and all manner of scientific and military instruments" together with "industries manufacturing capital goods for domestic and foreign producers" (Harrison, 1984, p. 69). These three groups, together with services, make up the regional economy. Although there is no doubt the New England economy has been restructured, and the type and rates of pay for work have deteriorated for a share of the workforce, manufacturing still remains a key element in the region's economic structure, and the knowledge-intensive or high-technology element is important not only in new industries but in old ones like clothing and printing.

Approaching the issue from a different tack, some researchers have shown that service growth has actually followed the development of manufacturing. Yago and McGahey (1984) reporting on New York State quote work by Gurwitz: "without the increase in manufacturing employment, total employment growth in New York State might have been 40 percent smaller than it was" between 1974 and 1981. They go on to comment: "Manufacturing jobs are more likely to be export-oriented, stimulating more local jobs in producing production inputs and services for the exporting firms and their workers. Understanding such sectoral linkages in the state's economy is critical for our economic future."

In Boston, Doolittle (1985) has analyzed the recovery of that economy and observed: "as the regional manufacturing economy regained its strength, employment in the city's business service, finance, insurance and real estate firms grew" (p. 84). "Despite the city's success in creating export services that offer their output in the national or international market, the city's fortunes are still tied closely to the regional manufacturing economy" (p. 86). At the city scale, Mullin *et al.* (1986) have shown how Maynard, Massachusetts has been transformed from woollen mill to computer industry town, so maintaining a role for manufacturing in its economy. Pittsburgh has also attracted attention. Berry *et al.* (1987) showed how manufacturing-based jobs in Pittsburgh have been replaced by service jobs, and laid the foundation for a high-technology base for long-term growth. Clark (1989), however, is more sanguine about this change, noting that the high-technology growth may be rapid, but the base is small.

The upshot of this work is that manufacturing's role in urban and regional development needs to be reinterpreted. That perspective is also reached by recognizing that manufacturing has a new style of organization which can stimulate development in new ways. Working on this new perspective, Scott (1986b) has shown that interindustry and service linkages now have a new and powerful local geography. This involves the vertical disintegration of industrial processes, and the development of subcontracting. Scott's work has shown that part of this reorganization and restructuring can involve rapid development of manufacturing in certain regions; a case study of Orange County (Scott, 1986a) has shown that new approaches and new systems in manufacturing have an important urban impact and created major clusters of activity, and of jobs. On an international scale, manufacturing is the driving force in the economy of a number of regions (Scott, 1988). Stepping back from the detail Scott has remarked that "industrialization continues to be as significant for an understanding of the late twentieth century city as it was for the nineteenth century city" (Scott, 1986b, p. 26).

One characteristic that the areas identified by Scott (1988) have in common is a strong research and development base. This has been recognized as an important new locational force for modern or high-technology industry, and considerable information has been assembled about this sector, for example by Hall and Markusen (1985) and Castells (1985). This work generally involved analyses of manufacturing activity, and also research and development expenditure and employment. In fact it is sometimes difficult to differentiate between the roles of these two activities, and identify the main sector of the regional economy. In some cases, the links between research and manufacturing are strong and both are part of the regional economy. The early growth of Silicon Valley fits that model (Saxenian, 1984, p. 171), while much of the activity in the M4 corridor involves both research and production activity (Hall *et al.*, 1987). Work on selected sectors – such as that by Scott and Angel (1988) on semi-conductors – has shown that some manufacturing can move away from the research and development locations to achieve cost savings. Saxenian (1984, p. 189) indicates this has happened in Silicon Valley, too, with "the dispersion of semi-conductor and electronics manufacturing to ... new hubs of regional growth ... throughout the South and the West". This spatial separation means that research and development emerges as the foundation of a region's economy with the manufacturing taking place elsewhere. Illustrating this stage in Silicon Valley's growth, Saxenian (1984, p. 189) observes that the region is gradually being transformed into a "high level control center – the site of corporate headquarters and sophisticated research, design and development activities".

Generalizing this experience, Knight (1987) has suggested that a new form of manufacturing city will emerge. "As the global economy expands and manufacturing operations are expanded around the world, the demand for knowledge intensive activities needed to support these manufacturing activities increases" (p. 202). As organizations internationalize "they are upgrading and expanding the more knowledge intensive functions such as administrative, research and associated professional, technical and specialized business services that are required by the growing world wide networks of manufacturing operations" (p. 205). Knight's approach sees the emergence of a new form of manufacturing or industrial city, where the management, control, product development, and research and development work would be undertaken. In the spirit of the present paper, the important point to make is that these activities may be counted in industries like finance, marketing, education, business services, research and the like, and be regarded as services, rather than as manufacturing. Certainly most activities will be located in office buildings rather than factories, which can give a mistaken impression of the economic activity of a region.

This research has made clear that manufacturing needs to be reconsidered as a sector in the development of modern regions. To take this approach a little further, the present paper looks at manufacturing in new ways, emphasizing the number of establishments, the construction of factories and the investment in plant and equipment, as well as the expenditure on R&D, rather than simply focusing on the level of employment. This approach complements the work of Harris (1987) which has looked at output measures of manufacturing and services. The paper also looks at the importance of a sector within the national context, on the understanding that national leadership can provide the grounds for development in a variety of ways that would not be apparent solely in terms of size of employment. The present paper explores these issues in Australia, by showing the strong role that manufacturing has played in the recent recovery of the Victorian economy, and relates that to a spatial concentration of research and development activity.

3   Economic Problems and Recovery in Victoria 1970–1988

Victoria has always been an important manufacturing center in Australia, dating from the early settlement of the country. Victoria's manufacturing base expanded and deepened through a time period when high tariffs were used to assist industrial development by restricting imports, protecting the local Australian market for Australian firms, or for subsidiaries of overseas firms. This approach produced rapid growth during the two decades leading up to 1970, but the increased international exposure of the national economy meant that it provided a difficult heritage to manage (Rich, 1987). Analysis by the state government in 1982 showed that the two largest employment sectors (motor vehicles and parts, and clothing) had protection levels of 51% and 73% (Ministry for Economic Development, 1982).

The decline in Victoria's importance relative to other states in Australia's development was variously ascribed to factors such as national shifts in tariff policy (which had a marked negative impact on Victoria because of the substantial concentration of industries with high levels of protection in the state). Simultaneously, other parts of the country grew rapidly owing to resource development and retirement migration. These two forces meant that Victoria seemed badly placed as a declining state within a changing national context that favored other areas. For some, Victoria's fortune provided an antipodean parallel to the US situation: a cold south lost in competition to a warm north and west (O'Connor, 1984).

This poor performance emerged as a major political issue in the early 1980s, as it became apparent that the state was slipping behind, and major redevelopment was needed. The greatest publicity centered around the extent to which outmigration was taking place. Victoria has experienced a net loss of people due to internal migration within Australia from 1977 onward. Related to that fact, Victoria began to lose part of its share of national population; between 1971 and 1988 this fell 1.3 percentage points. Perhaps the most important single item at the time was the decision by the largest property development firm not to spend on a single major project in Victoria in 1981. That public announcement, more than any other commentary, made clear the difficulties faced by the Victorian economy. In summary, it was saddled with a large share of internationally non-competitive industries, a falling share of national population, and provided few opportunities for the development industry. In distinct contrast to that prospect, the development in the 1980s has been strong and rapid.

The strong performance of the Victorian economy relative to other states of Australia has been documented in O'Connor (1990). One measure of economic improvement was a falling unemployment rate. Whereas during the middle 1970s unemployment was at times among the worst in the country, by the late 1980s it was the lowest in the nation and has kept at that level for a considerable time. In housing, too, there was clear evidence of recovery. Victoria's share of new house building fell to below

20% in 1980/81, but by 1987 it accounted for 28% of the national total, making Victoria the most important state for this activity. In summary, the state now has the highest shares of building of factories and houses and the lowest level of unemployment in the country. The following section will explore the role played by manufacturing in that recovery.

4 Manufacturing and Victoria's Growth

The first broad question to be addressed here is to measure the extent to which manufacturing has participated in Victoria's recent economic recovery. To test this idea, data on the national share of building, commercial investment, and new capital equipment expenditure for factories and for the finance and property sector are compared in a series of graphs. In the finance and property sector (see Fig. 10.1), Victoria's share of the range of indicators has rarely risen above 30%, and more commonly runs around 26–28%. In one area – finance for property and business services – the share rose after 1987, but that is an exception. On the other hand, in activities involving manufacturing (see Fig. 10.2), Victoria's national share has risen steadily, and in factory construction rose sharply since 1983. Also, the measures on these indicators run at higher levels – approaching 50% of the nation's activity in two measures.

Even though the levels of expenditure in the tertiary sector are larger than those in manufacturing (office building in Victoria is twice the value of that of factories, for example) it is clear that in terms of national influence and leadership, Melbourne's manufacturing role is stronger than its tertiary sector role. In this sense, manufacturing has been more important in the recovery than one would expect given an analysis based solely on employment. The second broad question is to identify what types of manufacturing have been involved, and what links exist between this activity and research and development. Research reported below will explore the significance of research and development in the Victorian economy, and its links with the growth of manufacturing.

5 Research and Development in Victoria

The purpose of this section is to explore the characteristics of research and development activity in Victorian manufacturing, and look in particular at the state's role as a center for industrial research and development. Ideally the analysis should be structured to show the links that exist between Victoria's obvious leadership in factory construction and general manufacturing identified earlier, and its role as a research and development center.

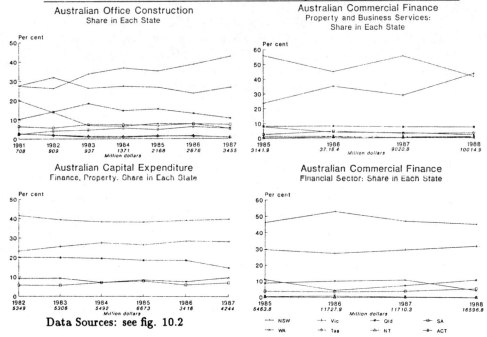

Data Sources: see fig. 10.2

Figure 10.1: Measures of recent change in Victorian tertiary industry.

Direct links like that are difficult to make, however, and the analysis needs to rely on implied associations between these variables.

Research and development in Australia is reported from statistical surveys that are carried out by the Australian Bureau of Statistics. These surveys follow OECD-derived definitions of activity, and report both dollar expenditure and man-hours worked. Much research and development activity is carried out by government agencies such as the Commonwealth Scientific and Industrial Research Organisation. In addition, research and development effort has been smaller than in many other countries, and recent government initiatives have been taken to lift activity, and its contribution to national economic change.

Looking first at the government expenditure on manufacturing research, Table 10.1 shows that Victoria's share of national expenditure is substantial and rose considerably between 1981 and 1986 at the expense of most other states. This suggests there is a solid infrastructure for manufacturing-related research and development in Victoria, something that private firms may be able to utilize.

In the private sector, manufacturing is the main focus of research and development, and this has grown rapidly from a small base in recent years. Within manufacturing, Australia's research and development expenditure

Table 10.1: Location of general government research and development expenditure on manufacturing (share of national total in each state)

State	1981/82 %	1986/87 %
New South Wales	48.4	41.9
Victoria	38.4	46.1
Queensland	8.8	4.7
South Australia	1.9	1.6
Western Australia	0.1	3.7
Tasmania	0.9	0.1
Northern Territory	–	1.9
ACT & Territories	1.6	–

Source: ABS 8109. Research and Experimental Development: General Government, Organisations, Table 13 (1981), Table 11 (1986).

Table 10.2: Research and development in major industry categories in Australia 1984/85

ASIC	Description	Expenditure
335	Appliances & Electrical Equipment	228,191
275/276	Basic Chemicals and other Chemical Products (Veterinary & Pharmacy)	99,608
323	Motor Vehicles and Parts	84,725
330	Industrial Machinery & Equipment	57,916
334	Photographic Scientific & Professional Equip.	27,786
294	Basic Iron & Steel	20,771
295/296	Basic Non Ferrous Metals	19,236
324	Other Transport Equipment	16,180
214/217	Margarine, Oils and Other Food Products	13,434
347	Plastic & Related Products	8,238
	Total in Leading Groups	576,085
	Share of Total Expenditure	88.9%

Source: ABS 8104. Data is research classified by product field, i.e. end result of research.

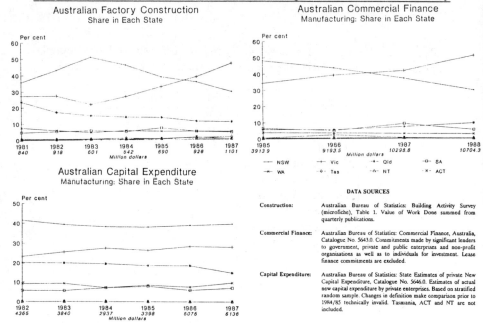

Figure 10.2: Measures of recent change in Victorian manufacturing industry.

is concentrated in appliances and electrical equipment (largely computers), basic chemicals (largely veterinary and pharmaceutical products) and the motor vehicle industry (see Table 10.2). These three groups accounted for almost two-thirds of expenditure in 1984/5; together with seven others they account for almost 90% of the expenditure on research and development; they will be referred to as "research oriented industry" in the analysis that follows.

The role of this activity in the development of Victorian industry can be analyzed in two ways. First, it is possible to identify Victoria's role in the ten groups identified in Table 10.2, and the information is displayed in Table 10.3. Second, it is possible to study the actual geography of expenditure on research and development by industry groups in Victoria. Regrettably the information available for that task, shown in Table 10.4, is not quite as detailed.

In seven of the categories of research-oriented industry shown in Table 10.3, Victoria's share of national employment has increased between 1980 and 1984, though its share of establishments has fallen in about half of the groups. In the two leading categories, Victoria's share of national employment is only equivalent to its overall share of national manufacturing, so the state's new found role in the nation is unlikely to be based

Table 10.3: Victoria's performance in research-oriented industry

ASIC	Share of National					
	Employment		Establishments		Fixed Capital Expenditure	
	1980/1	1984/5	1980/1	1984/5	1980/1	1984/5
335	29.1	32.6	31.4	31.5	37.0	35.2
275/276	33.9	34.5	31.6	34.5	35.6	43.3
323	53.8	54.8	37.1	34.4	22.8	62.7
336	29.1	33.7	34.0	32.1	32.8	42.9
334	43.9	41.7	26.7	24.2	56.4	66.9
294	13.6	14.3	33.7	34.4	10.5	15.8
295/296	16.9	14.1	31.5	30.8	12.8	3.8
324	29.8	30.4	18.5	18.8	42.6	44.6
214/217	NP	15.5	28.0	29.8	NP	22.2
347	41.9	40.6	38.1	36.9	41.8	39.6
Share of Total	34.0	34.1	31.5	30.7	24.7	32.2

Source: ABS 8205.2 Victoria; 8202.2 Australia.

Table 10.4: Victoria's share of research and development: expenditure in major industry groups 1984/85

ASIC		Industry Group	Victoria's Share
33		Other Machinery:	
	334	Photographic & Scientific Equipment	38.8
	335	Appliances & Electrical Equipment	45.0
	336	Industrial Machinery & Equipment	37.0
32		Transport Equipment	67.9
27		Chemicals Petroleum	53.3
	2763	Pharmaceuticals &	
		Veterinary Products	41.5
29		Basic Metal Products	32.6
21		Food, Beverages	37.5
34		Miscellaneous Manufacturing	34.6

Source: ABS Catalogue 8104.0 Table 13.

Table 10.5: Increase in number of establishments: by industry class 1980/81–1986/87

ASIC	Description	Change	
		%	Number
334	Photographic, Professional and Scientific Equipment	84	64*
285	Glass and Glass Products	81	9
278	Petroleum and Coal Products	50	3
216	Bread, Cookies and Biscuits	45	151
295	Basic Non Ferrous Metals	43	6*
348	Other Manufacturing	37	89
254	Furniture & Mattresses	32	134
217	Other Food Products	21	31
294	Basic Iron & Steel	20	21*
215	Flour, Milk & Cereal	18	4
314	Structural Metal Products	14	44
287	Cement & Concrete	12	28
275	Basic Chemicals	11	10*
213	Fruit & Vegetable Products	10	4
264	Printing & Allied Industries	7	55
347	Plastics & Related Products	6	21*
245	Clothing	5	37
246	Footwear	3	3

Source: ABS Publications 8202.2 Manufacturing Establishments

* Included in research oriented industry category.

on these sectors. However, in some other groups, notably transport and scientific equipment, the state's share of national activity is high. Several of these industries have shown big increases in national shares of fixed capital expenditure, rising to over 60 percent in the case of motor vehicles and photographic and scientific equipment, while Victorian firms in the industrial machinery and equipment industry accounted for over 40 percent of national fixed capital expenditure in their industry group.

The second measure of the part that research and development activity has played in Victoria's manufacturing involves details of the location of actual expenditure. Table 10.4 shows that Victorian firms accounted for more than half the national expenditure in research and development in two classes, and over 40% in two more. Because the industry classes are not the same as in the previous table it is difficult to make direct comparisons, however it is obvious that Victorian industry has a strong role in research and development in a wide range of sectors.

It remains to show that the national role in research and development activity is reflected in the strong recovery in manufacturing, identified earlier in terms of factory building and capital investment. It is not possible to do that in a direct way from published statistics as the construction and investment data is not disaggregated in sufficient detail. It is possible to follow the change in the number of establishments, and to look at that information to find the role played by the research-oriented industries. Table 10.5 shows the industrial categories that recorded an increase in the number of establishments between 1980 and 1986. Over this period, there was an increase in the number of establishments in 18 categories. As indicated by the asterisk, five of these groups were in the research-oriented category. The leading category, photographic, professional, and scientific equipment, was also prominent in analyses of Victoria's research and development activity as outlined in Tables 10.3 and 10.4. Many of the other changes relate to local market-related activities. In terms of employment, research oriented activities are prominent in the top employment groups in Victoria, and the relative position of the category "appliances and electrical equipment" (which is the leading activity in terms of research and development expenditure) has improved between 1980 and 1986, as shown in Table 10.6. This data shows that the research-oriented groups have become prominent in the industrial structure of Victoria. The expansion of manufacturing that has been so important to the state obviously derives a considerable part of its momentum from the research-oriented activities identified earlier.

6 Overview

Research reported here has demonstrated insight on a range of issues. Concerning analysis of urban and regional growth, the work shows that the significance of manufacturing can be underestimated if analysis looks simply at employment trends. Other measures like factory construction, fixed capital expenditure, and research and development expenditure can provide a broader base to understand the role of modern manufacturing in urban and regional development. Certainly in the Victorian case, a general economic recovery and a stronger role in the national economy were both coincident with an increase in the state's performance on these measures of manufacturing.

That understanding raises some questions about the relative importance of the service and manufacturing sectors in urban and regional development, and implies that the bias in favor of service-sector employment in most advanced countries is evidence of the underlying importance

Table 10.6: Employment by industry class, Victoria 1980/81 and 1986/87:
Ten largest groups

1980/81			1986/87		
323*	Motor Vehicles	41,347	323*	Motor Vehicles	37,251
336*	Industrial Machinery	25,945	335*	Appliances & Electrical Equipment	21,705
245	Clothing	25,495	264	Printing	27,338
335*	Appliances & Electrical Equipment	23,403	245	Clothing	24,326
264	Printing	23,832	336*	Industrial Machinery	18,027
316	Other Fabr. Metal	18,443	316	Other Fabr. Metal	14,307
324*	Other Transp. Equip.	15,443	347*	Plastics	12,981
234	Textiles	13,520	234	Textiles	12,900
347*	Plastics	13,876	324*	Other Transp. Equip.	12,470
211	Metal Products	13,277	253	Wood Products	11,875

* Included in Research Oriented Industry Category

of that sector. The interpretation overlooks some definitional concerns.
Much of the work in modern manufacturing – product design and development, quality control, testing, negotiation on government standards,
and design of systems to incorporate new products and processes – may
appear in some data classification systems as services, especially where
work is carried out by consultants. Yet it is very directly involved with
manufacturing, though it may not take place in a factory in the old sense.
It is important to be more precise on this aspect, and occupationally based
analysis could provide more insight in the future, as it will look at the type
of jobs, rather than the industry category.

Apart from these definitional concerns, there is a need to recognize
new interdependencies between services and manufacturing. In very early
approaches to this issue it was considered that the change in employment
in manufacturing would lead to a change in the service sector, something
that emerged from the old economic base philosophy. Recent work, which
has tended to focus on producer services, has found different reasons for
the growth of the sector, with particular emphasis on the scale of operation
and the impetus given by international markets. In individual regions
and cities, the diversity of the service sector has become to be seen as
a facilitating factor for manufacturing growth, especially where the latter
involves new firm development. Marshall (1982) has put the key questions
here, and found that the availability of services can be a stimulus to the
development of manufacturing firms. In this perspective, the availability

of services has a part to play in the incubation of firms, and a range of producer services is needed to nurture the new firms that emerge in a region. This approach has led to the call for a services component in regional policy (Marshall, 1985). Movement in that direction will be facilitated by detailed empirical understanding of the linkages between the two sectors at the local and regional scale.

This approach provides a new understanding of the growth of the service sector in an urban or regional economy. In short, service sector development is connected in complex ways to the vitality of a regional economy. It is not simply a reorientation in favor of new activities, or a response to international scale of operation. The latter may be behind the growth of services in centers like New York and London, but in many other locations the interdependencies with manufacturing are the key to understanding service sector growth.

Another issue to emerge from this research is the strength of linkages between research and development effort and manufacturing activity in a region. As outlined earlier, original interpretations of this issue implied that the connection was a strong one, with the model of Silicon Valley as the usual example of the process. Recent understanding, however, recognizes research and development as an international activity, not necessarily closely tied to local production. There seems to be scope to extend Malecki's (1980) approach to the analysis of corporate research and development activity, to incorporate a world market perspective. Approaches based on the international division of labor and "world sourcing" could be relevant here, as multi-locational organizations utilize research from any one of their locations worldwide, and apply it in another place.

In the Australian context an approach along those lines seems justified. With a well developed education and research community, Australia is well placed to contribute to research and development, and perhaps has a stronger comparative advantage in this area than in manufacturing. National policy favors the location of both the research and the production in Australia, but in many circumstances the latter may not be economically possible, so that more of the former could be an achievable objective. A pilot survey of research and development units of several major manufacturing companies in Australia has shown that some local operations were part of the world network, while others dealt only with local market factors.

This preliminary work showed that the organizational structure of a company – especially the local autonomy granted a subsidiary – was an important influence on the degree of research and development carried out in Australia. In sectors where Australia does have a strong production advantage – like aluminum production and processing – the local research and development function has begun to emerge as a significant undertaking and has expanded substantially.

To strengthen this aspect in Australia's growth, so that the benefits of both research and development and manufacturing jobs are felt within a state like Victoria, will require some new and innovative policy. Shaping this policy will require information on the location of industrial research and development facilities, the role of interplant transfers of research results and the extent to which research activity is linked with manufacturing in particular locations. This would complement the work of the GREMI group, which has identified conditions associated with the location of innovative manufacturing.

Approaches to this issue would make an important contribution to the understanding local economic development, especially in metropolitan areas. Research and development activity is recognized as a key factor in future metropolitan development, so that understanding its location, and circumstances underlying its interaction with manufacturing, would sharpen insight on the likely future of individual metropolitan areas.

At another level the research results presented here contribute to understanding of recent economic change in Australia. The latter has been spatially constrained within the major south-east states, on an even greater scale than in earlier periods. This has led to rapid development in the two main cities, after a time in which growth there seemed to slow. Apart from creating local problems in terms of house prices, this concentration has provided a new perspective in which national development policy can be shaped. The latter has attempted to cope with the distribution of services and facilities across a massive land area with small population. The present results suggest that national infrastructure policies could have greater impact if focused substantially in the south-east part of the nation, reinforcing the concentration of research and manufacturing activity.

At the time of writing, Australia has entered a period of slower growth which has been felt disproportionately in Victoria. The recovery outlined here has crumbled quickly, showing that the manufacturing sector is especially vulnerable to national demand trends. This shows that efforts to increase the international focus of the economy have had only a limited impact, and the Australian economy faces a long haul to develop an advanced manufacturing sector with international markets. Part of that journey will involve effort to strengthen the international role of research and development activities.

References

Bell, D., 1976. *The Coming of Post-Industrial Society*. Basic Books: New York.

Berry, B.J.L., S.W. Sanderson, S. Sterman, J. Taar, 1987. The Nation's Most Livable City: Pittsburgh's Transformation, in G. Gappert (ed.), *The Future of Winter Cities*. Urban Affairs Annual Reviews, Vol. 31. Sage, Beverly Hills, pp. 173–195.

Bluestone, B., B. Harrison, 1982. *The De-industrialisation of America.* Sage, New York.

Buss, T.F., F.S. Redburn, 1983. *Shutdown at Youngstown*. Suny Press, Albany.

Castells, M. (ed.), 1985. *High Technology, Space and Society*. Volume 28, Urban Affairs Annual Reviews. Sage, Beverly Hills.

Cohen, S.S., J. Zysman, 1987. *Manufacturing Matters: The Myth of the Post Industrial Economy*. Basic Books: New York.

Clark, G.L., 1989. Pittsburgh in Transition: Consolidation of Prosperity in an Era of Economic Restructuring, in R.A. Beauregard (ed.), *Economic Restructuring and Political Response*. Urban Affairs Annual Reviews, Vol. 34. Sage, Beverly Hills.

Doolittle, F.C., 1985. Metropolitan Employment Change in OECD Countries and the Policy Implications for Inner Cities. In *Research in Urban Economics*, Vol. 5, pp. 75–96.

Gans, A., 1985. Where Has the Urban Crisis Gone?, *Urban Affairs Quarterly*, Vol. 20, pp. 449–468.

Hall, P., A. Markusen, 1985. *Silicon Landscapes*. Allen & Unwin, Boston.

Hall, P., M. Breheny, R. McQuaid, D. Hart, 1987. *Western Sunrise*. Allen & Unwin, London.

Harris, R.I.D., 1987. The Role of Manufacturing in Regional Growth, *Regional Studies*, Vol. 21, pp. 301–312.

Harrison, B., 1984. Regional Restructuring and Good Business Climates: The Economic Transformation of New England since World War II, in L. Sawers, W. Tabb (eds.), *Sunbelt/Snowbelt: Urban Development and Regional Restructuring*. Oxford University Press, New York.

Knight, R.V., 1987. City Development in Advanced Industrial Societies, in G. Gappert, R.V. Knight (eds.), *Cities in the Twenty First Century*. Urban Affairs Annual Reviews, Vol. 23. Sage, Beverly Hills.

Malecki, E.I., 1980. Corporate Organisation of R & D and the Location of Technological Activities, *Regional Studies*, Vol. 14, pp. 219–234.

Marshall, J.N., 1982. Linkages between Manufacturing Industry and Business Services, *Environment and Planning A*, Vol. 14, pp. 1523–1540.

Marshall, J.N., 1985. Business Services, the Regions and Regional Policy, *Regional Studies*, Vol. 19, pp. 353–364.

Mullin, J.R., J.H. Armstrong, J.S. Kavanagh, 1986. From Mill Town to Mill Town: The Transition of a New England Town from a Textile to a High-Technology Economy. *Journal of the American Planning Association*, Vol.

52, pp. 47–59.

Ministry for Economic Development, 1982. *Economic Development Strategy for Victoria*, Paper 1, The Economic Scene, Melbourne, Ministry for Economic Development.

O'Connor, K., 1984. Urban and Regional Change in Australia: An Empirical Introduction, *Environment and Planning A*, Vol. 16, pp. 993–1002.

O'Connor, K., 1987. The Restructuring Process under Constraints: A Study of Recent Economic Change in Australia, *Australian Journal of Regional Studies*, Vol. 1, pp. 23–36.

O'Connor, K., 1990. *The State of Australia*. National Centre for Research and Development in Australian Studies, Monash University, Clayton.

Rich, D, 1987. *The Industrial Geography of Australia*, Croom Helm, London.

Saxenian, A., 1984. Urban Contradictions of Silicon Valley: Regional Growth and the Restructuring of the Semiconductor Industry, in L. Sawers, W. Tabb (eds.), *Sunbelt/Snowbelt: Urban Development and Regional Restructuring*, pp. 163–197.

Scott, A.J., 1986a. High Technology Industry and Territorial Development: The Rise of the Orange County Complex 1955–1984, *Urban Geography*, Vol. 7, pp. 3–45.

Scott, A.J., 1986b. Industrialisation and Urbanisation. A Geographical Agenda, *Annals AAG*, Vol. 76, pp. 25–37.

Scott, A.J., 1988. Flexible Production Systems and Regional Development: The Rise of New Industrial Spaces in North America and Western Europe. *International Journal of Urban and Regional Research*, Vol. 12, pp. 171–186.

Scott, A.J., D.P. Angel, 1988. The Global Assembly Operations of US Semiconductor Firms. A Geographical Analysis, *Environment & Planning A*, Vol. 20, pp. 1047–1067.

Stanback, T.M., 1985. The Changing Fortunes of Metropolitan Economies, in M. Castells (ed.), *High Technology, Space and Society*. Urban Affairs Annual Reviews, Vol. 28. Sage, Beverly Hills.

Yago, G., R. McGahey, 1984. Can the Empire State Strike Back? The Limits of Cyclical Recovery in New York. *New York Affairs*, Vol. 8, pp. 19–29.

11

Producer Service Networks in the Metropolitan Region of Vienna

Johannes Traxler, Manfred M. Fischer, Anna Nöst, Uwe Schubert*

1 Introduction

1.1 Basic concepts and definitions

In the 1980s the producer service sector has grown more rapidly than most other sectors in advanced economies, and today producer services form an important part of the service sector. The growth and increasing importance of producer services is part of a wider global transformation of economic systems towards what may be called a service economy (Gershuny and Miles, 1983). The growing demand for producer services is the result of several fundamental changes and trends taking place in the economy (see Marshall, 1988; Marshall *et al.*, 1988) such as:

- the internationalization of capital and the growth of more complex, larger and multi-site firms enhancing the demand for (new) services which have to be provided by service firms on a national and even international scale,
- the increasing integration of services with production (services are no longer simply dependent on manufacturing demand),
- the growing importance of subcontracting out and the changing balance between the internalization and externalization of producer services (i.e. for reasons of cost and economies of scale firms which used

---

*University of Economics and Business Administration, Vienna, Austria.

to produce services themselves are increasingly using specialist suppliers),

- the increasingly dynamic and complex context for business in general and the increasing complexity of production processes and market functions in particular, requiring new, more specialized, services and management methods which are frequently computer-based,
- considerable structural changes in the service markets (e.g. the rapid growth in new telecommunications and data processing services).

It is difficult to define the producer service sector unambiguously. From a pragmatic point of view producer services may be defined as those services which supply business and government organizations, rather than private individuals, whether in agriculture, mining, manufacturing, or service industries, and which can be traded either commercially on the open market or internally within organizations (see Marshall *et al.*, 1988). They are concerned with:

- goods-related services (such as distribution of goods, transport management, installation, maintenance and repair of equipment, communications networks, building and infrastructure networks),
- personnel support services (such as cleaning, catering, security, safety, welfare services), and
- information processing services (such as R&D, engineering and architectural design, marketing, market research, management consultancy, administration, computer services, financial planning, banking, insurance, legal counseling services, property management, office services).

This classification of producer services is of course rather broad in scope, and thus contains a considerable degree of variation within the categories. A somewhat more sophisticated classification scheme may be obtained by distinguishing additionally between producer services which serve markets internal or external to the firm. These subcategories evidently reflect the different markets served by producer service activities.

1.2   The role of producer services and their interaction networks in local development

Despite a general interest in producer services and much rewriting of research agenda there has been little substantial research into the dynamics of producer service activities and the role of producer services in regional economic development. This paper makes a modest attempt to contribute to the understanding of the role of producer services in regional economies and reports some preliminary results of ongoing research based on survey work in the metropolitan area of Vienna.[1] About 200 interviews were conducted by students, predominantly with younger firms in the producer service sector in the metropolitan area of Vienna. The survey focused solely on the external provision of particular information processing services, and thus neglects both goods-related services and personnel support services as well as "in-house" information processing services.

The major objective of this contribution is to present some preliminary empirical evidence on the role of producer services in the agglomeration of Vienna. First, some recent trends will be described using aggregate data. Then their economic significance due to forward and backward linkages with the regional (local) economy will be described. The study is partial and considers some major categories of producer services: advertising, marketing, management consultancy, electronic data processing (EDP), and engineering design.

2 Recent Trends in Service Employment in the Metropolitan Region of Vienna

One of the most significant features of the development of the modern Western economies during the post-war decades has been the growth of service activities. When measured in terms of employment or nominal output value in Austria this process was accompanied by a growth of the secondary sector until the mid-1960s, but since then a secular decline has set in (see Clement, 1988, pp. 77–79). This trend represents predominantly the secular increase in service-related prices *vis-à-vis* the prices of industrial products. Measured in constant prices the expansion in service output peaked around 1970 and has actually been decreasing steadily since (see Clement, 1988, p. 95).

These trends are also clearly reflected in the changing composition of the labor force in terms of profession. The top five professions in terms of employment growth between 1971 and 1981 (managers; electronic data processing; natural scientists, researchers and education; banking and insurance) clearly point to the increasing importance producer services play in the economy. This growth in importance may partly be explained by the changing input requirement of manufacturing industry. Essentially, increasing competition required firms to be adaptive and responsive, de-

---

[1]This research was carried out in the framework of interdisciplinary seminars at the Vienna University of Economics and Business Administration (jointly organized by the IIR and the Department of Economic Geography) and the Department of Geography at the University of Vienna.

pending upon the ability to gather, process, and act upon specialized information effectively. Certain producer services provide the appropriate source of this change. But this view is not the complete picture because some of the change in producer services is likely to be merely indirectly related to goods production.

The most distinctive feature of the location of services in Austria is their spatial concentration in the metropolitan region of Vienna, a concentration which has been maintained despite a recent decentralization to rural regions (measured in terms of growth rates). Unlike many private consumer services producer service activities are major contributors to the spatial concentration of service activity in the metropolitan region of Vienna.

A large share of the increase in service activities is due to new firm formation where producer services play a dominant role. Table 11.1 illustrates the development of the most important producer service subsectors (in terms of the number of firms) in the city of Vienna ("core region") between 1973 and 1989. At the intra-regional scale the pattern of change involves a marked relative deconcentration, spilling over to the ring.

3 Networks of Producer Service Firms in the Metropolitan Region of Vienna

The structural role of producer services in the operation of regional and local economies is a key issue to any research progress. The service input to production can have a positive impact on the competitiveness of manufacturing. The contribution of producer service firms to innovation, the role of service firms in the organization and selling of goods production, the role of services to provide up-to-date and complete information are all emphasized in the literature (see, for example, Freeman *et al.*, 1982; OECD, 1983).

At present, there is only a very limited understanding of the contribution of producer services to the performance of manufacturing and other sectors in the Austrian economy in general and in the metropolitan area of Vienna in particular. Clearly, the economic role of producer services in national, regional, and local economies needs to be analyzed in more depth.

Regionally and locally based producer services tend to be strongly embedded in regional and local networks, implying backward and forward linkages extending to all sectors of the economy, predominantly to the manufacturing sector. Three types of networks may be distinguished in this respect: client networks (output-oriented networks), intermediary

Table 11.1: Development of producer services in Vienna (1973-1985) measured in number of establishments

Producer Services	Urban Zone	Year		
		1973	1980	1985
Higher Services (advertising, business consultants, electronic data processing, R&D)	core region	579	648	1345
	CBD	132	136	271
	ring	447	512	1074
	outer region	318	439	1095
Routine Management	core region	291	341	353
	CBD	148	133	144
	ring	143	208	209
	outer region	134	224	236
Operative Services	core region	2070	1870	1688
	CBD	191	153	137
	ring	1879	1717	1551
	outer region	1647	1714	1736
Transportation Services	core region	658	526	612
	CBD	181	151	132
	ring	477	375	480
	outer region	619	576	681
Total	core region	3608	3385	3918
	CBD	652	573	684
	ring	2956	2812	3234
	outer region	2718	2953	3748

networks (input-oriented networks), and cooperation networks. It is important to mention again that the study is partial and concentrates on advertising, management consultancy, computer services (electronic data processing and software development services), and engineering consulting, which may be considered as information processing service activities.

Before we embark on the empirical side of this contribution a short overview of the main questions raised should be presented and the scheme of reporting survey results should be indicated.

- How intensive are backward and forward linkages of producer services in a local economy?
- How heterogeneous are the linkages within a local economy for different branches and sizes of information related high-ranking producer services?
- What role do networks play in the interaction patterns of producer service firms?

- Does location *within* an urban region (core, ring) influence the interaction patterns?

To answer these questions we adopt the following strategy of analysis (and reporting the results):

- First, for all types of services included in the survey the spatial interaction patterns of producer service firms are investigated, then differences by type of service are analyzed.
- The impact of the location of the firm (core, ring) on spatial interactions is investigated.
- Sectoral interactions with other service firms, with manufacturing, with the public sector are explored.
- The role of size of firm for the interaction pattern is assessed.

As the sample was not very large, only a very small number of observations is available in some of the disaggregations. For these cases we do not report any results. Furthermore, given the scope of the analysis, we report only the highlights of this research.

3.1   Client networks

The regional interaction patterns of the above-mentioned producer services are very distinct with respect to the location of the clients. Six different spatial categories of location are distinguished in the following analysis:

- the county/district,
- the core region of the metropolitan area,
- the outer region of the metropolitan area,
- other major urban areas in Austria,
- rest of Austria,
- foreign countries.

With respect to client networks the most important spatial category for all the producer services of the agglomeration – no matter where they are located – seems to be the metropolitan area. About three-quarters (two-thirds) of the producer service firms located in the core (outer region) of the agglomeration have their most important clients in the city of Vienna. The share of clients is slightly higher for firms located in the core, while short-distance interactions (i.e. clients located in the same county) seem to prevail for firms located in the ring. Moreover producer services in the core tend to be more nationally and internationally oriented (see Figure 11.1).

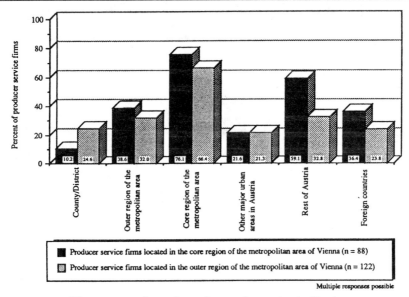

Figure 11.1: Location of most important clients.

Disaggregation by type of producer activity shows that for producer service firms located in the core region intra-regional customer interactions prevail for engineering firms (core area: 86%, ring: 57%). Clients in other areas of Austria are important for all types of service activity, for advertising/marketing and business consultancy/electronic data processing slightly more than for engineering. Engineering (50%) as well as business consultancy and electronic data processing (44%) exhibit international client interactions.

In comparison, the client networks of the producer services located in the outer region are similar, with only a few differences. Engineering firms are much less oriented to clients in the core region, but more strongly to clients in the same district. Advertising and marketing firms are also strongly oriented to the same district as well as to the core region, while business consultants and computer services have their markets above average in the core of the agglomeration (71%) and in the rest of Austria (37%).

In summary, it appears that by and large the interaction patterns resemble each other to a large degree. Business consultants, EDP and engineering firms tend to supply their services over wider markets than advertising and marketing firms.

It is worth mentioning that the producer services are predominantly supplied to manufacturing industries. A fairly large proportion, however, is delivered to other service firms. Commercial services are important

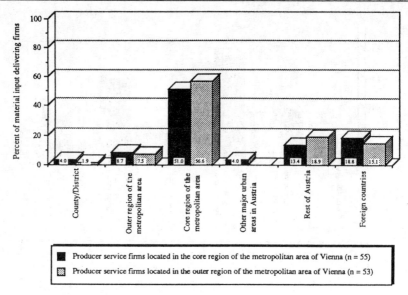

Figure 11.2: Location of material inputs delivering firms.

customers of advertising and marketing companies; engineering firms are the only significant service suppliers for the public sector.

Firm size plays a role insofar as smaller firms – as to be expected – are generally more locally oriented, and the international interactions increase with firm size. Nevertheless, there are no really striking differences between the different size classes and locations.

3.2   Intermediary networks

With the exception of engineering firms, material inputs play only a minor role in the transactions of producer service firms. Most of the material inputs are purchased from firms located in the city of Vienna. It is interesting to note that other Austrian regions as well as foreign countries are more frequently the source of deliveries than the outer region of the agglomeration. Producer service firms situated in the ring tend to be slightly more locally and regionally oriented, those located in the centre slightly more nationally and internationally oriented (see Figure 11.2). Disaggregations by types of producer service firms and size classes do not show any significant differences.

Figure 11.3 summarizes the services purchased from other service firms. The main factors mentioned by the interviewees as important to externalize service activities were lack of know-how required to carry out the activities, cost advantages (especially in the case of marketing and ad-

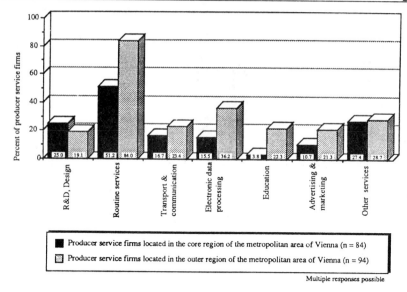

Figure 11.3: Services purchased from other firms.

vertising firms), and time constraints. The highest demand is for routine
services like counseling, financing and management. Regarding locational
differences, the following pattern may be observed: producer service firms
located in the ring generally tend to buy more services than firms in the
core region do. The most striking difference can be identified with respect
to the above mentioned routine services. About 84 percent of the firms in
the ring versus 51 percent of those in the core area demand such services
externally. The external purchase of computer services and education and
training also shows significantly higher values for the firms located in the
ring. On the other hand these firms demand fewer R&D-related services
than those located in the core.

Disaggregation by type of producer service, which is possible only for
the subsample of the ring, shows that the engineering and consulting/EDP
firms purchase routine services, advertising, and training more often than
advertising and marketing firms do.

Firm size (again the disaggregation is possible only for the subsample
of the outer region) plays a role as far as external purchases of services
are concerned. Larger producer service firms show a higher propensity
towards externalization of routine services as well as high-grade services
than smaller ones do. Thus, the larger firms seem to be more involved in
a division of labour than the smaller ones.

Concerning the spatial pattern of intermediary linkages, it is evident
that the lion's share of these inputs are purchased in the city of Vienna

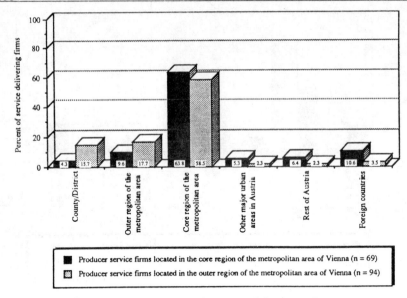

Figure 11.4: Location of service-delivering firms.

followed by the ring of the agglomeration. The firms located in the core region purchase only few services locally (i.e. in their own district), but most in the rest of the core region (city of Vienna). Foreign countries play a slightly more important role than the ring of the Vienna agglomeration. The firms located in the ring show a different pattern. They are even more locally and regionally oriented. The short-distance interactions are significantly higher than for the core firms; interregional and international interactions are not relevant (see Figure 11.4).

The disaggregation by sector does not yield any new striking results. Advertising and marketing companies seem to be the most locally oriented, while engineering firms, consultants and computer service firms have wider interaction ranges.

Size seems to play some role. As already seen, the small firms are extremely locally oriented and some of them (especially in the outer region) do not have interregional interactions at all. With firm size these interregional and international contacts increase.

These results corroborate the close regional link hypothesis for the producer service industry on the input side much more than for the output markets.

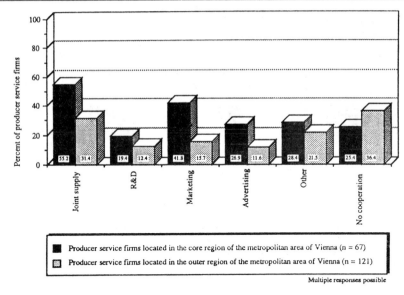

Figure 11.5: Cooperation of producer service firms with other firms.

3.3 Cooperation and contact networks

Looking at cooperative networks yields the following results. Producer service firms tend to cooperate intensively, particularly those located in the core region. About three-quarters of the firms located in the core area and about two-thirds of those in the ring have indicated cooperation links (see Figure 11.5). The majority of cooperation partners are within the agglomeration. This pattern is similar to that of the client networks and does not show striking differences between core and ring. The most important cooperation activities involve joint marketing strategies and joint sales packages (see Figure 11.6). The data, however, reveal additional interesting insights.

Engineering firms cooperate more intensively (with manufacturing and other service firms) than the other types of producer services considered; business consultants and EDP firms are the least cooperative. If producer services are located in the core (see Figure 11.6), their cooperation in the case of advertising and marketing firms concerns joint supply, advertising and marketing, while for engineering firms the R&D cooperation seems to be rather important; marketing and advertising co-operations tend to be more infrequent. Consulting and EDP firms cooperate first of all in matters of joint supply and marketing; the rest is comparatively less important. The firms in the ring (see Figure 11.7) are much less cooperative than those in the core. Cooperative activities of advertising and market-

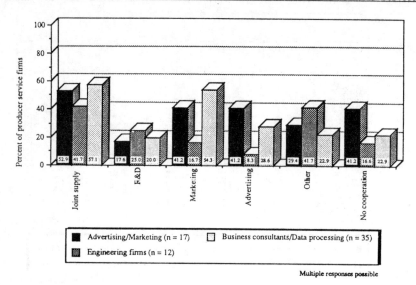

Figure 11.6: Cooperation of producer service firms with other firms disaggregated by different types of producer services located in the core region of the metropolitan area of Vienna.

ing firms (50% do not cooperate at all) are concentrated in advertising, marketing, and joint supply, very little in R&D.

Firms located in the city of Vienna are much more oriented towards cooperation with national and international partners than those in the outer region of the agglomeration (see Figure 11.8).

Differentiated by type of producer service activity, for firms located in the city of Vienna (core region) it can be seen that engineering firms show a stronger interregional and international orientation in their co-operation, while advertising and marketing firms are clearly more locally and regionally oriented (see Figure 11.6). The firms in the ring show a different pattern by type of activity (see Figures 11.7 and 11.9): only 6 percent of the engineering firms do not have any technical-scientific contacts; the advertising and marketing companies have the least frequent contacts in the subsample. But the engineering firms located in the ring are completely differently oriented than those in the core. Their major contacts are in the agglomeration; short-distance interactions are most important. Business consultants and EDP firms are the only firms to exhibit a stronger interregional and international orientation, often via partnership arrangements. In contrast to the intermediary networks, small firms, especially those located in the core, tend to cooperate more intensively than larger firms. Thus, it seems that small firms substitute (market) input links

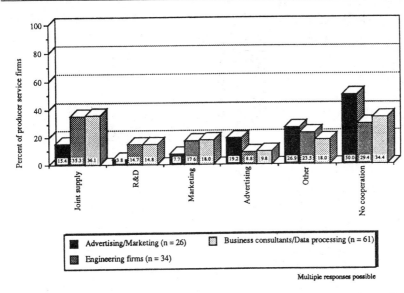

Figure 11.7: Cooperation of producer service firms with other firms disaggregated by different types of producer services located in the outer region of the metropolitan area of Vienna.

by cooperation links. Internationalization increases with firm size; small firms are more locally oriented.

Figure 11.10 reveals that contacts with universities, public research institutions and counseling services are rather infrequent, and the the counseling service provided by the chambers is not being used much either. The most important partners are the firms of the same sector and manufacturing as well as other service firms. In general, firms located in the core tend to have more intensive contacts than those in the ring. As to be expected, computer service and engineering firms tend to retain regular and frequent contacts with universities and especially with the Technical University of Vienna, while firms providing other producer services report only infrequent contacts with such institutions.

4   Conclusions

The producer service industry is the most dynamic component of service activities in Austria and even more so in the metropolitan region of Vienna. The rate of foundation of such firms in this area has substantially increased in the 1980s. Compared to other advanced economies the producer service market is still comparatively small and might grow considerably in future.

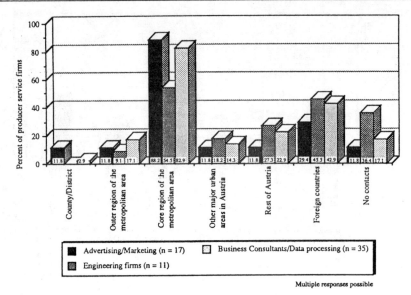

Figure 11.8: Location of contacts of producer service firms disaggregated by different types of producer services located in the core region of the metropolitan area of Vienna.

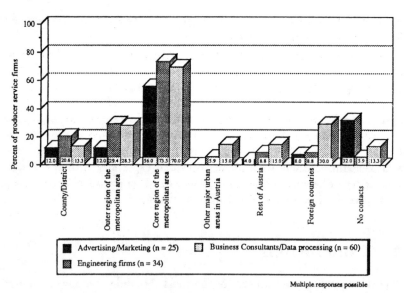

Figure 11.9: Location of contacts of producer service firms disaggregated by different types of producer services located in the outer region of the metropolitan area of Vienna.

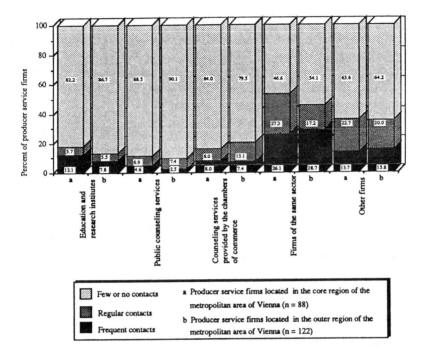

Figure 11.10: Contacts of producer service firms with research institutions.

The market is largely dominated by small firms which typically offer a general all-round service within their field. Concentration tendencies seem to be insignificant as yet.

Despite the fact that the sample-based results reported in this contribution are of a very tentative nature, the following conclusions can be drawn from the empirical analysis.

1. Producer services have a high degree of local/regional economic significance owing to intensive forward and backward linkages with the local/regional economy. But export orientation of the highest-ranking producer services is also significant.
2. Input purchasing networks are more locally and regionally oriented than output and marketing networks.
3. The networks of advertising, marketing, consultancy, and EDP rather than engineering service companies tend to be more locally and regionally oriented.
4. All types of networks tend to be highly correlated. Once the investment into the build-up of a network is made, it is often utilized for input purchase and cooperative activities as well as sales.

Because of its strong backward and forward linkages to the local economy the producer service sector seems to be of strategic importance to enhance economic welfare of cities. This sector should hence become a stronger focus of economic policy in Vienna. Additionally, it could be argued that the availability of local producer services is a prerequisite for the future industrial development in the region.

References

Clement, W., 1988. *Die Tertiärisierung der Industrie.* Signum Verlag, Vienna.

Freeman, C., J. Clarke, L. Soete, 1982. *Employment and Technical Innovation.* Frances Pinter, London.

Gershuny, J., I. Miles, 1983. *The New Service Economy.* Frances Pinter, London.

Marshall, J.N., 1988. *The Changing Organisation of Modern Western Society.* Geographisches Institut, ETH Zürich, Zürich.

Marshall, J.N., P. Wood, P.W. Daniels, A. McKinnon, J. Bachtler, P. Damesick, N. Thrift, A. Gillespie, A. Green, A. Leyshon, 1988. *Services and Uneven Development.* Oxford University Press, Oxford.

OECD, 1983. *Industrial Services.* Industry Committee, Directorate for Science Technology and Industry, Paris.

Part IV

Development Concepts
Reconsidered

12

Spatial Differentiation of Innovation – Locational and Structural Factors: Results of an Austrian Study

Franz Tödtling*

1 Introduction

The differentiation of innovation across space has been a topic of regional analysis from its beginnings: the work of Hägerstrand on innovation diffusion and François Perroux's growth pole theory are early cornerstones. In these early contributions the notion of a spatial hierarchy emerging from the process of innovation generation and diffusion was established, and was taken up also in later related works (Friedmann, Hermansen, Lasuén) as well as in the product cycle and the "filtering down" approach.[1] Location factors for innovation generation and diffusion were considered as central factors leading to such a spatial hierarchy in the innovation process.

Recent approaches, however, point to a more complex spatial pattern of the innovation process: socioeconomic characteristics of firms, entrepreneurs, the labor force and of other regional actors (e.g. local politicians) are conceived of as important in the innovation process. Many of these factors reveal their historical relation to the industrialization process in more complex patterns than the urban hierarchy or a "simple"

---

*Interdisciplinary Institute for Urban and Regional Studies, University of Economics and Business Administration, Vienna, Austria.

[1]According to this concept manufacturing products or industries are "filtering down" the urban hierarchy in the course of their aging process (Erickson and Leinbach, 1979; Norton and Rees, 1979; Suarez-Villa, 1983).

core–periphery structure. With regard to relevant characteristics of the labor force Storper and Walker (1983) as well as Massey (1984) argue that there is a "mosaic of unevenness" rather than a clear hierarchical spatial pattern. Studies on "innovative milieus" (Aydalot, 1986; Stöhr, 1987; Aydalot and Keeble, 1988) as well as studies stressing structural and behavioral factors of innovation (Ewers *et al.*, 1980; Thwaites et al., 1982; Bade, 1984; Brugger and Stuckey, 1987) point to the fact that there are special conditions leading to regional innovation activities, which may not correspond to the urban hierarchy or to a core–periphery pattern.

In the following, theoretical aspects concerning the spatial differentiation of the innovation process will first be discussed, then several empirical results of an Austrian study will be presented.

2 Spatial Differentiation of Innovation – Conceptual Background

2.1 Hierarchical approach

A spatial hierarchy of the innovation process underlies the product-cycle theory as well as the innovation diffusion approach. These concepts stress the "location factors" of innovation generation (product innovation) and the diffusion process (adoption of innovations, mostly process innovations). They assume a "linear model" of innovation, namely a certain sequence of phases in the innovation process that runs from basic and applied technical research (invention) to product development, construction, and prototype production, culminating in the introduction of the new product into the market. Then the diffusion process starts, in the course of which some firms adopt early, some late and some not at all.

It has been argued that each stage of this process has specific locational requirements (Utterback, 1979; Erickson and Leinbach, 1979; Davelaar and Nijkamp, 1987; Stöhr, 1987). For the generation of innovation (early phase, product innovation) the following requirements are considered important:

- a highly qualified workforce: these qualifications are "produced" by good education facilities and/or attracted by a good living environment;
- technical and economic universities and research institutions;
- producer services (management and technical consulting, marketing, legal services);
- potential suppliers of (varying) inputs;
- good access to a sufficient large market and to customers;

- infrastructure for rapid transport (air and rail) as well as telecommunication facilities.

These requirements are usually better fulfilled in the largest agglomerations (Lasuén, 1973; Hansen, 1981), so the early phases of the innovation process are considered to be concentrated there.

For the adoption of innovations (process innovations) the following locational requirements are regarded as important (Brown, 1981; Kleine, 1983; Gibbs and Edwards, 1983; Rees *et al.*, 1984; Müdespacher, 1987):

- a high density of plants in the same or in related industries (information and demonstration effects);
- existence of supply and service firms familiar with the new technologies;
- access to facilities for technology transfer;
- availability of specific technical qualifications on the labor market (personnel for the introduction / operation of the new techniques);

The locational requirements for the adoption of innovations (process innovations) are generally considered to be less important than for the innovation generation and product innovation, so process innovations should exhibit a less concentrated spatial pattern. For more complex process innovations, however, early adoption is still expected more often in the largest agglomerations, while late adoption should be more at the lower end of the urban hierarchy and in peripheral areas.

2.2   Non-hierarchical approaches

More recent approaches have pointed out that there may be systematic deviations from the hierarchical pattern of innovation:

- Storper (1986) has argued, in the context of the location of new industries, that these might try to avoid the highest-ranking agglomerations, because the latter are considered to have structures which are predetermined by the old successful industries. This refers to the fact that production factors, skills, suppliers, infrastructure, and local politicians may be strongly oriented to the older industries and that there may be factor monopsonies.
- Studies on "innovative milieus" and "territorial innovation complexes" in addition point to the fact that a complex set of factors, their interaction and synergy is playing a role in the regional innovation process, and that these conditions need not necessarily be in the largest agglomerations (Aydalot, 1986; Perrin, 1986; Stöhr,

1987; Aydalot and Keeble, 1988). Important factors in this context are entrepreneurial traditions and skills, technical skills of the labor force, strong interactions between innovation-relevant functions and firms ("regional networks" for the exchange of products, services and information).

- Furthermore, there are studies that see innovation activities of regional plants as more related to their structural and behavioral characteristics than to their location (Ewers *et al.*, 1980; Capellin, 1983; Taylor, 1983; Bade, 1984; Brugger and Stuckey, 1987; Tödtling, 1990a and b).[2] Plants which have strong "boundary-spanning functions" (Aldrich, 1979; Coombs *et al.*, 1987) or which are integrated into larger enterprises or networks of firms (Camagni, 1989; Rothwell, 1989) may easily overcome obstacles to innovation at seemingly unfavorable locations. On the other hand, there is a considerable segment of plants in large agglomerations which, because of their structural features, do not perform innovation activities (market-oriented industries, small-scale artisanal industry in old city areas).

A different conception of innovation underlies these latter approaches (particularly the "milieu approach"). Innovation is not seen as running necessarily through the stages from invention to diffusion in the suggested sequence of the "linear model" outlined above, but is conceived of more as a continuous and highly interrelated process which contains many feedback loops (Kay, 1979; Freeman, 1982; Dosi, 1988). Existing products and processes are continuously modified (incremental innovation), sources of innovation are not only formal technical research (R&D), but also customers, suppliers, the production level or the marketing function (von Hippel, 1988). Learning by doing and using (Malecki, 1988) is considered to play an important role. Whereas the linear model regards the innovation process as a sequence of specialized functions and activities, the latter conception stresses the importance of the "coupling" of functions (Sorge, 1986) as well as of feedback loops.

In addition to location factors behind innovation activities, the structural characteristics of plants, as well as social and cultural features of regional actors (entrepreneurs, labor force), are considered important. Structural characteristics of significance are the industry, size, organizational status, boundary-spanning functions and the qualification of the labor force. "Network characteristics" (technical contacts and cooperations) and the strategic orientation of the plant are also relevant. Location factors interact with these structural and behavioral factors in the

---

[2]Although in many cases the innovation-relevant structural characteristics may also exhibit a spatial hierarchy or a core–periphery regularity, this is not necessarily the case.

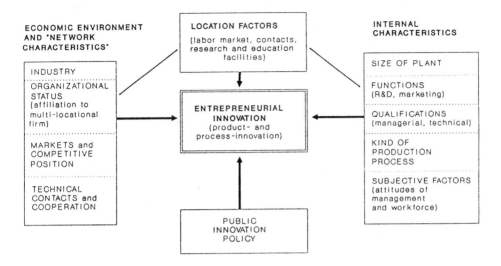

Figure 12.1: Factors influencing entrepreneurial innovation.

long run, however, which is leading to an economic specialization of regions (spatial division of labor: Massey, 1984). Because of the historical evolution, the innovation-relevant characteristics of firms do probably not show a "simple" spatial structure (e.g. core–periphery or according to the urban hierarchy), but a more complex one that is basically shaped by the past industrialization process.

In the following we suggest that the innovation activity of regional plants is the result of (Figure 12.1):

- internal characteristics of plants (size, functions, skills, and production processes),
- characteristics of the economic environment of the plant (industry and markets),
- network features (organizational status, technical contacts, and cooperations),
- the locational environment, as well as
- public innovation policies.

From the internal characteristics, the functional structure of the plant, as well as the skills, is considered as highly relevant. The "boundary-spanning functions" (Aldrich, 1979: R&D, marketing, management) are at the interface of the environment and internal processes: they have the task of searching, selecting and screening the relevant information in the innovation process. The qualification of the workforce reflects the "competence" and skills available for the innovation process (both for the technical development and for the introduction into the production and market: Andersson and Johansson, 1984). Other internal factors are the size of the plant, the existing production processes as well as attitudes of management and workforce to innovation.

The external factors refer to the locational environment (discussed above), to the economic environment and network characteristics of the plant as well as to public innovation policy.

The "industries" define the relevant economic environment of plants and they differ with regard to the growth of demand, the degree of competition and of market concentration (Scherer, 1980; Porter, 1980). They also differ in the technological opportunities and dynamics and thus in the average amount of R&D spent and the general importance of innovation. High technological dynamics have been observed in the past years, e.g. in the sectors penetrated by microelectronics (Freeman, 1982).

From the network features, the affiliation of plants with larger multi-locational enterprises (organizational status) is relevant in the innovation process. These plants on the one hand have access to resources of the larger enterprise (financial resources, R&D, market networks, planning departments, and information networks). On the other hand they are subject to an internal division of labor in the firm, which may be detrimental particularly to peripheral branch plants (Watts, 1981; Thwaites, 1982; Gibbs and Edwards, 1983; Massey, 1984; Tödtling, 1984; Holst, 1987). In general branch plants are expected to have low levels of product innovation. With regard to new production processes, however, they are – owing to their integration into a larger enterprise – considered to be earlier adopters than the single-plant enterprises. Single-plant enterprises on the other hand are much more dependent on the quality of their immediate locational environment. It is argued that they face disadvantages particularly in old industrialized and in peripheral rural areas (Thwaites and Oakey, 1985; Goddard *et al.*, 1986; Grabher, 1988).

Technical-economic contacts and cooperation with other partners reflect additional network characteristics of the plant and the "outward looking" behavior of the management: particularly for small firms these contacts and cooperations are considered increasingly important in the innovation process (Camagni, 1989; Rothwell, 1989).

Public innovation policy is another factor having an impact on the innovation activities of firms. In most market economies (e.g. in Austria), the state tries to promote and stimulate innovation activities in the economy by giving financial or informational support to firms or by promoting the development and diffusion of specific technologies. Firms that receive support from these programs may find it easier to overcome financial and other bottlenecks in the innovation process.[3]

The following conclusions may be reached with regard to the spatial differentiation of innovation. From the location-factor approach, a bias favoring innovation activities towards large agglomerations can be expected. They have better preconditions for the early phases and the generation of innovation (product innovations) as well as for the early adoption of process innovations. Low-innovation activities, as well as a predominance of the late phases (process innovations and their late adoption), are to be expected particularly for peripheral rural areas.

Modifications of this pattern are to be expected according to the approaches stressing structural and behavioral features of plants in a region: a high share of industries with "technological opportunities", plants with well articulated boundary spanning functions, strong technical contacts and with a skilled labor force (both technical as well as management skills) are regarded as favorable for innovation. It is difficult to determine *a priori* the regions with such an activity mix, but it seems probable that these activities are more highly represented in agglomerations – though not necessarily the largest ones. An unfavorable activity mix for innovation is to be expected again for rural areas (predominance of labor-intensive industries, branch plants or very small plants) as well as for old industrialized areas (capital-intensive branch plants "late" in the product cycle, lack of boundary spanning functions, low contact activities, a labor force specialized in traditional skills and with a low flexibility). These expectations, however, are less "deterministic" in the structural and behavioral approach. By deliberate and strategic actions, a plant may improve its potential for innovation: such actions are the building up of a qualified labor force (e.g. by internal training), the strengthening of boundary spanning functions (R&D and marketing, planning) and the establishment of cooperations and technical contacts with other firms.

In the following pages empirical evidence from Austrian regions with regard to innovation activities, as well as their relation to structural characteristics of plants and to locational factors, will be presented.

---

[3]In Austria there exist several programs and institutions which provide financial support to the development and introduction of new products: within the "TOP" program soft loans for the introduction of new products are given; a fund for research and development ("FFF") provides subsidies to R&D activities of firms; there are also institutions concerned with the information transmission in the innovation process (at the federal level e.g. "Innovationsagentur"); and there exist programs for the development and application of specific technologies (microelectronics, biotechnology).

3 Empirical Results for Austrian Regions

Three datasets have been analyzed to address these questions: (1) A survey on the R&D activities of Austrian manufacturing industry collected by the Federal Chamber of Industry for the year 1981 (R&D study); (2) a survey of broadly defined innovation activities carried out by the Austrian Institute for Economic Research for 1985 (innovation study);[4] and (3) a case study of selected industries and regions in Austria, covering innovation activities between 1981 and 1986. While the first two investigations were based on postal questionnaires, the latter was based on personal interviews. Only a summary of the results will be presented here – more detailed results can be found in other publications (Tödtling, 1987, 1990a, b).

3.1 R&D activities of manufacturing firms (1981)

The study was focused on spatial differences of R&D activities of Austrian manufacturing industry during 1981 as well as their sectoral, organizational and locational determinants (Tödtling, 1987). The questionnaires from about 650 plants were analyzed, representing 10 percent of Austrian manufacturing plants ("Industrie") and 45 percent of employment. R&D activities were measured both by expenses and by employment (full-time equivalents: Bundeskammer, 1981).[5] The study revealed that R&D was highly concentrated in certain industries, types of plants, and regions:

- A high share of R&D expenses and employment was concentrated in the electrotechnical industry, chemical industry, vehicle industry, metal industry and machinery; and in large plants[6] as well as in headquarters and main plants of multiplant firms.

- The plants in the region of Vienna had the highest shares of R&D expenses and employment, in particular of the highly skilled R&D personnel. Other areas with above average R&D activity were industrialized areas, but not the "old" industrialized areas (particularly

---

[4]Neither of these data sets was originally analyzed from the regional perspective. The regionalization was done at the request of the author for the R&D survey by W. Hackl and for the innovation survey with the help of G. Palme and L. Kubacek.

[5]The definition of R&D was based on the Frascati Handbook for statistical surveys.

[6]A considerable share of small plants did not undertake R&D activities; those that did, however, had an above average share of R&D expenses and employment.

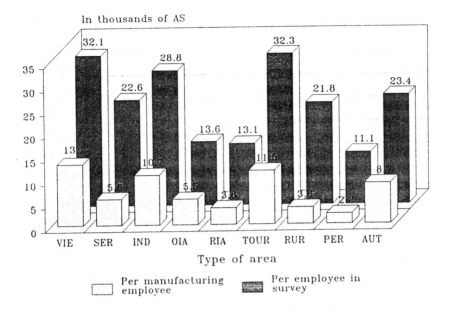

Figure 12.2: R&D expenditures 1981 by type of area (per employee in AS 1,000) – see p. 239 for key to regions.

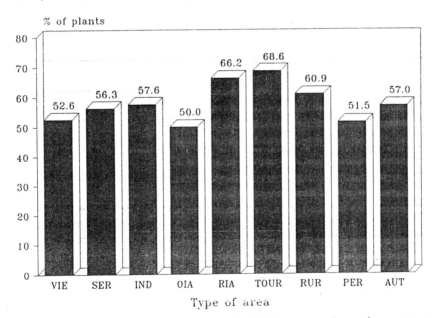

Figure 12.3: Innovation activity of plants 1985 by type of area (percentage of plants with innovation activity) – see p. 239 for key to regions.

the region of Linz) as well as "tourist areas".[7] R&D activities were very low in the peripheral rural as well as in the old industrialized areas (see Figure 12.2).

- As was shown by shift analysis as well as by analysis of variance (Tödtling, 1990) the larger share of the regional differences was due to the industrial mix as well as the organizational status and the size of plants; the locational influence (residuum in the shift analysis, "type of region" in the analysis of variance) was rather low.

To summarize the results, the study showed a high concentration of R&D in the largest agglomerations Vienna and Linz, basically confirming the hierarchical spatial pattern of innovation. On the other hand, the relatively high R&D activity found in the tourist areas (they have no large agglomerations and are in "intermediate" locations) points to the fact that non-central locations of R&D are feasible. The spatial differences of R&D which were found seemed to be due more to the structural characteristics of plants (industry, size, and organizational status) than directly to locational factors.

3.2   Innovation activities of Austrian manufacturing firms (1985)

This postal survey also addressed the manufacturing industry of Austria. The database was collected by the Austrian Institute of Economic Research; the methodological details as well as the results for all of Austria are published in Volk (1988).[8] About 570 plants returned questionnaires; they covered 10 percent of firms and 36 percent of the employment in Austrian manufacturing industry. The innovation activities studied included a broader spectrum than the above R&D study, thus providing a more complete picture of the innovation process. "Innovation activities" (and the related expenses) were defined to cover internal and external research, development, design work, patents and licensing, investment for the preparation of production and market introduction, as well as investment for the rationalization of production and office work. For some indicators, a different spatial pattern of innovation activities was found as compared with the R&D study (Tödtling, 1990a):

---

[7]The tourist areas have a mixed economic structure of tourist, service, and manufacturing industries.

[8]I have to thank the Austrian Institute of Economic Research, particularly E. Volk, for granting me access to the data, and G. Palme and L. Kubacek for help in the regionalization of the database.

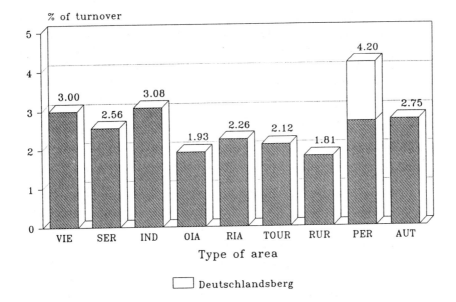

Figure 12.4: Innovation expenditure 1985 by type of area (as a percentage of surveyed plants) – see p. 239 for key to regions.

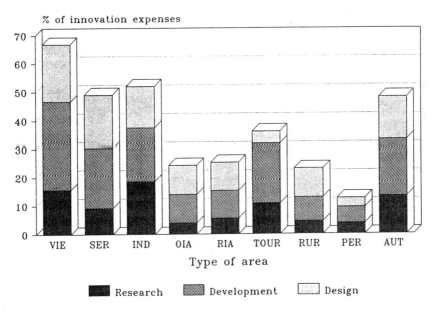

Figure 12.5: Expenditure for research, development, and design (as a percentage of innovation expenditure) – see p. 239 for key to regions.

- With regard to the share of plants undertaking innovation activities in the broadly defined sense, the industrialized-rural areas as well as the tourist areas had the highest values (66% and 69% of the responding plants: Figure 12.3). Both types represent areas in "intermediate location", with a rather mixed economic structure. In the region of Vienna the share of innovative plants was surprisingly low (53%). A low share of innovative plants was also found in the old industrialized areas (50%) as well as in the peripheral rural areas (52%).

- The expenditure on innovation activities was spatially much more concentrated than the innovative plants: above average shares could be found in the industrialized areas (including the region of Linz; 3.1% of the turnover) and the region of Vienna (3%: Figure 12.4). A surprisingly high share of these expenses, however, was also found in some parts of the peripheral rural areas (Südsteiermark).[9] In other areas of this type (Waldviertel, Burgenland) innovation expenditure was as expected very low: the rural periphery is thus very heterogeneous in this respect. Both in the agglomerations and in the rural areas the innovation expenses are fairly strongly concentrated in specific sectors and plants and not broadly distributed.[10]

- Strong regional differences could be found for the relative importance of early and late phases of the innovation process. The region of Vienna as well as the other agglomerations had much higher shares of activities in the early phase (research, development, design work: Figure 12.5) as well as for expenses on product innovation (Figure 12.6). The old industrialized areas as well as the rural areas had a much higher share of expenses on the late phases (production and marketing related phases) and on process innovation.

To summarize, the second study showed that innovation activities, when broadly defined, are not confined to large agglomerations. Plants undertaking innovation activities were even more highly represented in "intermediate" areas with mixed economic structures, namely the rural industrialized and the tourist areas, than in the agglomerations. The rural areas showed a strong heterogeneity with regard to innovation: some parts of them, particular those not too peripheral from a regional center

---

[9]A considerable share of the innovation expenses in this area was concentrated in one district (Deutschlandsberg: see Figure 12.3).

[10]In the agglomerations high shares of the innovation expenditure are in the electrotechnical, machinery, vehicle, and chemical industries. In the rural areas high shares of the innovation expenses are in the ceramics, textile, machinery, chemical, wood manufacturing, and food industries.

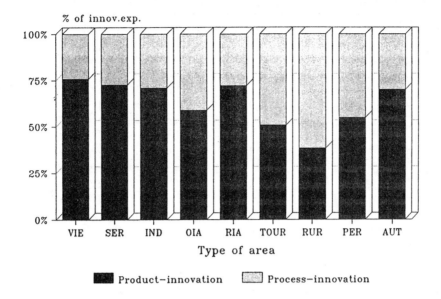

Figure 12.6: Expenditure for product and process innovation (as a percentage of innovation expenditure) – see p. 239 for key to regions.

(e.g. the Südsteiermark) had a fairly high share of expenditure on innovation activities (the latter being very often subsidiaries or branch plants of multiplant firms). Other rural areas, in particular the more peripheral ones, had very low innovation activities (Waldviertel, Burgenland). A spatial hierarchy corresponding to the product-cycle theory was observable for the kinds of innovation activities and projects, whereby the agglomerations specialize more on the early phases and on product innovations, the old industrialized areas and rural areas more on late phases and process innovations.

3.3   Case study of selected industries and regions

To gain more insight into the details and the determining factors of the regional innovation process, a case study of selected industries and regions was undertaken in 1987: 149 plants in metalworking, machinery, electrotechnical and electronic sectors and in five Austrian regions were investigated by means of interviews (Tödtling, 1990a, b).[11] The industries

---

[11]The interviews were done by H. Hofer (Wald- and Weinviertel), A. Strasser (Vöcklabruck), M. Weinrother and R. Bürger (Wien-Süd). The author developed the questionnaire and did the interviews at the plants in the Südsteiermark. The

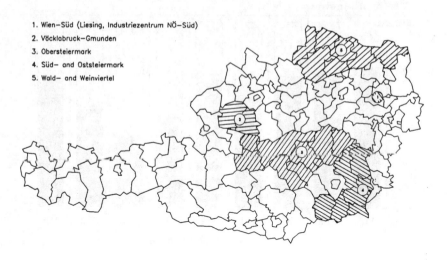

1. Wien–Süd (Liesing, Industriezentrum NÖ–Süd)
2. Vöcklabruck–Gmunden
3. Obersteiermark
4. Süd– ond Oststeiermork
5. Wald– ond Weinviertel

Figure 12.7: Investigated areas.

were chosen with regard to the importance of technological change: all of them are penetrated by new information technologies and by microelectronics both as products and for processes.

The regions cover only parts of the Austrian classification, particularly those areas with strong expected differences in the conditions for innovation. The areas selected were (1) an area within Austria's largest agglomeration, Vienna (Wien-Süd), (2) a more dispersed but dynamic industrialized area (Vöcklabruck),[12] (3) an "old" industrialized area (Obersteiermark), and (4)/(5) two peripheral rural areas (Südsteiermark and Waldviertel: see Figure 12.7). Important results of this case study were the following.

The plants investigated showed strong regional differences concerning relevant structural characteristics (organizational status, functional structure, qualifications of the workforce). In Wien-Süd and in Vöcklabruck the plants were to a higher degree headquarters or autonomous plants of multiplant firms, they had more management and boundary-spanning functions (Figure 12.8), and they had a more highly qualified workforce than in the old industrialized areas and the rural areas. Of the latter, rural Südsteiermark was strongly penetrated by branch plants and subsidiaries

case-study area of Obersteiermark was investigated by H. Glatz in a related study (Glatz and Moser, 1988; Glatz and Tödtling, 1988).

[12]In contrast to the Obersteiermark industrialization in Vöcklabruck is younger: most of the plants were established since the Second World War.

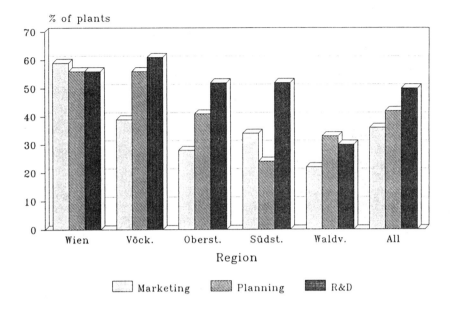

Figure 12.8: Functions performed by region: percentage of plants performing marketing, planning and R&D.

of multi-locational firms, established in the 1960s and 1970s.

Concerning innovation activities, significant regional differences were found, particularly for product innovations considered as "new to the market", less so for product innovations "new to the plant" and for most of the process innovations. The highest product innovation activity occurred in the plants of Wien-Süd, followed by those in the industrialized area of Vöcklabruck and those in the rural Südsteiermark (Figure 12.9). Clearly below average were the peripheral rural Waldviertel as well as the old industrialized region of Obersteiermark.[13] In the case of the process innovations "hierarchical" regional differences were found just for those which were considered as "new to the Austrian market" and the more recent CAD technology (Figure 12.10), not for the others (process innovation in general, CNC, automation techniques, computers, and new communication technologies).

The determining factors were investigated by PROBIT analysis (Tödtling,1990a, b):[14] factors were different for the various kinds of innovation

---

[13]In the case of product modifications, the regional differences were smaller but basically similar: the highest shares were again Vöcklabruck and Wien-Süd, the lowest in the Obersteiermark.

[14]G. Maier gave advice with regard to methodological aspects of the PROBIT

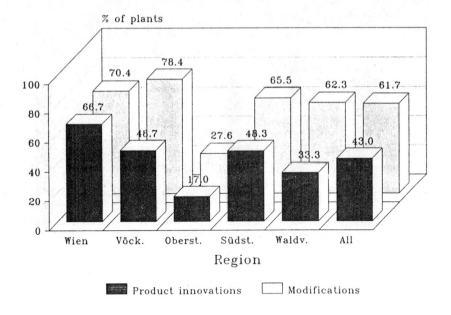

Figure 12.9: **Product innovations and product modifications (percent of plants).**

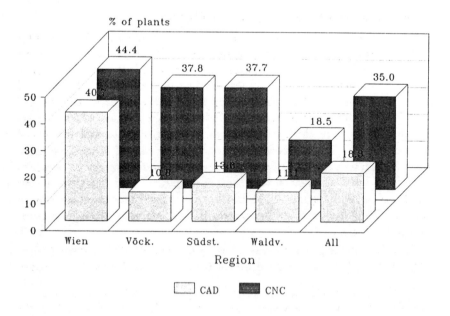

Figure 12.10: **Introduction of CNC and CAD (percent of adopting plants).**

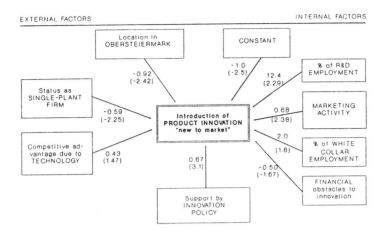

EXTERNAL FACTORS   INTERNAL FACTORS

Starting value. -0.16, Rho-sq. - 0.32, corr. Rho-sq. - 0.23

Figure 12.11: Introduction of product innovations "new to the market" (PROBIT analysis: coefficients and t-values).

activity. For the product innovations considered as "new to the market", the following factors turned out to be significant (Figure 12.11): the degree to which the plant had internal R&D and marketing activities, the share of white-collar employees, the facts that the plant was part of a multiplant firm and had already a competitive position based on technological advantage. In addition, the fact that the plant had received assistance from the public innovation policy was significant. From the locational factors (introduced as a dummy variable) the location in the old industrialized Obersteiermark had a negative influence.

The introduction of CAD depended partly on the same and partly on a set of different factors (Figure 12.12): the size of the plant, the share of technicians in the workforce as well as the share of other white-collar employees were significant internal factors. Among the external factors, export activity, a market position based on technological advantage, as well as technical-economic contacts to universities and to research institutions were significant factors.

The innovation activity of plants thus depended on a complex set of factors: the majority were structural and behavioral features of the plants; only a few of them were directly related to the location. The structural and behavioral characteristics, however, are in the medium and long run related to location via the process of regional specialization and the spatial division of labor (specialization by industry, functions and qualifications:

---

analysis (see also Maier, 1987).

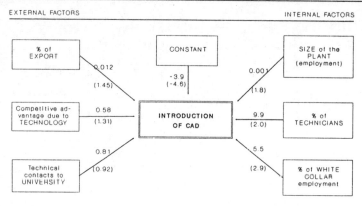

Figure 12.12: Introduction of CAD (PROBIT analysis: coefficients and t-values).

Massey, 1984; Tödtling, 1983; Bade, 1984).

Technical contacts as well as "sources" of innovation were investigated in more detail, since they reflect network characteristics and might be strongly influenced also by the regional environment. It was found that most of the innovations investigated correlated positively with the number of external technical contacts the plant had.[15]   These correlations were stronger for the more specialized contacts (to technical universities, research institutions, private consulting) but did not vary with distance. The majority of these contacts were to partners outside the respective regions (either at the national or international scale). The contacts at the regional scale were of some importance only for the plants in Wien-Süd and those in the Südsteiermark (to the province center of Graz); they were of minor importance for the plants in the other regions.

With regard to the sources of innovation it was found that internal functions/activities, external links to customers and suppliers, and the imitation of competitors were all important. There was also a regional differentiation (although not very strong) concerning these sources of innovation that corresponded to the respective structure of the plants and the locations: in Wien-Süd internal R&D and marketing as well as regional customers and competitors were relatively more important. In the rural areas linkages to multi-locational firms as well as to extra-regional partners (customers, suppliers, competitors) were relevant sources of innovation.

---

[15]These relations were analyzed by contingency tables and the related statistics.

4 Summary and Conclusions

From traditional theories of regional innovation a spatial hierarchy of the innovation process is to be expected. The innovation process is seen as running in a certain sequence from invention to the diffusion. The large agglomerations have, owing to their location factors, a comparative advantage in the early phases of the product cycle and of the innovation process (R&D and product innovation); the rural periphery is more involved in the late phases (process innovation or non-innovators).

More recent approaches offer a different view. The innovation process is seen as a continuous process having many interdependencies between early and late phases and feedback loops. Sources of innovation are not just technical research; they also arise from relations with customers, suppliers, competitors or internal marketing and production. Socioeconomic structures of the regions, which are shaped by the history of their industrialization (entrepreneurial traditions, characteristics of the workforce) as well as the structural and behavioral characteristics of the respective plants (their activity mix), are conceived of as important factors influencing the innovation activity in addition to location factors.

Empirical research on Austria revealed for all data sets investigated that both hierarchical and non-hierarchical spatial structures of innovation exist. Results in line with the hierarchical model were the following:

- R&D activities (expenditure, employment and its qualification) were high in the agglomeration of Vienna and the industrialized areas (Linz), low in the peripheral rural areas (R&D study).
- Early phases of the innovation process and product innovations also were relatively higher in the agglomerations (Vienna, other service centers, industrialized areas) than in the rural areas (innovation study).
- In the case study, plants in Wien-Süd and the industrialized region of Vöcklabruck had more innovation-relevant functions (R&D, marketing, planning) and skills (technical personnel) than the rural and old industrialized regions. They also had relatively more plants with product innovations "new to the market" as well as of selected process innovations (CAD as well as processes "new to the market").

The studies on the other hand also show non-hierarchical structures of the innovation process:

- R&D activities in Vienna and other large agglomerations are not carried out by a large number of innovative plants but are strongly concentrated in a few industries and firms. Thus there is no broad participation in innovation and there are large non-innovative segments in the high-ranking agglomerations.

- The highest share of plants undertaking innovation activities was in the industrialized rural areas and the tourist areas, which are in intermediate locations without large agglomerations. Innovation activities in these areas were less concentrated on the early phases and the large plants than in the agglomerations, involving small and medium-sized plants too. They concentrated more on late and applied phases of the innovation activity.

- Also, some of the rural areas showed remarkable segments of innovative plants both in the innovation study and the case study (Südsteiermark). They were often plants of multi-locational firms in modern sectors which took advantage of the rural labor market but were not confined to a strict spatial division of labor.[16] There were also innovative single-plant firms, which benefited from the technical skills of the owner or the workforce.

- The old industrialized areas in all three studies had very low innovation activities:[17] they had low levels of R&D, of early innovation phases, and of product innovations. This fact is difficult to explain by the static location factors approach of the hierarchical model, but is strongly related to the socioeconomic transformation those areas have experienced in the past.

The old industrialized areas represent the earliest locations of industrialization and they have been innovation centers in the past. They have lost much of their innovative capacity in the course of their industrialization process and the related socioeconomic transformation (see also the contribution of Friedmann in Part III). The past success of basic and mass production industries has led to a high employment share for these sectors, to an increase in the scale of plants and firms, and to the emergence of strong internal labor markets. Because of the dominance of the large firms there were no favorable conditions for the formation of new firms (low entrepreneurial skills, factor monopsonies, lack of producer services: Storper, 1986; Tichy, 1987). In the process of economic concentration, the plants in basic and mass production industries lost their headquarters and the boundary-spanning functions to the large agglomerations (Vienna and Linz) and became more and more confined to the production func-

---

[16]Although these plants clearly were integrated into an internal division of labor they were not all confined to production activities only, some of them had also applied R&D activities.

[17]This result is in line with studies by Keil and Schneidewind (1987) and Grabher (1988) for old industrial areas in Lower Austria.

tion. Also, the existing small and medium-sized firms suffered from lack of management and technical personnel and of producer services.

To sum up, it can be said that location factors and related spatial hierarchies do play a role in the entrepreneurial innovation process. Their impact, however, is less direct, being strongly related to the process of regional specialization ("spatial division of labor"). The importance of structure and behavior reduces the "locational determinism" and leaves scope for strategic action, both for firms and for regional policy. Under certain conditions (these can be either internal structures or network characteristics of the plants) there can be considerable innovation activity at "objectively" unfavorable locations, just as there can also be considerable segments of non-innovative plants in large agglomerations.

Former innovation centers may lose their innovative dynamic if the actors are not able to adjust internal structures to new external and global challenges. What seems to be required for a region to stay innovative in the long run is a culture of "rooted cosmopolitanism" (Friedmann). In economic terms this implies strong participation in large-scale networks (Johansson, Kamann) as well as "local embeddedness" and integration into the local milieu (Maillat, Garofoli), aspects which have been discussed intensively in previous sections of this book.

References

Andersson, A.E., B. Johansson, 1984. Knowledge Intensity and Product Cycles in Metropolitan Regions, IIASA, *Metropolitan Study* 8, Laxenburg.

Aldrich, H.E., 1979. *Organizations and Environment*, Prentice Hall, Englewood Cliffs.

Aydalot, P. (ed.), 1986. *Milieux Innovateurs en Europe*. GREMI, Paris.

Aydalot, P., D. Keeble (eds.) 1988. *High Technology Industry and Innovative Environments: The European Experience*, Routledge, London.

Bade, F.J., 1984. *Die funktionale Struktur der Wirtschaft und ihre räumliche Arbeitsteilung*, Deutsches Institut für Wirtschaftsforschung (DIW), Berlin.

Brown, L.A., 1981. *Innovation Diffusion: A New Perspective*, Methuen, London and New York.

Brugger, E.A., B. Stuckey, 1987. Regional Economic Structure and Innovative Behaviour in Switzerland, *Regional Studies*, Vol. 21, pp. 241–254.

Bundeskammer der Gewerblichen Wirtschaft, 1981. *Forschung und Dokumentation in Österreich*, Vienna.

Camagni, R., 1989. Space, Networks and Technical Change: An Evolutionary Approach, Paper presented to GREMI round table, Barcelona, March 1989.

Cappellin, R., 1983. Productivity Growth and Technological Change in a Regional Perspective. *Giornale degli Economisti ed Annali di Economia*, Vol.

42, pp. 459–482.

Coombs, R., P. Saviotti, V. Walsh, 1987. *Economics and Technological Change*, Macmillan, London.

Davelaar, E.J., P. Nijkamp, 1987. The Urban Incubation Hypothesis: Old Wine into New Bottles?, *Mitteilungen des Arbeitskreises für neue Methoden in der Regionalforschung*, Vol 17.

Dosi, G., 1988. The Nature of the Innovation Process, in G. Dosi, C. Freeman, R. Nelson, G. Silverberg, L. Soete (eds.), *Technical Change and Economic Theory*, Pinter, London, pp. 221–238.

Erickson, R.A., Th.R. Leinbach, 1979. Characteristics of Branch Plants Attracted to Nonmetropolitan Areas, in R.E. Lonsdale, H.L. Seyler (eds.), *Nonmetropolitan Industrialization*, John Wiley, London and New York, pp. 57–78.

Ewers, H.J., R. Wettmann, J. Kleine, N. Krist, F.J. Bade, 1980. Innovationsorientierte Regionalpolitik, *Schriftenreihe des Bundesministers für Raumordnung, Bauwesen und Städtebau*, Nr.6.42, Bonn–Bad Godesberg.

Freeman, C., 1982. *The Economics of Industrial Innovation*, MIT Press, Cambridge, Mass.

Gibbs, D.C., A. Edwards, 1983. Some Preliminary Evidence for the Interregional Diffusion of Selected Process Innovations, in A. Gillespie (ed.), *Technological Change and Regional Development*, London Papers in Regional Science, Pion, London.

Glatz, H., H. Moser, 1988. Innovationsorientierte Regionalpolitik – Eine Strategie für alte Industriegebiete? *Wirtschaft und Gesellschaft*, Vol. 14, pp. 197–226.

Glatz, H., F. Tödtling, 1988. Industrieller Strukturwandel und Regionalpolitik – Unterschiede der betrieblichen Innovation und regionalpolitische Handlungsmöglichkeiten. *Schriftenreihe Raumplanung für Österreich*, Nr. 15, Bundeskanzleramt, Vienna.

Goddard, J., A. Thwaites, D. Gibbs, 1986. The Regional Dimension to Technological Change in Great Britain, in A. Amin, J. Goddard (eds.), *Technological Change, Industrial Restructuring and Regional Development*, Allen & Unwin, London.

Grabher, G., 1988. De-Industrialisierung oder Neo-Industrialisierung? Innovationsprozesse und Innovationspolitik in traditionellen Industrieregionen. *WZB Berlin*, Edition Sigma.

Hansen, N.M., 1981. Development from Above: The Centre-Down Development Paradigm, in W. Stöhr, F. Taylor (eds.), *Development from Above or Below? The Dialectics of Regional Planning in Developing Countries*, John Wiley, New York, pp. 15–38.

Holst, M., 1987. External control and innovation activities in manufacturing industry. Paper presented at the 27th European Congress of the RSA in Athens.

Kay, N.M., 1979. *The Innovating Firm, A Behavioural Theory of Corporate R&D*, Macmillan, London.

Keil, D., P. Schneidewind, 1987. Strukturschwache Industriegebiete in Österreich – Problemgebiet St. Pölten Traisental. *ÖROK-Schriftenreihe*, Nr. 57, Vienna.

Kleine, J., 1983. Investitionsverhalten bei Prozeßinnovationen – Ein Beitrag zur mikroökonomischen Diffusionsforschung, *WZB Berlin*.

Lasuén, J.R., 1973. Urbanisation and Development: The Temporal Interaction between Geographical Clusters, *Urban Studies*, Vol. 10, pp. 163–188.

Maier, G., 1987. Die Schätzung diskreter Entscheidungsmodelle mit Hilfe der SAS Prozeduren BROBIT und MNLOGIT, *IIR-Discussion* 27/2, Institut für Raumordnung, Wirtschaftsuniversität Wien.

Malecki, E.J., 1983. Technology and Regional Development: A Survey, *APA Journal*, Vol. 50, pp. 262–269.

Malecki, E.J., 1988. Research and Development and Technology Transfer in Economic Development: The Role of Regional Technological Capability, Paper presented at the European Summer Institute of the RSA in Arco.

Massey, D., 1984. *Spatial Divisions of Labor: Social Structures and the Geography of Production*, Macmillan, London.

Müdespacher, A., 1987. Adoptionsverhalten der Schweizer Wirtschaft und regionale Aspekte der Diffusion der Neuerungen der Telematik. *Jahrbuch für Regionalwissenschaft*, Vol. 8, pp. 106–134.

Norton, R.D., J. Rees, 1979. The Product-Cycle and the Spatial Decentralization of American Manufacturing, *Regional Studies*, Vol. 13, pp. 141–151.

Perrin, J.C., 1986. Les synergies locales – éléments de théorie et d'analyse, in P. Aydalot (ed.), *Milieux Innovateurs en Europe*, GREMI, Paris.

Porter, M.E., 1980. *Competitive Strategy: Techniques for Analysing Industries and Competitors*, Free Press, New York.

Rees, J., R. Briggs, R. Oakey, 1984. The Adoption of New Technology in the American Machinery Industry, *Regional Studies*, Vol. 18, pp. 489–504.

Rothwell, R., 1989. SMFs, Inter-firm Relationships and Technological Change, Paper presented to the European Conference on Strategies for Local Economic Development, Dublin.

Scherer, F.M, 1980. *Industrial Market Structure and Economic Performance*, Rand McNally, Chicago.

Sorge, A., 1986. *Informationstechnik und Arbeit im sozialen Prozeß: Arbeitsorganisation, Qualifikation und Produktivkraftentwicklung*, Campus, Frankfurt and New York.

Stöhr, W., 1987. Regional Innovation Complexes. *Papers of the Regional Science Association*, Vol. 59, pp. 29–44.

Storper, M., 1986. Technology and New Regional Growth Complexes: The Economics of Discontinuous Spatial Development, in P. Nijkamp (ed.), *Technological Change, Employment and Spatial Dynamics*, Springer-Verlag, Heidelberg, pp. 46–75.

Storper, M., R. Walker, 1983. The Theory of Labor and the Theory of Location, *International Journal of Urban and Regional Research*, Vol. 7, pp. 1–43.

Suarez-Villa, L., 1983. *Dynamics of manufacturing and the theory of location,*

University of California, unpublished paper, Irvine.

Taylor, M., 1983. Technological Change and the Segmented Economy, in A. Gillespie (ed.), *Technological Change and Regional Development*, London Papers of Regional Science, Pion, London.

Thwaites, A., 1982. Some Evidence of Regional Variations in the Introduction and Diffusion of Industrial Products and Processes within British Manufacturing Industry, *Regional Studies*, Vol. 16, pp. 371–382.

Thwaites, A., R. Oakey (eds.), 1985. *The Regional Economic Impact of Technological Change*, Frances Pinter, London.

Tichy, G., 1987. Das Altern von Industrieregionen: Unabwendbares Schicksal oder Herausforderung für die Wirtschaftspolitik, *Berichte für Raumforschung und Raumordnung.*

Tödtling, F., 1984. Organizational Characteristics of Plants in Core and Peripheral Regions of Austria. *Regional Studies*, Vol. 18, pp. 397–412.

Tödtling, F., 1987. The Regional Pattern of Industrial R&D in Austria: Sectoral, Organizational and Locational Determinants. *Revue d'économie régionale et urbaine*, No. 2, pp. 239–256.

Tödtling, F., 1990a. *Räumliche Differenzierung betrieblicher Innovation – Erklärungsansätze und empirische Befunde für österreichische Regionen*, Edition Sigma, Berlin.

Tödtling, F., 1990b. Regional Differences and Determinants of Entrepreneurial Innovation - Empirical Results of an Austrian Case Study, *IIR-Discussion* No. 40, Institut für Raumordnung, Wirtschaftsuniversität Wien.

Utterback, J.M., 1979. The Dynamics of Product and Process Innovation in Industry, in Ch.T. Hill, J.M. Utterback (eds.), *Technological Innovation for a Dynamic Economy*, Pergamon Press, New York.

Watts, H.D., 1981. *The Branch Plant Economy – A Study of External Control*, Longman, London and New York.

Volk, E., 1988. *Die Innovationsaktivitäten der österreichischen Industrie – Technologie und Innovationstest 1985.* Österreichisches Institut für Wirtschaftsforschung, Vienna.

Von Hippel, E., 1988. *The Sources of Innovation.* Oxford University Press, Oxford.

Appendix:
List of Variables in the PROBIT Models

DEPENDENT VARIABLES (binary variables):

product innovation "new to the market": plant has introduced between 1981 and 1986 one or more product innovations considered as "new to the Austrian market"

introduction of CAD: plant has introduced CAD technology

EXPLANATORY VARIABLES:

location in Obersteiermark: dummy variable for location of the plant in the case-study area of Obersteiermark

single-plant firm: dummy variable for single-plant firm

% export: percentage of exported sales

technological advantage: dummy variable for indication of the plant of a competitive advantage via "technology"

innovation promotion: dummy variable for plant having received financial support from public innovation policy

size of plant: number of employees of the plant

R&D: percent of employment concerned with R&D activities (full-time equivalents)

marketing: dummy variable for indication of plant of full performance of marketing activities

% technicians: percentage of engineers in the workforce

% white collar: percentage of other white-collar employees

financial obstacles: dummy variable for indication of financial obstacles in the innovation process

Region indicators

VIE	Region of Vienna
SER	Other service centers
OIA	"Old" industrialized areas
IND	Other industrialized areas
RIA	Industrialized rural areas
TOUR	Tourist areas
RUR	Non-peripheral rural areas
PER	Peripheral rural areas
AUT	Austria

13

Growth Center vs. Endogenous Development Strategies: The Case of Research Parks

Harvey Goldstein*

1   Introduction

In the United States as well as in western Europe, there has been a great deal of interest and investment in research (or science) parks as an instrument for stimulating regional economic development. Since 1982 the number of research parks in the United States has tripled. More than two-thirds of the state governments have invested in research parks through public, state universities or through economic development or technology development agencies of state government.

While stimulating regional economic development is invariably the overall objective of states' investment in research parks, there appear to be clear differences in the strategies, or processes, by which research parks are to achieve the overall objective.[1] A growth center strategy lies un-

*University of North Carolina at Chapel Hill, Chapel Hill, USA. The author is grateful to the Ford Foundation for partial support of this research, to Sukchan Ko, Judy Barnet, Dawn Donaldson, and Sarah Flaks for their valuable research assistance, and especially to Mike Luger, collaborator on the overall research project, for his many fruitful ideas that are imbedded in much of the paper.

[1]States vary in the importance placed on achieving particular objectives such as creating new jobs, the formation of new businesses, raising average wage/salary levels, diversifying the state economy, stemming the "brain-drain", and increasing the technological capacity of the region for attracting innovative activity. We are not including in this discussion, for instance, those research parks that were

derneath a majority of research park initiatives, in which the recruitment of the research and development (R&D) branch plants of multi-locational firms is emphasized. In a smaller number of cases research parks are based on the generation of new, small, innovative businesses from the latent pool of entrepreneurs already within the region. These two strategies, of course, reflect often sharp differences at the level of regional development theory between neoclassical and Schumpeterian traditions, or between the ideologies and practices of top-down versus bottom-up development (see, for instance, Stöhr and Taylor, 1981; Malecki, 1983; Rees and Stafford, 1983; Friedmann and Weaver, 1979). In recent years there has been a shift away from the domination of the practice of economic development as business recruitment cum locational incentives towards the "bottom-up" approach (e.g. Luger, 1984; Bergman, 1986).

In this chapter we assess each of these strategies when applied to research parks, using what are widely considered to be two of the most highly successful research parks in the United States. The next section is a brief review of growth center and endogenous strategies of regional development, emphasizing how each strategy is "supposed" to work in the case of investments in research parks. The third section provides background descriptions of the two cases of the Research Triangle Park in North Carolina and the University of Utah Research Park in Salt Lake City, Utah, while the fourth section presents results of analyses of the milieus and economic development outcomes of each park. In the fifth section we assess the two strategies by addressing the questions of (1) to what extent is each case successful in terms of the expected results of the respective strategy? (2) was the respective strategy the "correct" one, given the prevailing conditions and resources? We also reflect on possible lessons for the design of technology-led economic development policies from the examination of these two cases.

2   Two Alternative Strategies

2.1   Growth center strategy

Growth center strategy is based upon the theoretical work of Perroux (1950, 1987) and also upon applications of the theory offered by Boudeville (1966), Hansen (1972) and many others. In the 1960s development economists optimistically adopted this strategy for industrial development in lagging regions in both the Third World and industrialized countries (e.g. France, the United States). The strategy lost favor in the 1970s

---

created as primarily land development projects or as revenue enhancements for private (or public) universities.

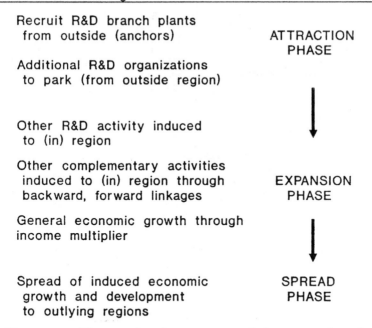

Recruit R&D branch plants from outside (anchors)	ATTRACTION PHASE
Additional R&D organizations to park (from outside region)	
Other R&D activity induced to (in) region	
Other complementary activities induced to (in) region through backward, forward linkages	EXPANSION PHASE
General economic growth through income multiplier	
Spread of induced economic growth and development to outlying regions	SPREAD PHASE

Figure 13.1: The growth pole strategy applied to research parks.

(see critiques by Friedmann and Weaver, 1979), but in the late 1980s is regaining interest, at least implicitly.

Figure 13.1 illustrates how growth pole strategy is supposed to work in the context of the use of research parks for stimulating regional economic development. R&D branch plants are recruited to serve as anchors in a newly created research park, which along with related local research universities represents the actual growth pole. The concentration of R&D activity should attract other R&D facilities to the research park or adjoining area, based upon the realization of localization economies. Other activity such as manufacturing and producer services will be induced to locate in the region through the development of backward and forward linkages. All of these activities will contribute to growth of the residentiary and consumer services sectors through the usual income multiplier applied to the increment in local spending from enhanced aggregate payroll in the region.

The strategy implies the provision of rather large, up-front, public investments in the form of the park itself for land and infrastructure, and/or financial incentives to the corporations to locate branch plants in the park or adjacent areas. It is also assumed generally in growth pole strategy that some reasonable proportion of the economic activity stimulated by the propulsive industries in the growth center will spread

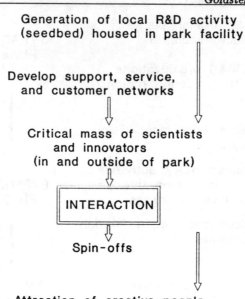

Figure 13.2: The endogenous development strategy in the case of research parks.

out to more peripheral regions. More specifically in this case it is assumed that the manufacturing and support activities related to, and induced by, the R&D activity will locate in the outlying areas. Here, the location of a concentration of a highly educated, professional labor force and the amenities thought important to attract such people are neither necessary nor (for reasons of labor cost) desirable.

2.2 Endogenous development strategy

This type of strategy, also commonly referred to as entrepreneurial, fertility, seedbed, or indigenous, is more eclectic in both theory and practice than growth pole strategy. Nevertheless it focuses on fostering self-generated growth and development rather than importing capital, investment, expertise, labor, or other resources. The theoretical bases are found in Schumpeter (1934, 1950), and were applied to urban development by Thompson (1965) as early as the mid-1960s. The practice of the strategy waited until the 1980s when a conducive political culture that was more conservative but also more populist arose, and when the "successes" of "dynamic" regions such as Silicon Valley, Route 128, Baden-Württemberg, the Rhone Valley, and the "Third Italy" became more widely known. A larger number of cases of endogenous development initiatives in Europe are documented and analyzed in Stöhr (1990). More recent work on what makes a region "creative" or "dynamic" has been performed by Shapero (1981), Andersson (1985), Sweeney (1985, 1987), Johansson (1987) and reviewed by Malecki (1987, 1988).

The creation of a research park will often be a response to the needs of local entrepreneurs (e.g. inventive university faculty) for facilities, services, networks, and a creative milieu (see Figure 13.2). The park will then serve as a seedbed of creativity for the region, by helping to provide a critical mass of scientists, engineers, and other innovative individuals (along with research universities and government research institutes and labs). It would also be instrumental in helping to: develop support services, sources of capital, and networks; spin off new businesses from successful ones already in the park; and give innovative activity greater visibility within the region, possibly leading to the emergence of local "latent" entrepreneurs. Over time the region would attract creative people from outside, further enhancing the density of entrepreneurial talent. The theories underlying the strategy make no claim about any spatial spread of the development to adjacent or peripheral regions, unlike growth center strategy.

3 Comparative Case Studies – Background

3.1 The Research Triangle Park

Created in 1959, the Research Triangle Park (RTP) in North Carolina is the largest, and considered to be one of the most successful, research parks in the United States.[2] There are now about 50 R&D organizations on 7,000 acres of land with a combined workforce of approximately 32,000 employees. From its beginning, RTP has deliberately sought the R&D branch plants of major national, and more recently, foreign and multi national corporations. Indeed, the list of branch plant organizations in RTP reads like a "Who's Who" of the corporate world – IBM, Data General, General Electric, Dupont, Northrop, BASF, Ciba-Geigy, Burroughs-Wellcome, Rhône-Poulenc, Northern Telecom, and so on.

In the mid-1950s the state of North Carolina had the second lowest

---

[2]For a complete and detailed history of the Research Triangle Park see Linda Sellars, An Oral History of the Research Triangle Park, unpublished dissertation, Department of History, University of North Carolina at Chapel Hill. Other useful historical references include Louis R. Wilson, *The Research Triangle of North Carolina* (Chapel Hill: Louis R. Wilson, 1967), and W.B. Hamilton, 'The Research Triangle of North Carolina: A Study in Leadership for the Common Weal, *South Atlantic Quarterly*, Vol. LXV, No. 2, Spring 1966, pp. 254–278.

per capita income of any state. Its employment base was concentrated in three low-wage, declining industries: tobacco, textiles, and furniture. There was little or no R&D activity in the state except for that in the three research universities (University of North Carolina at Chapel Hill, Duke University, and North Carolina State University). Yet the combination of high-quality universities and the lack of job opportunities for highly skilled scientists and engineers had led to a "brain drain" from the state of serious proportion (Little, 1988).

These conditions, and projections of a continued downward statewide economic trend relative to the nation as a whole, led state political, business, and educational leaders to form a committee to investigate how the strengths of the state's research universities could be used to help restructure the economy. The committee produced a report proposing that the combined resources of the three universities could induce the location of a concentration of industrial research laboratories to the region where the three universities were located. This was based on the premise that the industrial labs could take advantage of access to faculty expertise in particular scientific and technological fields of strength. Economic development would subsequently spread to other parts of the state, according to the report, because corporations would want to locate high-tech production facilities in general proximity to the concentration of R&D facilities, but in locations where labor costs were not as high as in the region that became known as the Research Triangle.

Not much happened until about two years after the report was issued, when a retired industrialist from New York decided to invest in the general concept proposed by the committee. He proposed to build a private research park on 4,000 wholly undeveloped acres near the (at the time) small airport in the center of the triangle formed by the cities of Chapel Hill, Durham, and Raleigh, also the locations of the three research universities. This private investment initiative was unsuccessful, but a group of private citizens and civic-minded corporations bought out the assets of the (empty) private research park and formed a private, non-profit foundation to own, develop, and manage the research park (Little, 1988). A $500,000 grant and gift of about 170 acres of land in the middle of the park from the newly formed Research Triangle Foundation were used to create a non-profit contract research organization, the Research Triangle Institute, the park's first occupant.

University faculty and business leaders in the state who had good contacts with research managers of well-known corporations became active in trying to recruit R&D branch plants to the park. The results of these efforts were slow until 1965. But then, to the surprise of many, IBM bought a large site for a major facility. Shortly thereafter state political leaders with strong ties to the Kennedy and then the Johnson administrations were instrumental in getting the National Institutes of Health to locate its first branch facility of the National Institute of Environmental Health Sciences (NIEHS) in the park as well. IBM and NIEHS served as anchors for the struggling park by giving it legitimacy among the corporate world at a time when the South as a whole was not considered a suitable region for locating R&D facilities. Over the next twenty-two years the growth of RTP swelled with a string of corporate and federal government announcements of the decisions to locate R&D facilities in the park. Not until 1987 did the growth of the park falter in terms of attracting new organizations, as competition among other regions also vying for R&D branch facilities became highly intensified and as the growth of the overall amount of corporate investment in new R&D facilities stabilized.

3.2 The University of Utah Research Park

In contrast to the Research Triangle Park, which relied on the recruitment of R&D branch plants of large multilocational organizations, the University of Utah developed its park in response to the needs of local (faculty) entrepreneurs. Much of the ensuing growth of the park has occurred through the spinning off of new businesses from existing park organizations.

The park opened in 1970 and occupies a 320 acre site adjacent to the main University of Utah campus in Salt Lake City, Utah. As of 1988 some 57 organizations with a combined workforce of about 4,200 employees were located in the park.[3]

The Salt Lake City region now has a diversity of high-technology businesses that span a variety of industry sectors. Yet twenty years ago the regional economy was lopsidedly dependent upon the federal government (mostly for defense- and aerospace-related contracts) and the minerals and energy sectors, all relatively volatile. In other ways the region suffered from some of the same problems as the Raleigh–Durham area of North Carolina. These problems included being located in a peripheral area far from major metropolitan centers and markets, and a brain-drain from the region and state due to the narrowness of employment opportunities for university graduates (Brown, 1987). Like Raleigh–Durham, one of the few strengths of the region for attracting high-technology development was the research university, which was particularly strong in the physical and health sciences as well as engineering. Unlike Raleigh–Durham though, there was also a strong tradition of entrepreneurial activity within the university and in the larger region, and a very well educated and skilled

---

[3]These organizations include some University of Utah departments as well as some service functions including a hotel, child care facility, bank, etc.

labor force. Both of these strengths were (and still are) closely related to the large influence of the Mormon culture in the region.

In 1965 the US Department of Defense designated federal land under its control near the University of Utah campus as superfluous and made it available to the state government. Opportunistically, the university proposed that the land be given to it for the purpose of building a research park. Several prominent faculty members and administrators had observed first-hand, as students or faculty at Stanford, how a university could help create an entrepreneurial milieu that later could stimulate high-technology development for an entire region. The university's initial proposal to the state governor for the use of the excess federal land cited the "brain-drain" that the state was experiencing, arguing that the research park could help generate a large number of job opportunities for scientists, engineers, and managers for the region. An additional interest of the university for the park was to solve a chronic need for "crunch space" when large contract research projects were awarded to the university.

A consulting firm, Arthur D. Little, Inc., was hired to conduct a feasibility study for the park. The consultant's report was pessimistic about the chances of success. Difficulties in attracting a sufficient number of industrial research facilities to the region, *vis-à-vis* other regions such as northern California and Boston/Cambridge with superior locations and business infrastructure, were cited in the report. Implicit, though, was the warning that the Mormon culture might be a disincentive for firms to locate an R&D facility there because of the perceived unwillingness of the requisite highly educated professionals to locate in the region if they were not Mormon.

In spite of the report the university pursued the acquisition of the land and authority from the state legislature to develop the park, which it received. A set of negotiations between the university, the state, and the city resulted in the city providing the necessary utilities and roads for the park in exchange for a stream of "in lieu of taxes" contributions by the university to the city.

The first tenant to locate in the park about two years after it was formed was the university itself. It had a need for crunch space to perform a contract for the federal government to evaluate the artificial heart, first invented at the university. Somewhat earlier, a professor in the computer science department, David C. Evans, and a colleague from MIT formed their own company that grew out of their university-based research on computer graphics. Evans and Sutherland Computer Co. moved into temporary building space on land adjacent to the park in anticipation of the park's development.

The first private tenant, Terra Tek, Inc., was to have a significant influence on the future of the park. Wayne Brown, a professor and chairman of the mechanical engineering department, had previously established a very successful business, Kenway Engineering, Inc., that again had grown out of university-based contract research. Encouraged by his success, Brown started an additional business, Terra Tek, Inc., that grew out of still other university-based research on rock mechanics. Terra Tek located in the park, and soon developed a business strategy of expanding its corporate influence by spinning off viable groups as separate, new technology-based businesses. Terra Tek retained a share of the equity ownership of these spin-off businesses, along with their own management and outside investors. Many of the Terra Tek spin-offs also located in the park, including NPI, Inc., now a world leader in plant biotechnology products.

Much of the subsequent growth of the park has stemmed from faculty spinning off businesses to extend contract research begun in the university, or alternatively from second- and third-generation spin-offs from businesses that first located in the park. Indeed, the park director[4] has estimated that over one-half of the current employment in the research park can be traced to two faculty members/entrepreneurs, Wayne Brown and David Evans. The university's policy of "academic capitalism" has been a critical ingredient for the success of the research park as well as serving as a symbol of this model of research park development.

4 Comparative Case Studies – Park Milieus and Regional Outcomes

We now examine the extent to which the two parks, representing the two different strategies outlined above, differ in certain key attributes that help to describe the milieu of the park. After this we look at how they differ in the regional development impacts that can be attributed to the respective research parks.[5]

4.1 Comparison of park milieus

First, the two different strategies are defined, in part, on recruiting branch plants of corporations located outside the region versus the development of locally based businesses. Thus the two parks should differ in the percent-

---

[4]Interview with Charles Evans, University of Utah Research Park director, 8 July 1988.

[5]Data reported in this section was collected through a questionnaire administered in the spring and summer of 1988 to the population of R&D organizations located in the two research parks, and to a sample of high-technology business that had located in the respective metropolitan areas.

Table 13.1: Single-plant vs. branch plant in RTP and Utah Research Parks

Plant type	RTP	Utah
Single plant	29.3%	56.7%
Branch plant	70.7%	43.3%

age of branch plant and single-plant organizations located in the respective parks. Table 13.1 shows that the difference is considerable and in the expected direction. Moreover, of the branch plants in the Utah park, over 60 percent are headquartered in the state of Utah, indicating that many of these are still locally based, but have a headquarters function in a separate facility. On the other hand, only 38 percent of the branches in RTP are headquartered in North Carolina.

Because locally based, start-up businesses are less likely to have a large number of specialized facilities for separate functions, we would expect that parks following the endogenous development model would have organizations with a greater variety of functional activities, i.e. would be less "pure" R&D, than parks following the growth center strategy. From Figure 13.3 we can see that the organizations in the Utah park engage in considerably less basic research and considerably more product development and prototype development than the organizations in RTP. The respective proportions of applied research, routine production, and administration are surprisingly similar, though.

We expect differences in the respective occupational mixes of the parks' workforces to reflect the expected differences in the mix of functional activities above. That is, there should be a smaller percentage of scientists and engineers in the Utah park and a larger percentage of technicians, semi-skilled and low-skilled production workers, managers, and clerical workers, compared to RTP. Figure 13.4 indicates that the Utah park does have a smaller percentage of scientists and engineers compared to RTP and a larger percentage of skilled technicians (presumably for product and prototype development), but the two parks do not differ much in the percentage of the other occupational groups.

The factors that are considered most important by park organizations for locating in the park *vis-à-vis* other sites within the region provide insight into what the park provides for the region in terms of milieu that is special or unique. A key aspect of the endogenous development strategy is the creation of a synergistic or dynamic milieu. One of the most important functions of a research park in this strategy is to provide oppor-

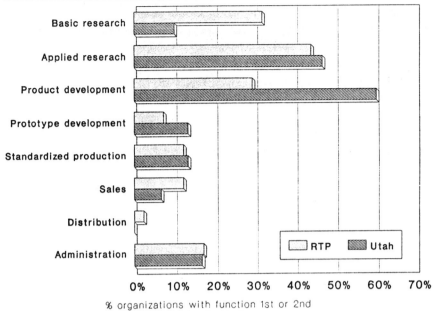

Figure 13.3: **Functional specialization of RTP and Utah park organizations.**

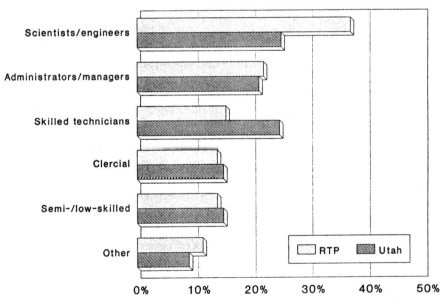

Figure 13.4: **Occupational mix in RTP and Utah.**

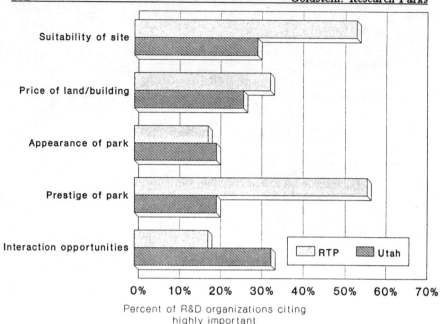

Figure 13.5: Factors for locating in research park.

tunities for interaction among entrepreneur scientists and engineers. More generally, greater emphasis would be placed on the function of providing agglomeration economies. Figure 13.5 and Table 13.2 indicate the relative importance of various research park functions from the point of view of organizations that had located in the two respective parks.

From Figure 13.5 we see that opportunities for interaction with professionals from other organizations in the park are considered the most important factor for locating in the Utah park, while this was considered among the least important factors in the case of RTP. Prestige of the location and the address, on the other hand, is considered among the most important factors for locating in RTP. These results are consistent with the hypothesis that prestige of location is more important when attracting branch plants to a region than in attempting to stimulate the development of locally based businesses.

Organizations that have located in RTP place considerably less importance on park management playing a liaison role with universities, providing technical or managerial assistance, and providing opportunities for interaction compared to Utah (see Table 13.2). More importance is attached to the provision of physical infrastructure, the provision of workplace amenities, and overall land use planning within the park by RTP organizations. This data suggests that a custodial and "public goods"

Table 13.2: Functions park management should provide

Function	Rank RTP	Rank Utah
Amenities	2	4
Infrastructure	2	5
Business assistance	6	6
Liaison with universities	5	2
Interaction opportunities	4	3
Physical planning	1	1

provision role for the research park is consistent with the growth center strategy, while a more interventionist role (i.e. providing services that are internal to the operations of the business organizations) may be more consistent with the endogenous development strategy.

4.2   A comparison of regional development outcomes

We finally come to the question of what regional development outcomes can be attributed to the respective research parks. Here we focus on regional employment growth and labor supply effects, but we also examine the extent to which the parks stimulated innovative activity in the region and stimulated regional output by park organizations purchasing inputs from local suppliers.

Figure 13.6 presents the responses from park organizations to the survey question, "What is the likelihood that this organization would have located in the region if the research park had not existed?" Roughly, over 70 percent of the organizations that located in the Utah park would have located at some other site in the region even if the park had not existed. About 50 percent of the organizations in RTP would have located in the region anyway.[6]

These results are reinforced when we examine the responses to the same question sent to a sample of high-technology organizations that located in their respective regions at some time after each research park was founded (see Figure 13.7). RTP has been responsible for over 16 percent of the high-technology organizations locating in its region while the University of Utah Research Park has been responsible for only about 4 percent of the

---

[6]These percentages were calculated by applying the probability figures of 0.9, 0.7, 0.5, 0.3, and 0.1 to the percent of responses "very likely", "likely", "maybe", "unlikely", and "very unlikely", respectively, and summing the products.

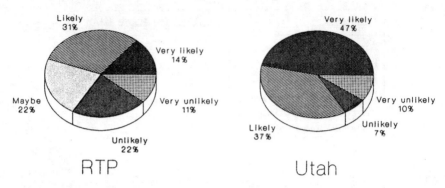

% of park R&D organization respondents

Figure 13.6: If the park did not exist, would you have located in the region?

high-technology businesses locating in the Salt Lake City region. RTP's net contribution to the global economy, i.e. organizations that would not otherwise exist anywhere, is represented by 7.9 percent of all out-of-park high-tech organizations in the region, while the comparable figure for the Utah park is 2.8 percent.

These results on the employment growth impacts that can be attributed to the respective research parks generally are consistent with the prior expectations of the two strategies. In growth center strategy one attracts capital to the region that would have been invested somewhere else. In the endogenous strategy there is rarely a locational decision, but only whether or not to start a business *in situ* (Sweeney, 1985; Cooper, 1985). So we would have expected a very small percentage of high-tech organizations in Salt Lake City to have said they would have located in some other region if the research park had not existed. On the other hand, we also would have expected a larger percentage of the organizations to have responded that they would not be in existence at all if not for the park.

The sources of labor supply for the two research parks differ considerably. Over 67 percent of the professional workforce of the Utah park come from local sources, versus 52 percent for RTP (see Figure 13.8). The proportion of professionals recruited from other businesses in the region versus the proportion transferred from corporate branches outside the re-

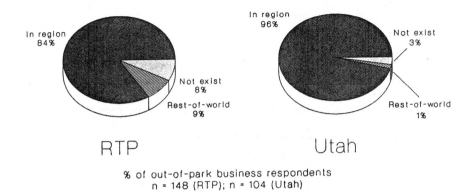

RTP   Utah

% of out-of-park business respondents
n = 148 (RTP); n = 104 (Utah)

Figure 13.7: If the park did not exist, where would you be?

gion in large part accounts for this difference. The difference between the two parks in their respective distribution of sources of the non-professional workforce is less than for the respective professional workforces.

The park as a source of innovation, or ideas, to other high-technology businesses that located in the region after the park was created is a relatively minor role for both research parks (see Figure 13.9). RTP's primary benefits to the region's high-tech businesses primarily are as a stimulant of economic growth and vitality, and as a source of prestige for the region. The University of Utah Research Park, in general, is valued less by other businesses in the region compared to RTP but, similar to the RTP case, its stimulation of economic growth and enhancement of the region's prestige are cited as the most significant benefits. On the other hand, RTP is considered "very important" or "somewhat important" as a source of R&D inputs by 7.7 percent of the sample businesses in the region and the Utah park by an even smaller 4.3 percent.

Finally, the proportion of local purchases made by park organizations in RTP is 32.5 percent of total non-labor purchases compared to 44.7 percent for organizations in the University of Utah Research Park. Although these results are consistent with those expected from the two strategies, the difference in industrial structure of the two regions at least partially accounts for the differences in proportion of local purchases between the two parks.

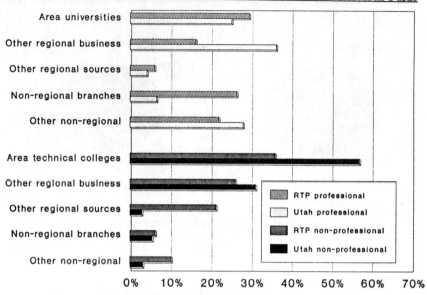

Figure 13.8: Sources of park workforces.

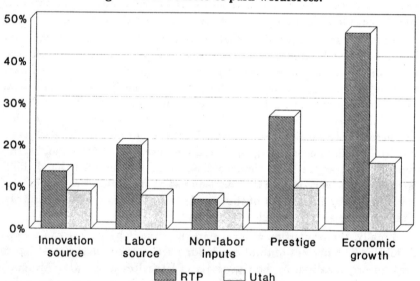

Figure 13.9: Benefits of the park to other high-tech businesses in the region.

5 Assessment of the Strategies and Conclusions

Here we address the questions of (1) to what extent has each case followed the expected outcomes of its respective strategy; and (2) was the strategy the "correct" one, given the conditions at the time the strategy was chosen? We then summarize what we have learned from these cases that might have more general relevance for technology-based regional economic development policies.

5.1 To what extent were the outcomes consistent with the expectation of the strategies?

For the case of the Research Triangle Park, the outcomes have followed those expected by growth center strategy to a large degree, but by no means fully. The park was highly successful in attracting anchors that would have otherwise located elsewhere. The anchors then led to the further growth and expansion of the park by, in turn, attracting other R&D branch plants of outside corporations. Some amount of additional R&D activity has been induced to the region by the localization economies created by the park in combination with the area's three research universities. On the other hand, complementary activities that would be expected to be linked backwardly or forwardly to the R&D "pole" have not developed to the degree that the strategy assumes. This has limited the range of the types of job opportunities stimulated by the park to mostly high-level professional ones. Similarly, the spatial spillover, or spread effect, of the park has been quite limited. To date, the induced development, concentrated as it has been in other R&D activity and consumer services (from the normal multiplier effect), has been largely within the three-county Triangle area. The spread of induced development in the form of high tech manufacturing to adjacent and peripheral areas of the state has been hindered by a poorly educated labor force outside the major metropolitan areas (see Rosenfeld, Malizia and Dugan, 1988).

The University of Utah Research Park case also to a large degree has followed the path and process of development anticipated in the endogenous strategy. Yet as in the RTP case, it also has fallen short in some important aspects. First, the creation of the park was in response to local entrepreneurial demand, consistent with the strategy. It succeeded in helping to increase the density of entrepreneurs and, with the university itself, to develop a critical mass of scientists and engineers. The park and the university have provided a milieu for interaction and creativity that has spawned a significant number of patents by university faculty and a significant number of spin-off businesses directly from the university and from existing park businesses. The park and the university combined have also begun to provide the region with an image of dynamism and high-technological/innovative capacity outside the state including foreign countries. This is important for attracting creative people to the region, particularly non-Mormons.

Yet, the strategy in the case of Utah has fallen short in extending and integrating the milieu created in the park and the university into the rest of the region. The development of networks and other elements of an agglomeration economy, considered by many to be requirements for the endogenous development strategy to succeed (e.g. Brusco, 1986; Sweeney, 1987; Gruenstein, 1984; Miller and Cote, 1987), has not occurred to any appreciable degree outside the immediate environment of the university.

5.2   Were the respective strategies the "correct" ones?

To evaluate the correctness of the strategies chosen we must take into account the regional conditions prevailing at the time the respective parks were conceived rather than the present conditions.

In the case of RTP, the principal objectives were oriented to statewide economic development, and specifically increasing job opportunities in growing industries, raising earned per capita income levels by stimulating higher-wage jobs, and stemming the brain-drain of university graduates from the state. In a strategic sense, the strength of the state for technology-led economic development lay almost entirely with its research universities, all of which were located in the Raleigh–Durham region. Other conditions, or factors, that the literature on high-technology location consistently cites as important – large metropolitan areas, a strong base in durable goods manufacturing, concentration of headquarters functions, good air transportation access, and a well-educated resident labor force (e.g. Premus, 1982; Markusen, Hall and Glasmeier, 1986) – were either low or absent in the state in the late 1950s. The three research universities combined probably had the largest concentration of scientific and engineering talent in the South, but the level of entrepreneurial activity within the universities was rather low. For that matter, there was an absence of a strong entrepreneurial tradition in the state as a whole. On the other hand, key faculty had developed excellent contacts with researchers and research managers in many large technology-oriented corporations. Under all these circumstances, the choices of using the three research universities and a nascent research park as an R&D growth pole, and of focusing on recruiting the branch plants of established corporations were probably the only feasible ones. It is very difficult to conceive of a scenario based on the endogenous development strategy that had any remote chance of being successful for the RTP case at that time.

Several special factors existing in the Salt Lake City region at the time made the endogenous development strategy the "correct" one, and the growth pole strategy probably an infeasible one, despite the region having many economic development needs and objectives similar to those of the Raleigh–Durham area and North Carolina. First, the University of Utah had a very strong entrepreneurial tradition (Brown, 1987). Second, the region had a well-educated and highly skilled non-professional labor force and an existing concentration of high-technology industry, albeit only in defense-related industries. Third, the region's political and cultural life was (and is) dominated, or at least strongly influenced, by the Church of Latter-Day Saints (the Mormons). The first of these factors provided the initial impetus for the park and accounts for much of the subsequent growth of the park itself. The second factor provided start-up businesses with a requisite labor force for advanced manufacturing, since start-ups are rarely able to afford a spatial division of labor between R&D and production functions.

The third factor had at least two effects. It supported the endogenous development strategy, by providing a powerful inducement for Mormons who had left the region for lack of job opportunities in scientific and engineering fields to return and possibly start new businesses once the "milieu" had begun to be developed. Thus the strongly influential Mormon culture of the region helped to increase the potential pool of entrepreneurs. But it also posed a critical disadvantage for successfully implementing a growth pole strategy. The Mormon culture was perceived as having a negative effect on the willingness of outside technology-oriented corporations to locate R&D branch plants in the region, because of difficulty in recruiting highly sought-after, non-Mormon scientists and engineers to relocate there.

For all of these reasons, we conclude that the endogenous development strategy was a "correct" one for the University of Utah Research Park while the growth pole strategy most likely would not have worked.

5.3 What have we learned about technology-led regional economic development strategies?

The cases described and evaluated above represent two alternative strategies for regional economic development designed around stimulating a spatial concentration of R&D activity. While it is not possible to make any generalizable conclusions from a sample of two, we can, nevertheless, state some insights gained from these two cases that may be useful in developing regional policy.

First, we found that the success of technology-led regional development strategies, in general, is difficult to predict. Few experts would have predicted in the late 1950s that the region now known as the Research Triangle would become one of the largest concentrations of R&D activity in the United States. Perhaps even fewer would have predicted in the late 1960s that the University of Utah and its research park would become a model of scientific/technological entrepreneurialism with the second largest number of patents of any academic institution in the country.[7] Neither region had many of the conditions and locational factors that are now considered critical for becoming centers of successful high-technology development. Instead, so-called "soft factors", including imagination and leadership by some key individuals in negotiating for necessary resources and in building necessary political support, were critical to the success in each case. To the extent that such "soft factors" are still as important, then accurate prognoses of the potential of a region to achieve technology-led economic development success must be able to take into account more than "objective" regional conditions. On the other hand, we need to be careful not to be swayed in our assessments by mere local boosterism and unfounded optimism.

Second, the particular conditions in a region matter in selecting an appropriate strategy. We do not assert that the respective strategies chosen in the case of RTP and Utah were based upon systematic analysis of "what will work best". Rather, the choices seem to have been pragmatically based and within the realm of experience of a few key leaders. Yet it is clear that had RTP adopted a strategy of encouraging start-ups and locally based small businesses, it would not have been successful. The same goes for the University of Utah had it focused on trying to attract the R&D branch plants of corporations headquartered outside the region. This leads to the suggestion that technology-led economic development strategies be based upon a careful analysis of local conditions, both strengths and weaknesses, rather than on a prior ideological commitment to "development from above", versus "development from below". Our results also underline the foolhardiness of the economic development practice of policy imitation, in which the successful strategies of another state or region are adopted with the expectation of similar success.

Third, and closely related to the second point, is that regional conditions change, and strategies may need to adapt accordingly if the process of development is to continue. In each of the two cases, recent development

---

[7]Cited by Dr. Norman Brown, director of the University of Utah Technology Transfer Office.

arguably would have been enhanced had officials started to diversify their respective strategies starting approximately five years ago. That is, by the mid-1980s when announcements of new openings in RTP had just started to slow, the maturing of the region since the park was created had led to conditions much more favorable for the development of new, technology-oriented small businesses. Yet park and state government officials have, for the most part, continued their emphasis on industrial recruitment, and have not responded well to changed conditions and new opportunities. An analogous tale could be told in the case of the University of Utah Research Park.

Finally, the length of time that it takes for a region without a prior concentration of R&D or other high-technology activity to restructure its economy seems to be grossly underestimated by many policy officials, even when the most appropriate strategies are chosen. In both RTP and Utah cases, it has taken considerable time for their respective local economies to develop the necessary infrastructure to support the technology-led economic development process beyond the initial investments and stimulations represented by the research parks. Only in the last several years, or since RTP's twenty-fifth birthday, has the predicted upswing of new, technology-oriented business start-ups based upon linkages with organizations in the park or with the universities started. Likewise, it may take a similar length of time for networks of suppliers, information exchange, and specialized services to materialize for the support of entrepreneurial activity outside of the University of Utah environs. One lesson here is that we may have a tendency to "write off" many cases of technology-led regional economic development strategies as failures or likely failures based upon short- or intermediate-term evaluations. The second lesson is that patience, long-term commitment, and hence deep "political pockets" by regional leaders are often critical success factors underlying such strategic initiatives.

References

Andersson, A., 1985. Creativity and Regional Development, *Papers of the Regional Science Association*, Vol. 56, pp. 5–20.

Bergman, E.M., 1986. Introduction: Policy Realities and Development Potentials in Local Economies, in E.M. Bergman (ed.), *Local Economies in Transition*, Duke University Press, Durham, NC.

Boudeville, J.R., 1966. *Problems of Regional Economic Planning*, Edinburgh University Press, Edinburgh.

Brown, W.S., 1987. Locally-grown High Technology Business Development: The Utah Experience, in W.S. Brown and R. Rothwell (eds.), *Entrepreneurship and Technology: World Experiences and Policies*, Longman, New York.

Brusco, S., 1986. Small Firms and Industrial Districts: the Experience of Italy, in D. Keeble and E. Weuer (eds.), *New Firms and Regional Development in Europe*, Croom Helm, London.

Cooper, A.C., 1985. The Role of Incubator Organizations in the Founding of Growth-Oriented Firms, *Journal of Business Venturing*, Vol. 1, pp. 75–86.

Friedmann, J., C. Weaver, 1979. *Territory and Function*, University of California Press, Berkeley.

Gruenstein, J.M.L., 1984. Targeting High-Tech in the Delaware Valley, *Business Review*, Federal Reserve Bank of Philadelphia (May–June), pp. 3–14.

Hansen, N. (ed.), 1972. *Growth Centers in Regional Economic Development*, Free Press, New York.

Johansson, B., 1987. Information Technology and the Viability of Spatial Networks, *Papers of the Regional Science Association*, Vol. 62, pp. 13–25.

Little, W.F., 1988. Research Triangle Park, *The World and I* (November), pp. 178–185.

Luger, M.I., 1984. Does North Carolina's High Tech Development Program Work?, *Journal of the American Planning Association*, Vol. 50, pp. 280–289.

Marcusen, A.R., P. Hall, A. Glasmeier, 1986. *High Tech America: The What, How, Where, and Why of the Sunrise Industries*, Allen & Unwin, Boston.

Malecki, E.J., 1983. Technology and Regional Development: A Survey, *International Regional Science Review*, Vol. 8, pp. 89–125.

Malecki, E.J., 1987. The R&D Location Decision of the Firm and "Creative" Regions, *Technovation*, Vol. 6, pp. 205–222.

Malecki, E.J., 1988. Theories and Policies of Technological Development at the Local Level. Paper presented at the Regional Science Association European Summer Institute, Arco, Italy, 17–23 July.

Miller, R., M. Cote, 1987. *Growing the Next Silicon Valley*, Lexington Books, Lexington, Mass.

Perroux, F., 1950. Economic Space, Theory, and Applications, *Quarterly Journal of Economics*, Vol. LXIV, pp. 89–104.

Perroux, F., 1987. The Pole of Development's New Place in a General Theory of Economic Activity, in Higgins, B., D.J. Savoie, *Regional Economic Development, Essays in Honour of François Perroux*, Unwin Hyman, Boston.

Premus, R., 1982. *Location of High Technology Firms and Regional Economic Development*, Government Printing Office, Washington, DC.

Rees, J., H. Stafford, 1983. A Review of Regional Growth and Industrial Location Theory: Towards Understanding the Development of High Technology Complexes in the United States. Paper prepared for the Office of Technology Assessment, US Congress.

Rosenfeld, S., E. Malizia, M. Dugan, 1988. *Reviving the Rural Factory: Automation and Work in the South*, Research Triangle Park, NC, Southern Growth Policies Board.

Schumpeter, J.A., 1934. *The Theory of Economic Development*, Harvard University Press, Cambridge, Mass.

Schumpeter, J.A., 1950. *Capitalism, Socialism, and Democracy*, 3rd edition, Harper, New York.

Shapero, A., 1981. Entrepreneurship: Key to Self-Renewing Economies, *Commentary*, Vol. 5, pp. 19–23.

Stöhr, W.B. (ed.), 1990. *Global Challenge and Local Response*, Mansell, London.

Stöhr, W.B., D.R. Taylor (eds.), 1981. *Development from Above or Below?: The Dialectics of Regional Planning in Developing Countries*, John Wiley, New York.

Sweeney, G.P., 1985. Innovation is Entrepreneur-Led, in G. Sweeney (ed.), *Innovation Policies: An International Perspective*, Frances Pinter, London.

Sweeney, G.P., 1987. *Innovation, Entrepreneurs, and Regional Development*, St. Martin's Press, New York.

Thompson, W.R., 1965. *A Preface to Urban Economics*, Johns Hopkins University Press, Baltimore.

14

Spread and Backwash in the Spatial Diffusion of Development

Edward M. Bergman,* Gunther Maier**

1 Introduction

The turbulence in regional development processes during the last two decades appears to have punctured (or at least partially deflated) some of the grand theory and policy expectations held earlier by many of us. At precisely the historical moment that all signs pointed toward continued spatial concentration of economic activity, it began to disperse convincingly to peripheral regions without benefit of explicit policy measures, particularly so for the US and several other advanced economies. This unexpected dispersal elicited a wide variety of wholly new theoretical perspectives on regional development (Stöhr and Taylor, 1981; Stöhr and Tödtling, 1977, 1978) that continue to develop along with questions of technological innovation and related topics.[1]

Just as the newest development trend became fully established and explanations of it began to enter the literature, evidence appearing in the

---

*University of North Carolina at Chapel Hill, Chapel Hill, USA.

**University of Economics and Business Administration, Vienna, Austria. An extended version of this paper has been published in *Jahrbuch für Regionalwissenschaft*, Vol. 9/10, pp. 75-93. The authors thank Vandenhoeck & Ruprecht for permission to use the paper.

[1]Still others sought to consolidate the principal lessons to be learned from previous research; Gaile's work in particular (1979, 1980) is relevant to this paper. He took stock of what had been learned from two dozen studies of spread backwash processes and synthesized both their accomplishments and their shortcomings as a guide to future research.

early 1980s registered yet another shift *away* from peripheral and again
toward metropolitan economies, often in conjunction with forces driven
by the emerging International Division of Labor (Stöhr, 1987; Muegge
and Stöhr, 1987; Maier and Tödtling, 1987). European scholars developed a meta-level view of shifts between concentrated periods of urban
and peripheral development quite similar to long waves (van den Berg *et
al.*, 1982; Schubert and Nijkamp, 1985). Particular phases of such waves
were said to affect regions roughly in accordance with their nation's overall level of development. Others, particularly in the US, remain frankly
puzzled by the data's clear depiction of a sharp reversal and despair of any
theoretical view that might offer a convincing account of these changing
events (Garnick, 1988).

Meantime, resources for subnational regional policy were withdrawn
by many central governments in Western countries, leaving local policy-
makers to fend for themselves (Bergman, 1986). Although studies of local
policy-making have improved our understanding (Stöhr, 1985, 1986, 1990),
the theoretical support to guide successful *regional* policies and their mea-
ger funding base remains contradictory or is insufficiently specified. In
such instances, applied research capable of *simulating* development processes with empirical evidence becomes valuable as a guide for policy making (Bergman, Maier and Weist, 1988a) and, as argued more fully in this
paper, research of the sort reported here may serve the equally valuable
purpose of stimulating further theoretical views of spread and backwash.
If considered successful, this paper may represent an atypical sequence in
which applied research efforts support improved regional theorizing.

2   Research Problem and Conceptualization

The research problem posed here was initiated by the Governor of Arkansas,
who required a sound basis for allocating exceedingly scarce resources to
alternative development policies that might increase overall growth of a
historically poor state. Since the state's poorest counties require the greatest attention, it was also important to focus induced growth in the peripheral, rural counties. In essence, the research needed to determine which
policies maximize spread effects of policies and which minimized backwash
(Bergman, 1989).

In reviewing two dozen studies of spread–backwash[2] to synthesize their
accomplishments and evaluate prospects for future improvement, Gaile
(1980) observed:

---

[2]Included, of course, are studies that employ a range of comparable terms:
polarized/trickle down, centrifugal/centripetal, concentration/diffusion, trickle
up(in)/trickle down(out), and so forth.

"the amount of empirical research which has been generated in testing the spatial aspects of the elemental processes of spread–backwash is disappointing."

He found the concept, although essentially spatial, dichotomized in all studies as applying to two prototypical development configurations: core/periphery, north/south, urban/rural, etc. Likewise, the spread–backwash concept was equally dichotomized as consisting solely of only one net effect, depending on which was dominant. Gaile proposed that the latter dichotomy be relaxed by consciously separating and identifying processes that contribute *independently* to spread and those to backwash effects, regardless of how such an effect is to be measured (e.g. economic growth, economic development, change or expansion, innovation diffusion).[3] Further, the mechanisms or processes that give rise to all such effects deserve to be evaluated in each instance: in some circumstances a given mechanism (e.g. government income, trade or commuting) may yield spread effects while in other situations it may instead produce backwash. This view is entirely consistent with that held by Myrdal (1957) concerning effects that may differ by general level of development:

"a high average level of development is accompanied by improved transportation and communications, higher levels of education, and a more dynamic communication of ideas and values – all of which tends to strengthen the forces for the centrifugal spread of economic expansion or remove obstacles for its operation." (p. 34)

Accordingly, there is little possibility that a wholly generalized set of effects will result from a given set of development mechanisms or policies. Conversely, one might well expect to identify the effects of certain mechanisms quite convincingly for any particular region at any given level of development. The model in this paper specifies several distinct policy mechanisms and development processes known to be at work in the Arkansas region and it adopts growth of non-farm-earned income as the most appropriate measure of economic development effects.

Closely related are spatial structural factors which Gaile argues act to condition *how* various development mechanisms produce alternative effects:

---

[3]Gaile argues that absolute – not relative – measures of spread–backwash effects are preferred if one wishes to remain consistent with the intent of the concept's developers and to anticipate development probabilities in typical core–periphery situations. He further argues that a dynamic view of effects is to be preferred to inferences derived from a static measure of effects.

> "Spread–backwash processes are not dichotomous, but are largely
> the same set of processes which may, depending on structural
> factors, yield [seemingly] dichotomous development results or
> impacts."

Several of Gaile's spatial structural factors are adopted in this model, e.g.
distances between spatial units, size of core, existing spatial distribution of
development, presence of small urban places in periphery and the structure
of transportation networks.

However, we argue these spatial factors should apply across the *continuous space* of contiguous units of analysis, not only to the special case of
dichotomously defined cores and peripheries. The very processes of spread
and backwash that resist simplistic and deterministic dichotomization also
imply that a given locality is so inter-nested with all its neighbors that
it simultaneously functions as "periphery" to nearby dominant centers
and as "core" to lesser units at its periphery. Further, as Gaile points out,
spread and backwash effects may differ markedly when reckoned across the
hierarchical elements of interregional scale versus the (perhaps) stronger
contiguous elements of intraregional scale.

These several points are readily resolved in our model of spread–backwash by incorporating a revised version of the economic potential formulation. "Models of individual spread backwash processes indicate that
the spatial impact expected follows the general form of a distance decay
curve..." (Gaile, 1980). The spatial factors and distance decay stressed
by Gaile can be neatly operationalized in a revised economic potential
formulation (see Bergman and Maier, 1989). Accordingly, our model is
capable of distinguishing spread from backwash effects for each contributing mechanism, based on the signs of regression coefficients estimated from
adjacent county effects (potential-type variables) and home county effects
(unit of analysis variables). This means that we evaluate evidence of
spread–backwash for all counties in Arkansas and in the contiguous margins of surrounding states, yet also include interregional effects that may
arise from processes underway in other US states and regions. In a sense,
spread–backwash effects are thereby generalized across space, not merely
estimated for the special case of the classic core–periphery development
dichotomy. To simplify the language of this generalization, we employ the
terms "home county" as a generic reference to county units of analysis
in which the *effects* (growth or decline of earned income) are registered
(Bergman, 1989) and in which key processes are typically thought, at least
partially, to be responsible for these effects. Spatially proximate effects
on home counties are further exerted through the influences of key processes underway in "neighboring counties" that attenuate in accordance
with empirically observed distance decay functions.

AK :   Arkansas

Figure 14.1: Road network: continental US.

Spread–backwash effects can be the result of a number of relationships
between agents in the various spatial units. Probably most important
are market relationships in the goods and labor market. Shopping trips,
commuting, flows of goods and services between enterprises are important
interactions that may lead to spread and backwash. Also, competition between counties for newly locating firms and other economic activities is an
important factor. But the more structured network type of relationships
between economic actors that play a prominent role in modern industrial
economics can also bring about spread/backwash effects. Because of the
higher stability of networks as compared to pure market relationships (see
Johansson, 1991; Kamann, 1991), spread and backwash resulting therefrom will also display greater stability.

The empirical investigation in this paper not only allows us to distinguish spread and backwash effects but also to analyze the spatial reach
of these effects and the factors contributing to them. Since we can use
two different distance decay functions with each variable and the model
structure also allows for the case of no influence from neighboring counties, we can test hypotheses about the spatial reach of interaction effects.
As it turns out, for most variables a distance decay function derived from
commuting data is most adequate. So, indirectly our paper indicates that
– at least in our case study area – in the aggregate networks and market
relationships do not reach out very far.

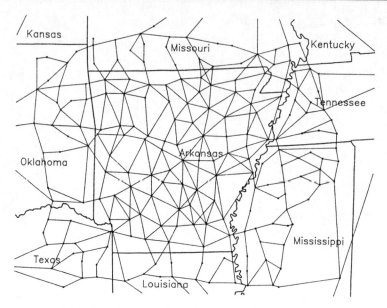

Figure 14.2: Road network: Arkansas and surrounding states.

3   Data, Variables, and Study Area

Our potential model is based on observations from 251 spatial units. A large proportion of these spatial units (201 units) reflect the interactions within the State of Arkansas and between it and its surrounding states. These 201 units are composed of all of the 75 counties in Arkansas and an additional 126 counties from the six surrounding states (Tennessee, Mississippi, Louisiana, Texas, Oklahoma and Missouri) that connect Arkansas with its region (see Figure 14.1). To account for national influences on potential interactions, we also include 50 other spatial units, comprising of 3 units for the state of Texas and 47 units for the remaining continental states and the District of Columbia (see Figure 14.2).

Counties were chosen as the unit of analysis for Arkansas and its surrounding states. Counties are a natural choice as a spatial unit because they are relatively homogeneous in terms of patterns of interaction, they are points of origin for important policy measures (e.g. elementary and secondary education), and they are the smallest unit of analysis with current and readily available data.

We used distance data between 251 cities in the counties or regions as a basis for estimating two types of potentials.

One problem associated with this approach is the derivation of the distance decay function. Ideally one would derive this function through the estimation process simultaneously with the parameters of the model (see, for example, Bröcker, 1984). This approach, however, leads to a highly complex estimation procedure for which no standard software is available. Also, this approach requires that the distance decay function be specified in parametric form with one or two parameters left to be estimated.

We chose the more traditional approach of deriving the distance decay function from external sources. With a distance decay function to hand we can then compute potentials for all variables and estimate the respective coefficients by standard regression techniques.

Since the primary reasons for using potentials are related on the one hand to commuting and shopping trip patterns, and on the other to shipments of products, we use information that is available about these interactions. The 1977 Commodity Transportation Survey is the most recent information about the volume and characteristics of commodity shipments by manufacturing establishments in the US. For household vehicle trips the most recent information is provided by the 1983–84 Nationwide Personal Transportation Study.

This data tells us the probability that the shipment of one ton of material or one household trip falls into a specific distance category. From this information we are able to derive distance decay functions to be used for computing the potentials.

We have tested both types of distance decay functions with our explanatory variables. In general, the distance decay function for household trips performs better for all of the population-related potentials while the distance decay function for commodities shipments seems to be more adequate for all of the income components for which input–output relationships are important. We use the data for all 251 spatial units in the data set to calculate the potentials. However, only the 201 counties in Arkansas and surrounding states are used in the estimation procedure.

The study uses data from three different sources.

- 1979 and 1986 income data, published by Bureau of Economic Analysis;
- 1980 population data, from the US Census Department;
- information about the existing highway network and proposed improvements provided by the Arkansas Highway and Transportation Department (AHTD).

Dependent variable in our analysis is the change in private non-farm income between 1979 and 1986. The explanatory variables are as follows:

- *Intercept and dummy variables:* Besides the standard INTERCEPT of regression analysis, we used a number of dummy variables. They

are either zero or one and have the effect of shifting the whole regression equation. SYSHI is one if the county has good access to
the interstate highway system, zero otherwise. We characterized the
county's industry mix by a set of dummy variables, which were set
to one if the county had an above-average income share from a particular industry. This (somewhat) indirect way of accounting for
the industry mix was used to avoid econometric problems associated with including a subcomponent of the dependent variable on
the right-hand side of the equation.

- *Population variables:* For each population characteristic (central city
  population, urban population, rural population, black population,
  population older than 25 with high school completed, and population
  older than 25 with four or more years of college completed) we used
  the home-effect variable and the potential. In addition the "number
  of non-farm proprietors in 1979" (home-effect and potential) was
  used from the BEA data set to account for the fact that proprietors'
  income is included in the dependent variable, and to represent an
  important policy variable.

- *Income variables:* This group encompasses all income components
  not included in the dependent variable, i.e. government, farm, retirement, and transfer income. The home effects and potentials of
  these variables enter the estimation procedure.

4   Evidence and Interpretation

To isolate the effects of each explanatory variable, we use multiple regression analysis in our estimation procedure.[4] The dependent variable

---

[4]This model's estimates are based on the 201 counties in Arkansas and the
six surrounding states. The model specification is the result of a long search
process in which various specifications and variable combinations were considered.
Throughout the many variants of the model that were estimated, we obtained
similar results. This finding gives us some confidence in the qualitative results of
the model. Our statistical modeling procedure included only those variables that
had the greatest impact on explaining differences in private non-farm income.
As a result, home and neighboring county versions of the explanatory variables
were not included for all variables. The results of this estimation procedure are
reported in Table 14.1. All variables in Panel B are significantly different from
zero, with 90 percent certainty, while most variables are significant at the 99
percent level. The overall performance of the model is very good. The corrected
R^2 is 0.98, indicating that nearly all the variance in regional income growth can
be explained by these variables.

is 1979-86 growth of private non-farm income, measured in thousands of dollars. Our operationalization produces two possible versions of each explanatory variable: a "home" effect variable, which reflects the impact of a county's variable on itself, and a "neighbor" effect variable, which measures the home county growth effect of this variable induced by other surrounding counties along the entire highway system. If the variable reflects some policy consequence, the model allows one, for example, to estimate the spatial impact of a hypothetical change in state policy. For example, what would the expected impact on a county's income growth be of increasing the number of high school graduates in home versus neighboring counties?

The differences between home effects and neighbor effects for each variable can be observed by examining the coefficient estimates from the model. In the following discussion of home versus neighboring effects, we will refer to a "representative" county in which a hypothetical change in level of policy or explanatory variables might be said to have an "average" impact.

Assuming that a given variable's effect on income growth is significant for both home and neighboring counties, there are four possible sign patterns of theoretical interest. The most familiar set of patterns reflects a homogeneous or balanced set of effects: a given variable in home and neighboring counties uniformly increases home county income (signs of both regression coefficients are positive) or decreases it (both signs negative). These patterns are consistent with development theories that posit the uniform spread effects of a development process or mechanism across adjoining territory.

The other set of patterns reveals opposite or unbalanced effects on income of a variable when measured in home and neighboring counties. In short, a given development mechanism in the home county might increase its income but that same mechanism operating from neighboring counties *reduces* home county income growth. (Its mirror image can also result: a neighboring county factor increases home income growth while that same mechanism at home reduces growth.) Myrdal and numerous others have emphasized the likelihood of polarizing or backwash effects in developing regions such as Arkansas, particularly those with primitive market structures. For purposes of schematic convenience, sign patterns can be represented as in Figure 14.3. Each type of effect on home county income growth is associated with one circle and arrow.

This paper categorizes these general patterns to detect spread–backwash effects across counties in one of America's poorest rural regions. We can also use Figure 14.3 to identify and label some direct policy meanings of coefficient sign patterns as well. Starting in the upper right-hand cor-

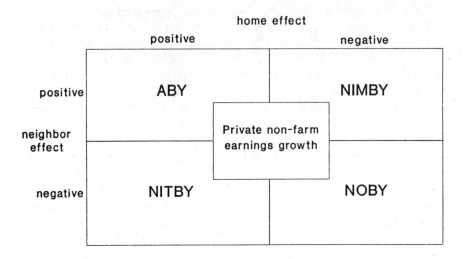

Figure 14.3: Types of Sign Patterns.

ner, any variable that exhibits this sign pattern implies that its greater presence in a home county reduced income but that home county income increases with higher levels of the variable in neighboring counties. We can appropriate the common term NIMBY (Not In My Back Yard) to summarize the typical policy viewpoint of this zero-sum type backwash effect.

The next clockwise effect – NOBY – applies to a variable that decreases home county income wherever it is found. No One's Back Yard is the obvious policy interpretation for this set of factors.

Next in order is NITBY: this type variable increases home county income if high levels are measured *only* in the home county. The variable reduces home county income growth as its level rises in neighboring counties. Not In Their Back Yard is the policy equivalent of this classic backwash effect.

Finally, Anybody's Back Yard (ABY) is the least controversial policy effect because high levels of a factor in home *and* neighboring counties spread out to raise income growth in every county. It of course is the classic spread effect. To determine which variables produce which effects, we must now examine the findings.

The principal findings are arrayed in Table 14.1: Panel A summarizes the coefficients for all variables tested and Panel B includes only those variables which remained significant in an edited model. Table 14.2 defines the variables. Several points deserve comment at the outset. First, the model fit is quite good: coefficients of variables included in both models

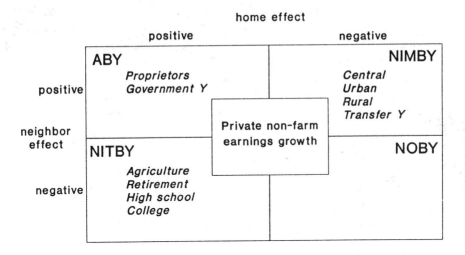

Figure 14.4: Types of sign patterns: results.

retain their signs and orders of magnitude. The list of variables is further grouped: the first major group includes dummy variables (Type = D) for industry concentration and interstate highway access. The second group includes home county variables and the third group lists the same variables for neighboring counties. These two are further subdivided into measurement types where the dependent variable (earnings growth in $) responds to a unit change in people (Type = C) or dollars (Type = $) associated with the independent variable. As examples, EPRNF in Panel B indicates that a unit change of one additional non-farm entrepreneur in the average home county would have raised its 1979–86 income growth by 37,364 dollars, or that each additional dollar of income from government sources in neighboring counties (PSIGOV) would raise home income by slightly more than one cent.

When coefficients in Table 14.1 are converted to the patterns suggested earlier as tests of interdependent development, results in Figure 14.4 reveal both spread and backwash effects operating simultaneously in our study region.

Spread effects (ABY) are clearly evident in the case of income received from government sources, although the effects from home county government income are considerably stronger (76 cents), thereby indicating relatively severe spatial attenuation of income received in neighboring counties (1 cent). Entrepreneurial activity (number of proprietors) in home and neighboring counties also spread beneficial growth effects, but in this case a unit increase in neighboring counties accumulates to yield

Table 14.1: Empirical results

Variable	Panel A Estimate	F	Panel B Estimate	F
INTERCEPT	-1327.01	0.00	-4532.89	0.04
DAGRS	-9505.48	1.71		
DCON	-10106.70	2.64		
DSER	-32697.17	2.25		
SYSHI	7886.18	1.58		
SYSLO	3833.04	0.15		
EPRNF	24.48	7.70	37.36	58.81
HIGHSL	18.19	27.57	17.43	57.07
COLLEGE	6.19	1.65		
CENTRAL	-0.87	0.51	-0.97	4.45
NOCENTR	-2.53	4.02	-2.52	20.32
NONURB	-1.98	3.89	-2.45	18.62
AGRI	0.15	0.11		
RETIR	0.30	0.19		
TRANSFER	-1.44	0.41		
IGOV	0.55	7.38	0.76	31.41
PSEPRNF	108.79	22.23	97.31	24.55
PSHIGHSL	-39.50	6.23	-25.41	19.56
PSCOLLG	-43.58	5.29	-17.19	6.78
PSCENTR	6.38	1.24		
PSNCENTR	4.00	0.44		
PSNONURB	5.04	1.29		
PSAGRI	-0.05	1.98	-0.07	5.34
PSRETIR	-4.32	5.59	-3.24	4.26
PSTRANSF	24.08	7.43	27.11	29.22
PSIGOV	0.01	1.18	0.01	3.31
R-square	0.9899		0.9892	
F	688.14		1312.87	
DF Error	175		187	

higher relative growth effects (97,310 dollars); perhaps a surrounding entrepreneurial culture boosts a home county's earnings growth more than the purely localized effect (37,364 dollars) of a home county's own proprietors. This finding lends considerable support to frequently stated but seldom documented assertions concerning the powerful development role of entrepreneurs (Gaile, 1980; Pedersen, 1970). Although these relative effects differ, development in a representative county tends to spread as

Table 14.2: Definition of variables

Name	Type	D.Dec.	Definition of Variable
INTERCEPT		-	Intercept
DAGRS	D	-	Above av. Share of Agri. Services, 1979
DCON	D	-	Above av. Share of Construction, 1979
DSER	D	-	Above av. Share of Services, 1979
SYSHI	D	-	High Access to Interstate system, 1980
SYSLO	D	-	Low Access to Interstate system, 1980
EPRNF	C	-	Number of Non-farm Proprietors, 1979
HIGHSL	C	-	People Older Than 25 with High School as Highest Education, 1980
COLLEGE	C	-	People Older Than 25 with College as hHghest Education, 1980
CENTRAL	C	-	Central Cities Population, 1980
NOCENTR	C	-	Urban Population (non-Centr. City), 1980
NONURB	C	-	Rural Population, 1980
AGRI	$	-	Agricultural Income, 1979
RETIR	$	-	Retirement Income, 1979
TRANSFER	$	-	Income from Transfer Payments, 1979
IGOV	$	-	Income from Government Services, 1979
PSEPRNF	C	HH	Potential of EPRNF
PSHIGHSL	C	HH	Potential of HIGHSL
PSCOLLG	C	HH	Potential of COLLEGE
PSCENTR	C	HH	Potential of CENTRAL
PSNCENTR	C	HH	Potential of NOCENTR
PSNONURB	C	HH	Potential of NONURB
PSAGRI	$	Shipm.	Potential of AGRI
PSRETIR	$	HH	Potential of RETIR
PSTRANSF	$	HH	Potential of TRANSFER
PSIGOV	$	Shipm.	Potential of IGOV

levels of government income or proprietors rise.[5] This type of spatial interdependence is usually assumed (or ignored) and seldom demonstrated with empirical evidence.[6]

---

[5]No evidence of systematic loss effects was revealed, despite the negative signs for central city, urban and rural populations. As discussed in a subsequent section on NIMBY effects, these signs are essentially "scaling" factors that adjust the expected earnings growth downward because of systematic overestimates from the effects of other included variables.

[6]Gaile (1980) comments on this absence as follows: "Spread is defined (often simplistically) in only about one-third of the studies surveyed. Backwash is

Backwash effects account for a majority of important variables. The NITBY version is particularly interesting because it captures the uneven effect of unit increases in an educated labor force. That is, every additional high school graduate in a home county boosts its income growth by 17,433 dollars whereas each additional graduate in neighboring counties within commuting range depresses home county income by 25,410 dollars. Apart from the potent effects on earnings growth produced by education, one policy interpretation suggests the possibility of highly specific targeting. That is, a better-educated labor force in counties near large labor markets will not necessarily raise locally generated earnings, but education in rural counties beyond the draw of metropolitan commutersheds may indeed raise local levels of earned income. Analogous findings of reduced income growth due to unit increases in college graduates from nearby counties add further support for this interpretation, although *local* college graduates appear to have no significant effect on their home county's earnings growth, perhaps owing to their even greater tendency to commute.

Not In Their Back Yard (NITBY) arguments also apply but with lesser force to retiree income and agricultural income received in neighboring counties. Put differently, home counties surrounded by neighbors that host more retirees and agriculture grow more slowly than otherwise expected. Lateral integration of adjacent economies is apparently harmed as income from external remittance or commodity agriculture deprives neighbors of potential growth spin-offs.

NIMBY patterns are at best suggestive because their variables lack the conclusive symmetry of significant home *and* neighboring county effects. One set of effects appears to show the uniformly negative influence of every type of settlement pattern: central cities, other urban and rural populations all appear to depress earnings growth, but in fact their coefficients serve as negative "scaling" factors that adjust estimated growth effects in settlements of varying urban density. The "penalty" associated with the coefficient for central city populations is less than half that of the others, thereby revealing the agglomeration advantages enjoyed by concentrated urban centers. Another asymmetric NIMBY effect results from transfer payments received as income in neighboring counties. Presumably, these funds leak out as their recipients shop in nearby market centers, but transfers do not significantly appear to stimulate (or retard) growth of earnings when received in the home county. The clear evidence of numerous backwash effects generalized over continuously defined space is a major finding of this study.[7]

---

defined less often. *The distinction between spread–backwash processes and their impacts on spatial development was not made in any of the studies surveyed."*

[7]The absence of such evidence in previous studies was pointed out by Gaile

5   Concluding Caveats

As the original product of a policy simulation model designed for Arkansas, the present findings are necessarily limited in terms of application. That is, if any remaining technical difficulties are eliminated, one must still remain cautious regarding both policy and theoretical inferences. At the policy level, we can only adopt the *what if* logic that simulation models allow. We are really asking the historical question: *what* income growth would you have expected in Arkansas *if* some policy outcome in the representative county (either home or neighboring) was marginally higher than its observed level in 1980? To the degree that the model successfully captures most of the processes at work between 1980 and 1986, our confidence in any answer to the "what if" formulation drops off rapidly as development is projected further into the future. *The very object of economic development policy is intended to change the relationships revealed in this model.* Therefore, one should apply these findings very cautiously to important policy-making and public expenditure decisions. It is, however, worth noting that even with such cautions, the information available from the model appears to be far superior to that available from other case-study methods, trend analysis or anecdotal sources upon which policy-makers typically rely.

On the question of spread–backwash or polarized–decentralized development tendencies, the model supplies tantalizing but similarly limited evidence. The problem here is one of specifying more rigorously the theoretically defined variables and of examining a representative body of evidence (not simply Arkansas counties and nearest neighbors). As many other researchers who have studied spatial development well know, there are always present a mixture of spread or backwash effects operating simultaneously in every region. The mixture itself may differ markedly in Arkansas versus Minnesota, for example, owing to widely differing levels of general development, degrees of market failure, unique institutional impediments or specific cultural/regional practices. And, of course, further development in Arkansas will likely change the way in which rural and urban counties become further interdependent. Accordingly, this type model should be replicated for several types of regions to test for stability of parameters that indicate the presence of spread or backwash effects.

Careful specification of a sound theoretical model would allow greater insight into the underlying development processes at work. Some of the

---

(1980): "The specification of processes which have a predominantly backwash impact has proceeded even less satisfactorily. Many studies do not even recognize this negative impact of growth center–hinterland interaction, and others that do make no new statements concerning it."

variables introduced in this study to examine policy effects may require further disentangling and tighter definition. The possibilities for designing a well-specified explanatory model are definitely improved with the provisional findings available here and work is now progressing in that direction.

References

Bergman, E.M., 1986. *Local Economies in Transition*, Duke University Press, Durham, NC.

Bergman, E.M., 1989. Interdependent Development: Evidence and Policy, Paper presented at the National Rural Studies Commission Meeting, Greenville, Miss.

Bergman, E.M, G. Maier, 1989. The Spatial Diffusion of Development: Spread and Backwash Reconsidered, *Jahrbuch für Regionalwissenschaft*, Vol. 9/10, pp. 75–93.

van den Berg, L., R. Drewett, L.H. Klassen, A. Rossi, C.H.T. Vijverberg, 1982. *Urban Europe: A Study of Growth and Decline*. Pergamon Press, Oxford.

Bröcker, J., 1984. Räumliche Querschnittsregressionen mit potentialisierten Variablen, *Seminarberichte Gesellschaft für Regionalforschung*, Vol. 21, pp. 55–99.

Gaile, G.L. 1979. Spatial Models of Spread–Backwash Process, *Geographical Analysis*, Vol. 11, pp. 273–288.

Gaile, G.L., 1980. The Spread–Backwash Concept, in *Regional Studies*, Vol. 14, pp. 15–25.

Garnick, D., 1988. Local Area Economic Growth Patterns: A Comparison of the 1980's and Previous Decades, in Committee on National Urban Policy, *Urban Change and Poverty*, National Academy Press, Washington D.C.

Johansson, B., 1991. Economic Networks and Self-Organization, this volume, Ch. 2.

Kamann, D.J., 1991. The Distribution of Dominance in Networks and its Spatial Implications, this volume, Ch. 3.

Maier, G., E.M. Bergman, 1988. *Economic Impacts of Highway. Educational and Entrepreneurial Policies: The Technical Report.* Submitted to William Clinton, Governor of Arkansas. UNC Institute for Economic Development, Chapel Hill.

Maier, G., F. Tödtling, 1987. International Division of Labor and Industrial Change in Austrian Regions. In H. Muegge, W.B. Stöhr (eds.), *International Economic Restructuring and the Regional Community*, Avebury, Aldershot.

Muegge, H., W.B. Stöhr, 1987. *International Economic Restructuring and the Regional Community*, Avebury, Aldershot.

Myrdal, G., 1957. *Economic Theory and Underdeveloped Regions*, Harper & Row,

New York.

Pedersen, P.O., 1970. Innovation Diffusion within and between National Urban Systems, *Geographical Analysis*, Vol. 2.

Schubert, U., P. Nijkamp, 1985. Structural Change in Urban Systems. In J. Brotchie and J. Newton (eds.), *The Future of Urban Form – The Impact of New Technology*, Croom Helm, London.

Stöhr, W.B., F. Tödtling, 1977. Evaluation of Regional Policies: Experiences in Market and Mixed Economies. In Hansen, N.M. (ed.), *Human Settlement Systems*, Ballinger, Cambridge, Mass.

Stöhr, W.B., D.R.F. Taylor (eds.), 1981. *Development from Above or Below? The Dialectics of Regional Planning in Developing Countries*, John Wiley, Chichester.

Stöhr, W.B., F. Tödtling, 1978. Spatial Equity – Some Antitheses to Current Regional Development Doctrine, *Papers of the Regional Science Association*, Vol. 38.

Stöhr, W.B., 1985. Towards a Conceptual Framework for Research on "Selective Self-Reliance" in Europe. In S. Musto (ed.), *Endogenous Development: A Myth of a Path – Problems of Economic Self-Reliance in the European Periphery*, German Development Institute, EADI-Book Series 5, Berlin.

Stöhr, W.B., 1986. Regional Innovation Complexes, *Papers of the Regional Science Association*, Vol. 59, pp. 29–44.

Stöhr, W.B., 1987. Regional Economic Development and the World Economic Crisis, *International Social Science Review*, Vol. 112, pp. 187–198.

Stöhr, W.B. (ed.), 1990. *Global Challenge and Local Response: Initiatives for Economic Regeneration in Contemporary Europe*, Mansell, London.

Weist, D., E.M. Bergman, 1988. *Economic Impacts of Highway Educational and Entrepreneurial Policies: The Policy Report*. Submitted to William Clinton, Governor of Arkansas. UNC Institute for Economic Development, Chapel Hill.

15

Reconsidering Regions

Edward M. Bergman,* Gunther Maier,**
Franz Tödtling**

In the Introduction to this volume we argue that regions will be of considerable and growing economic importance in the future. Economic and political integration as well as the recent breakdown of authoritarian state regimes will reinvigorate the emergence of subnational economic, social, and cultural entities and require them to make decisions more autonomously than in the past. At the same time, however, the guidance regional authorities can expect from regional development theory is contradictory, limited or inapplicable. Because of theoretically unexpected development trends in the 1970s and 1980s – some of which are documented and discussed in this volume – much confidence was lost in traditional concepts of regional development. This set off a lively discussion in the discipline, concentrating in part on proposed alternative regional development concepts, and partly on a re-evaluation and rethinking of traditional paradigms.

In this book we bring together some contributions that move the debate along in new directions. In doing so, we take a rather broad perspective and combine papers that reflect the rather distinct approaches and backgrounds of their authors. Just to mention a few, it ranges from a conceptual discussion of the economic network concept by Börje Johansson to John Friedmann's plea for a comprehensive approach to planning the industrial transition; from Harvey Goldstein's evaluation of two US research parks to a critique by Costis Hadjimichalis and Nicos Papamichos of the Third Italy regional development "paradigm".

The types of contribution to these debates now include industrial economics, as well as traditional regional science and development planning.

*University of North Carolina at Chapel Hill, Chapel Hill, NC, USA.
**University of Economics and Business Administration, Vienna, Austria.

Because of this broad perspective, some of the relationships and connections between the papers may remain hidden for the reader.[1] Therefore, it is the purpose of this chapter to arrive at a general assessment of discussions presented in the book, to evaluate the commonalities and connections between the various papers, and to underline the remaining open questions. This will be done while fully recognizing that several disciplines presently contribute to a new and improved understanding of regional development.

Firms reacted to the uncertain economic environment of the 1970s and 1980s with organizational changes within and between them. Corporations spun off some functions and deconcentrated others in ways that led to novel and tightly interwoven systems of interdependent firms and establishments – networks. These newly emerging forms of organization, i.e. intermediate relationships in the traditional distinction between markets and hierarchies, have attracted particular attention in recent years. Spatially, a parallel develoment occurred: the traditional dichotomy of core and periphery became blurred when policies tried to reflect this division. Intermediate zones showed remarkable dynamics. Their industry displayed features of strong internal specialization and key linkages appear to rely increasingly on well articulated forms of sociocultural embedding within communities. Technological change continues to play a strong role in the development of those "innovative milieus" or "innovative districts" as well as science or research and development parks.

The four main parts of the book drew first from critical reviews of these new ideas before moving to a re-evaluation of more traditional concepts in the light of recent theoretical develoments. In Part I ("Networks of Firms and Industries") the network concept was reviewed from multiple points of view. The idea of a network as a potentially flexible but at the same time structured connection between economic agents is fairly central to the whole book. This then set the stage for following contributions by Traxler *et al.*, Goldstein, and Bergman and Maier, which relate back to it.

In Part II we moved to an explicitly spatial view by looking at "Innovative Local Districts and Milieus". In particular, questions of how these new forms of economic organization manifest themselves in space and whether they represent a general model of regional development or a peculiarly specialized model suited to highly unique circumstances were raised.

---

[1]Despite the broad perspective attempted, the contributions to this book cannot cover the full scope of the regional development discussion in recent years. The full picture cannot be painted by a single volume; this more ambitious task would require the contributions of a much larger number of authors.

Part III examined possible outcomes for regions subject to economic restructuring from a traditional – i.e. sectoral – view of regional development. Particular emphasis was placed on the linkages between manufacturing and the producer service sectors of two regional economies as well as a general discussion of the various environments that influence the performance and development of old industrial areas.

Part IV, finally, introduced novel empirical evidence of traditional regional development concepts like growth poles, spread/backwash, and innovation generation and diffusion. In conducting these highly original research studies, all of the contributions in this part drew upon network concepts of Part I and by doing so reinterpret – at least in some sense – these older concepts. Spatial attributes are also featured as important aspects of the chapters, ranging from interregional distinctions down to time–distance dimensions of economic linkage between small communities. Re-establishing a strongly spatial flavor to development studies, which have tended recently toward aspatial abstractions of industrial economics, is an important contribution of these chapters.

In going all this way it becomes quite clear that a synthesis of the old concepts and the new ones can bring further progress in our understanding of regional development. We hope that our summary will help to sort out those parts of old and new ideas that will last and prove valuable in the long run for our understanding of regional development processes from the more transitional elements. In section 1 of this concluding chapter we briefly summarize the four parts of the book. The connections between these parts are discussed with an eye toward showing how the various contributions relate to some older elements of regional development theory. In section 2 we extract and explore some of the components of a "new" theory of regional development worthy of further development.

1 Integration or Replacement: The Challenge of New Concepts

Networks as organizing concepts in regional development have previously examined flows of production (e.g. regional input-output, backward or forward integration, etc.) or the spread of information (e.g. diffusion of technical information, innovations, market opportunities, etc.). In all cases, these served as amplifying or complementary adjuncts to one or more general views of development. Those more general views were highly dependent upon rather uneasy assumptions about regional economies that authored a comfortable fiction about two polar alternatives:

1. regions that host concentrated, scale-efficient corporate enterprises (either horizontally or vertically integrated in hierarchical organizations) in export industries, and

2. regions as homes to atomistic enterprises highly dependent on regional markets to distribute non-exported output, secure specialized or inexpensive factors of production, and share indirect efficiencies (localization, urbanization and transfer economies) via arm's-length transactions with other such enterprises.

These assumptions came steadily into question as the distinctions between types of enterprises began to blur – and as theories based on these distinctions became less reliable predictors of regional development – in the flurry of restructuring during the 1970s and 1980s. The basic organizing principles of business organizations and their distinct reliance on hierarchy vs. markets was first subjected to serious question in the early work of Oliver Williamson, although regional scholars did not examine its implications until later.

Attention to this work grew as major corporations gradually shed previous functions (often creating new market equivalents in business and technical service sectors, subsequently called "producer services", a sector analyzed for Vienna by Traxler, Fischer, Nöst, and Schubert), stressed R&D in specific regional complexes (see Goldstein's paper), constantly re-evaluated corporate decisions to "make or buy" (or acquire), and sent late product cycle manufacturing operations off-shore or thoroughly rationalized it at home (see O'Connor's chapter on manufacturing in Victoria, Australia). These restructuring events created very strong incentives for firms everywhere to go beyond markets and hierarchies in making key production decisions (see Grabher's paper).

The emergence of a vital literature on economic networks led to its rapid acceptance as an organizing concept in economics, industrial organization, labor relations and, eventually, regional development. However, the precise contribution that economic networks will eventually make to our understanding of regions remains open to question. Fortunately, we may draw upon the contributions to this volume in considering how regions and theories of develoment may be affected by a network logic. In retrospect, networks are a predictable form of hybrid that reduce the administrative burdens and loss of innovation arising out of hierarchical control, yet help reduce the uncertainty and instability of pure market transactions. The point is stressed by Johansson and Kamann that networks arise precisely to minimize and control expensive transactions costs.

In some ways, networks could be thought of as merely the extension of input–output relations between firms. In fact, Johansson defines an input–output coefficient as an index signifying the special case of relatively invariant flows among firms on contractural networks that give the appearance of intersectoral exchange. His more general approach is to study flows over newly established or contracted links, to understand how new nodes, links and networks arise. But networks in his view are also more than a generalized account of the relations between traditional buyers and suppliers of goods and services. The fact that corporate entities forfeited hierarchical controls from spin-offs of old units (eventually to become new firms) and established network agreements with them reveals much about forces that now account for certain types of network links. In this context, Goldstein's chapter can be seen to examine innovation-induced development of two regions with network features that reveal strong hierarchical or market origins.

In all circumstances where hierarchies or markets alone yield unacceptable transactions costs, firms join one or more networks through contractual understandings and make investments necessary to establish and service network obligations, investments that Johansson considers sunk costs. These costs and contracts are essential to secure what might be considered flow – rather than place – based scale economies. That is, scale arises from the expected flow of benefits and efficiencies delivered over networks; these are generally equivalent to agglomeration economies available through optimal location in geographic space. Networks are also considered by Kamann to be an increasingly useful – though not complete – substitute for simple agglomeration. However much networks may substitute for or complement key features of agglomeration, an understanding of network features promises further significant altering of our present concepts of spatial scale and location in regional development.

For Johansson, links in these networks can acquire the semi-permanent features of durable capital, much like roads or patterns of commuter travel behavior over the road networks, behavior that is formed by employment and housing contracts of workers. This concept of network was implicitly used in the Bergman and Maier chapter where relatively invariant travel behavior allows one to detect evidence of networked interdependence among subregional counties.

The relatively "hard" distance of space and pure economic perspective approximated by Johansson's durable networks is balanced in Kamann's view of the "soft" distance in complementary networks among actors formed on another plane of sociocultural distance in terms of attitudes, values, norms or culture. Kamann's layering of planes, softness of distance and non-market qualities implies a far wider range of network actors than firms acting to minimize transaction costs. Actors include all those "partners who can provide the latest products, machines, know-how and information. They must be reliable and trustworthy" (p. 38). The multiple and reinforcing networks with clients, input suppliers and collaborative contacts among Vienna's producer service firms are examples of Kamann's more general point.

This opens the door for a more generous view of potential network nodes and sources of economic advantage. One interpretation might apply the typically northern European view of economic networks to the southern European view of industrial districts or milieus. That is, the subtle and culturally bound factors that account for the success of flexible production in carefully niched product lines characteristic of small and informally organized production units might be seen as a tightened form of intraregional network. The production networks of such regions are themselves rather fluid and volatile, but the underlying sociocultural network is embedded much more firmly on a basic community plane. Pedersen's distinction between small firms as production units in developed countries and informal production units as extensions of family life and social reproduction in developing countries situates all such producers on rather different networks simultaneously. This view (and that of Helmsing, 1986) may point to one way of further integrating implications for regions from development studies in First and Third World contexts. There appears to be ample scope for a more careful examination of networks and milieus or districts that may together define a region's overall development prospects.

Part II of the book is focused upon new "models" of regional development which have appeared since the 1970s and are widely discussed today: innovative milieus and industrial districts. The background for this discussion is an observed shift from a Fordist to a flexible production paradigm as well as the related crisis of old industrial areas (see also Friedmann's paper) and the appearance of new "innovative" growth areas. Both concepts, that of "industrial districts" (e.g. "Third Italy" discussed by Garofoli and Hadjimichalis/Papamichos) and "innovative milieus", are related to the network concept introduced in the first few chapters. However, there are important differences as well.

The concepts differ from the network view in their explicit spatial component. Emphasis is placed on the territory rather than the firm and it is argued that its (favorable or unfavorable) "milieu" and the cultural and social background of the region determines its economic performance. "It is the milieu, not the enterprise, on which the analysis must focus" (Maillat, p. 113). At the same time Maillat argues that the milieu should not be identified with territorial space: "The notion of milieu does not, *a priori*, refer to a geographical unit, rather it corresponds to the notion of an analytical framework having an inside and an outside, where priority is given to what is going on inside" (Maillat, p. 114). The mechanisms which are thought to be at work in the economic sphere are similar to the network links discussed in Part I of the book. Maillat, for example, writes about "market and non-market links" (section 3.1 on p. 109). The milieu and industrial district, however, comprise more than just economic relationships, but also political, cultural, social, organizational, etc. components, factors which have been stressed more strongly in the papers by Kamann and Pedersen (see also Friedmann's paper). It is their joint appearance which distinguishes one milieu from another. Since it is innovation which is the major driving force of growth and development, qualitative aspects of the milieu are more important than quantitative ones. Advocates of the milieu concept would probably argue that the existence of a specific political climate in conjunction with entrepreneurial spirit and experience with flexible production systems is more important for the economic well-being of a region than the size of its capital stock and labor market.

To some extent the concepts of milieu and industrial district can be viewed as the spatial variant of the network idea. While the network literature starts at the enterprise level, traces the network connections therefrom and consequently has a hard time identifying the spatial dimension of the networks, the literature on industrial/innovative districts or milieus picks up the network links – be they economic, social, political, etc. – at a specific region and analyzes them from this territorial view point. Because of this perspective the milieu literature identifies a number of location specific factors which are considered to be key elements of the concept. However, a number of important questions remain open until now:

- Most important, the fundamental question of what are the necessary and sufficient conditions that constitute an innovative milieu has not been answered satisfactorily. Because of its case study character the literature tends to focus on regions that are innovative and performing well (Third Italy, Baden-Württemberg, Silicon Valley, etc.). Therefore, it has little to say about non-innovative milieus and what distinguishes the two. The investigations of the GREMI group (see Maillat) are a major exception. As Maillat claims, their case study regions were not *a priori* chosen with respect to their innovative milieus. However, their number of ten case study regions is way too small to identify any significant differences. This is not just a statistical argument but has an important policy component. If one cannot identify the constituting elements of an innovative milieu, a policy that tries to stimulate innovation by creating such a milieu must almost certainly fail. This problem is aggravated by the fact that for most innovative milieus a strong location specific component is acknowledged.
- The appearance of an innovative milieu as a territorial manifestation may depend upon the economic structure of the territory. It might

be the case that the components that are hypothesized to form an innovative milieu are more general and only appear to be territorial in local industrial districts because of the region's small-scale structure and the consequent need for interfirm and interorganizational links. The same links being incorporated in a large, multiregional or multinational corporation would reach beyond the region and implement the same function without a territorial manifestation.

- Although there seems to be consensus that the innovative district is the area where the global and national impulses for innovation meet with the local conditions (milieu), the respective importance remains largely unclear.

The discussion in Part III of the book provides some indication for answering some of these questions. The papers in this part view the development process from a more aggregate level and deal with the sectoral composition of an economy and its transition through time (O'Connor) and with the role of producer services in an urban economy as a supposed link between manufacturing and the service sector (Traxler *et al.*). The first paper, by John Friedmann, draws our attention to the fact that the sectoral composition of a region and its transformation is not an isolated phenomenon but closely related to political, institutional, physical, etc. structures. These relationships – in Part I some of them have been called networks, in Part II they constituted a "milieu" – form a stable system that is difficult to influence by regional policy. In the case of an "innovative milieu" this system favors innovation and restructuring, in an "old industrial region" – Friedmann's illustrative example – its rigidity severely hampers restructuring with all its negative consequences. In Friedmann's view the problem of restructuring an old industrial area is "far more complex than attracting a number of high-tech industries producing for export through a program of linked state and local subsidies" (p. 177). He calls for a "creative response to crisis" in the sense of seeing in it "new opportunities for acting decisively in unprecedented ways" (p. 177). To be able to respond in this way, regions need a local identity as well as a well developed sense for picking up new trends and developments at the global level. Because innovations originate in many different spheres, this challenge goes way beyond the economic relationships as they are underlined in the network concept. It requires a general attitude that Friedmann innovatively calls a "rooted cosmopolitan culture". By stressing the need to pick up developments at the global level ("outward looking behavior" as stressed in the network literature or Maillat's "external component") as well as local identity (stressed particularly in the milieu and district approach) Friedmann implicitly calls for an integration of network and milieu concepts.

The problems former strong economic heartlands dominated by manufacturing have experienced in many parts of the world have given rise to different hypotheses. They range from the old idea of a "law" of sectoral succession (e.g. Bluestone and Harrison, 1982; Stanback, 1985) to the hypothesis that much of the shift from manufacturing to services can be attributed to the creation of "business services", a relatively new part of the service sector that offers services which were once provided by manufacturing firms internally. The papers in Part III of the book indicate that the dynamics of the sectors and the relationship between them may be more complicated. O'Connor, for example, draws the conclusion that manufacturing and the service sector are interdependent and that more work is needed to clearly understand this relationship. Traxler *et al.*, on the other hand, note that producer services are not merely an appendix to manufacturing. To a considerable extent they sell their services to other producer service firms.

A second major point in O'Connor's analysis is the role R&D plays in the recovery of the Victorian economy and of manufacturing in particular. This relates his paper to the discussion in Part II of the book as well as to the papers by Tödtling and by Goldstein in Part IV. The major argument between these papers focuses around the question of how localized R&D effects are. While the concept of an "innovative milieu" implies that there is a considerable local component, O'Connor as well as Goldstein conclude that the local effects are rather weak. O'Connor adopts the view of "research and development as an international activity, not necessarily closely tied to local production" (p. 193). Goldstein notes that in the two cases of research parks he analyzes it took the local economy a long time to restructure in order to be able to take advantage of the park.

Innovation and R&D, it seems, can have quite different spatial implications according to whether they are performed within large, multinational corporations or in a network of small and medium-sized enterprises. Only in the latter may R&D activities generate an innovative milieu sending out development impulses to the region. This view is supported by the contribution by Traxler *et al.*, who note that the smaller a business service firm is the more locally it interacts. In the case of large corporations R&D functions are often located according to their own locational requirements, thus acting like branch plants from the point of view of the region. The innovation that originates from the R&D branch plant is implemented at production plants of the company usually located in different regions and countries.

In the final part three papers have been dealing with new perspectives and approaches to traditional but very central concepts of regional development. The concepts which are reconsidered are the spatial hierarchy of the innovation process (Tödtling), growth center strategy versus endogenous development (Goldstein) as well as spread and backwash (Bergman and Maier). All three papers are at least implicitly related to the concepts discussed in the first three parts of the book.

Innovation, its generation and diffusion was already of central importance in the 1950s and 1960s, particularly in growth pole theory (Perroux, Boudeville, Hansen and others), in diffusion theory (Hägerstrand and others) as well as in product cycle theory (Vernon, Norton and Rees). These traditional approaches, by focusing strongly on location factors for product and process innovation, imply generally a spatial hierarchy in the innovation process. In accordance with some of the former contributions, Tödtling's paper points out that the processes and structures involved are more complex. There may be systematic deviations from a hierarchical pattern, since:

- there are reasons for new industries to avoid the predetermined structures of the largest agglomerations which are strongly shaped by formerly successful industries (Storper);
- innovative local milieus might not coincide with the urban hierarchy, as they require the interplay of economic, technological, and cultural factors (see the contributions by Maillat, Garofoli, and Friedmann); and
- innovations do not just depend on locational factors but also on structural and behavioural features of the firm, such as its network characteristics.

The analysis at the firm level for Austrian regions has shown that adverse locational conditions can partly be overcome by strategic actions of the firm. Organizational changes like the strengthening of relevant functions (boundary-spanning functions: R&D and marketing) as well as the improvement of the qualificational structure are important examples. Participation in relevant networks like supplier and market networks as well as technical contacts and cooperations with other firms and regions also help to overcome locational obstacles.

Goldstein applies the established concepts of growth centers and endogenous development to research parks, an institution which has received considerable attention by policy-makers in recent years as an instrument to foster economic and technological development. He demonstrates that there are different forms and variants of research parks, depending on the – very often implicit – underlying strategy of regional development. He discusses these for research parks based on growth center strategy (Research Triangle Park) as well as those based on endogenous development (University of Utah Park). He shows that internal characteristics (type of establishments, type of functions and innovation activities, qualifications, internal linkages) as well as external network characteristics (corporate linkages, linkages to external firms and knowledge centers) differ strongly for these two cases. The paper also gives important insights for the evaluation of research parks as an instrument of regional policy. It shows that:

- The success of research parks depends not only on regional conditions but also on accidental factors. Dynamic personalities, decisions of key firms and institutions are such factors, and they make it difficult to predict the success of such parks (this result is in accordance with the findings of Maillat, Garofoli, and Tödtling).
- The length of time necessary for stimulating and evaluating technology-led regional development – particularly for regions which lack important locational conditions – is usually greatly underestimated.
- Effects of research parks appear spatially rather concentrated; the evidence of spread effects to outlying areas and the peripheral hinterland has been low.

A major conclusion of Goldstein's paper is that there is no general "best" model for research parks, since the underlying regional situations and conditions are of major importance for success. "This leads to the suggestion that technology-led economic development strategies be based upon careful analysis of local conditions, both strengths and weaknesses, rather than on prior ideological commitment to 'development from above', versus 'development from below' ". This conclusion also rules out the mere imitation of research parks and other policy instruments, which at present very often occurs.

The long-established concept of spread and backwash in regional development (Myrdal and Hirschman have given initial contributions in the late 1950s), which has only been touched in Goldstein's paper, is taken up by Bergman and Maier more systematically and approached in a new way. This contribution at the end of the book is an interesting complement to the network papers at the beginning. While most of the network papers made little reference to geographical space, the paper by Maier and Bergman explicitly investigates the spatial interdependence of the development process. It looks at the spatial macro results of underlying networks which connect regions and give rise to spread and backwash processes. Compared to existing studies their approach has new elements. They are not looking at spread and backwash between just one center and its hinterland (or between two types of regions) but are investigating the whole spatial system (in this case Arkansas), also linking it to the rest of the economy. Thus they look at these processes "across the continuous space of contiguous units of analysis" (Bergman and Maier, p. 268).

For the investigation of the spatial interdependence of development the authors chose a potential model: underlying networks of different spatial scales can be implicitly investigated by applying different distance functions. In the model chosen spread and backwash furthermore are not absolute concepts in the sense that they are tied to specific mechanisms or instruments, but they are relative concepts: the same mechanism or instrument can turn out as spread as well as backwash, depending on the local and other conditions. Spread and backwash are expressed in the sign of the respective parameters. The empirical analysis furthermore has shown that taking into account the spatial interdependence of the whole system can yield surprising and unexpected aggregate effects. In part they result from indirect effects and the aggregation of the underlying networks. The application of different distance functions points to the fact that networks of various scales differ in their impact on aggregate indicators of regional development. Networks up to the scale of labor markets have particularly strong aggregate effects.

2   A "New" Theory of Regional Development in the Making?

What conclusions can be drawn from relevant points in various chapters of this volume and identified for their contribution to a new regional development theory? The following ten elements to be considered in new theoretical approaches may be summarized as follows:

1. Processes of regional development are the result of many actors and protagonists, belonging to networks of quite different dimensions and planes (pointed out by Kamann, Friedmann, Maillat, Garofoli, Hadjimichalis/Papamichos). There are networks of essentially economic flows, although not exclusively output and financial (Johansson) but also networks across which cultural, technological, institutional, and political exchange occurs. Regional development thus can be broadened as a network-determined spatial concept that refers to local/regional nodes and intersections (or along common channels) of these networks. A capacity for network participation that ties a region to relevant external partners may therefore become a stronger determinant for development than many previously important internal factors, since network participation enables a region to mobilize resources and gives access to vital information and knowledge. However, the internal capacity to exploit and expand network connections may be an unrecognized factor of some importance.

To some, this stress on networks may appear merely to revive arguments for better communication and transportation systems. If so, it should be stressed that the points made here are considerably more subtle and important than simple upgrading and expansion of typical technologies would imply: the classes of nodes, range and type of actors, functions served by networks, layering and complexity of network architecture, interleaving of public and proprietary conduits, and rules of network access present a far more textured pattern of regional development than theory or policy now considers.

2. These networks imply new relations between partners but also the emergence of unequal power relations and, consequently, different kinds of dependencies (Kamann). Depending on the network position of its key actors, a region will in the aggregate be either a controlling or a dependent one (see also Sheppard, Maier, and Tödtling, 1990). This implies that the synergetic surplus of networks will be distributed unevenly across space (Kamann). If so, shaping the membership and privileges of network members might be an objective of regional policy measures that attempt to orchestrate equitable relations within an ensemble of regions and at the same time position its multilateral relations with other regional systems for maximum advantage. The European Community and former Eastern Bloc members will doubtless consider some position along these lines, as might the emerging North American regional system.

3. There is also a contradictory relationship between networks and the flexibility they are claimed to foster: as pointed out by Johansson, networks imply investment and sunk costs, and because of that they are quite resistant to rapid change, even though they permit rapid change within and among network nodes. Network changes among firms involve mostly innovations (new products, processes, organizations or markets). These innovations change the cost structures in such a way that the search for new network partners and the related investment is often more profitable than maintenance of the old ones, whether or not they are in close spatial proximity.

4. Network characteristics of firms and regions are of particular importance for innovation and technological change and thus for the continuous renewal and the future growth prospects of spatially defined regions (Johansson, Kamann, Grabher, Maillat, Garofoli). Networks sustain firms during difficult periods of restructuring since they represent a beneficial compromise between stability and flexibility: they

provide more stability than markets and more flexibility than hierarchies. The supply lines between buyers and sellers of intermediate
products may be mutually beneficial as "value added partner" chains
arise where the intermediate flows are mutually designed, produced
and delivered through a series of quasi-to-formal agreements. As
Grabher has shown, other network agreements link large, technically
advanced, and financially secure firms, acting as "general contractors", with smaller, nimble firms capable of generating a wide variety
of commercially viable applications that range from retained niche
markets to shared mass-market products. The full range of network
possibilities that bear on regional development prospects and useful
conceptual advances deserves future attention.

5. The logic of networks extends from subregional to meta-regional activities. Innovation activities of firms and, consequently, regional
   economic renewal rely on internal characteristics of firms (functions
   and qualifications), or local and regional networks (local milieu: density of face to face contacts, informal contacts, coherence between
   actors). As networks become new organizing frameworks available
   to enterprises, internal restructuring allows firms to reposition themselves further in a regional size distribution (or milieu) of same-sector
   firms, retaining for themselves some subset of functions while ceding
   different functions to other firms. Alternatively, network membership may allow firms to "slough off" internal functions, usually as
   reductions of middle management, that then enter the market as independently organized producer service firms that supply functional
   services, often back to their sectors of origination. Producer services
   have flourished everywhere recently and with particularly interesting effects in Vienna, as the chapter by Traxler *et al.* makes clear.
   How networks enable these adjustments to arise and new agglom-
   erating forces to define regional economies is a topic deserving far
   more attention in future.

   Similar processes are at work as well along large-scale networks.
   These networks establish links between regional firms and export
   markets, foreign knowledge centers and cooperation partners that
   provide special information and knowledge inputs. Friedmann describes the requirements of local embeddedness and outward-looking
   behaviour best by speaking of a "rooted cosmopolitanism".

6. The emerging importance of networks and milieus together draw
   the attention of regional development theory to questions of industrial economics and organization, particularly questions concerning
   the varying functions of firms and "regional" relations among them.

Development theory cannot remain fragmented by, on the one hand, neoclassical assumptions of atomistic market functioning (and "failure") so common to early regional science; nor can it simply ignore implicit assumptions about the "motor" functions of large export firms embedded in much growth pole theorizing. The time is ripe to examine functional and regional interdependencies among firms and their establishments that differ by size, age, ownership, control, factor dependency (i.e. technological vs. resource), function "shedding" (behind emergence of producer services), and so forth. Rapid restructuring of these characteristics in Western industrial economies is reason enough to re-examine these issues, but the fundamental rethinking now underway in Eastern European regional economies presents both added pressure and a living laboratory for those willing to make seminal contributions.

7. The developments leading to some of the theoretical innovations discussed here raise the question of short-term vs. long-term efficiency in regional structure and industrial composition. We know from system theory that the economy is a system that may display chaotic behavior (e.g. Day, 1982, 1983). In such a complex system, although it appears quite stable for some time, seemingly marginal changes in one of the parameters may yield dramatic changes in the overall structure. The system may jump from one form of internal organization to another. Such a transition requires the economic actors to adjust to the new situation. Actors who have been highly efficient under the old regime may find it more difficult to adjust than actors who were less efficient in the short run. In this sense there might be a trade-off between short-term and long-term efficiency. Economic actors and firms in particular face the problem of structuring their activities in such a way that they are profitable in the short run as well as flexible enough to be adjusted to structural changes in the system.

As pointed out by Grabher as well, network structures appear to be particularly well suited for balancing these short- and long-term requirements. In this sense the network approach to regional development relates to the growing regional literature on chaos, systems analysis, self-organization, bifurcation, etc. (see, for example, Wilson, 1981; Andersson et al., 1989).

8. There is an apparent conceptual gap between the firm-oriented analyses of networking and network development and the region-oriented analyses of milieus, innovative districts, etc. While network relations appear to be rather insensitive to physical distance we nevertheless

can observe spatial structures of development and relatively short-range interdependencies in the development process. When we try to base the concept of regional development on a network approach, the question why networks can be accessed more easily at some locations than at others remains largely open. Empirical studies offer case-specific explanations. The theoretical basis is still lacking.

9. There seem to be no general "success models" of regional development, a point stressed by Hadjimichalis/Papamichos, Friedmann, and Goldstein. Success stories such as Third Italy, Silicon Valley or other high-tech areas are often evidence of the localized outcome (phenotypes) behind more generic economic processes and determinants (changes in the production process, institutions, labor relations). While our earlier adoption of growth pole development assumptions would now be seen as simplistic, we are today more likely to acknowledge how generic processes interact with historically evolved local and regional conditions (economic, cultural, political conditions). It is out of these more complex interactions that regions are permitted to flourish or wane, depending on their enabling position along networks and within the international division of labor. From the policy point of view this implies that particular local and regional conditions require uniquely devised strategies and models. This places far more emphasis on the practice of regional economic planning, as Friedmann notes, a practice informed by development theory but driven by territorial interests. Large-firm-based growth center strategies may be successful in certain regions (example of the RTP), the stimulation of small firms and entrepreneurship as endogenous strategies in others (Utah Research Park). As the regional conditions change, however, policy must also change (Friedmann, Goldstein).

   Closely related is the problem of how to condense an inductive theory out of a set of case-study analyses. This question is at the heart of the implicit discussion between the contributions by Garofoli and by Hadjimichalis/Papamichos in this volume. How much of the specific situation in a particular case-study region can be ignored for the sake of theory building before the theory becomes inadequate? This question is particularly difficult to answer in social sciences where we cannot control the "experimental" setting that produces our observations.

10. "Stage models" of industrial succession in regional development and other simplified models (core–periphery, spatial hierarchy) no longer appear to capture adequately the unfolding of events (Parts III, IV).

As O'Connor has shown, despite the general decline of manufacturing employment in industrialized countries, it still is of major importance if one examines its output and linkages to other sectors. Also, a closer look at regional transformation shows that an old-established manufacturing base may – if it is renewed continually – retain its importance for a considerable time.

However, renewal may not result simply from diffusion of technological advance and innovation down a spatial hierarchy; this view is laid open to serious question by Tödtling's contribution. In the absence of hierarchically strong shaping factors, it may be that one or more rival endogenous explanations must be sought to understand the relations between firms' adoption and generation of innovations and their host regions' development prospects. Similarly, the complexity of spread and backwash processes is shown to arise among components of regions that do not conform to prevailing core–periphery analogies, a development typology as rare as the mythical "featureless plain" assumed by central place adherents. Rather, the Bergman–Maier simulation model reveals the close interdependence of development across the continuous space of adjoining counties and provocatively demonstrates the strong effects of transportation network properties and urban–rural differentiation. By re-examining these central propositions with fresh evidence and research designs, it becomes possible to see where our conceptual apparatus has totally broken down and which pieces might yet be salvaged.

There is much food here to nourish a healthy reconsideration of regional development theory and policy. The early clues and key insights provided by Walter Stöhr and others during the last decade or so have been followed up by numerous research findings reported here; these findings promise to fuel the next round of theorizing and policy experimentation. The very nature of such inquiry requires that theory be revised when its inadequacies are revealed in practice. The base of empirical and conceptual research that will trigger the next round of revised theorizing and testing has been advanced by authors of this book's chapters. They cordially invite other colleagues to join the important task of reconsidering regions.

References

Andersson, Å.E., D.F. Batten, B. Johansson, P. Nijkamp (eds.), 1989. *Advances in Spatial Theory and Dynamics*, North-Holland, Amsterdam.

Bluestone, B., B. Harrison, 1982. *The Deindustrialization of America*, Basic Books, New York.

Day, R.H., 1982. Irregular Growth Cycles, *American Economic Review*, Vol. 72, pp. 406–414.

Day, R.H., 1983. The Emergence of Chaos from Classical Economic Growth, *Quarterly Journal of Economics*, Vol. XCVIII, pp. 201–213.

Helmsing, A.H.J., 1986. *Firms, Farms and State: A Study of Rural, Urban and Regional Dimensions of Change*, Allen & Unwin, Winchester, MA.

Sheppard, E., G. Maier, F. Tödtling, 1990. The Geography of Organizational Control: Austria, 1973-1981, *Economic Geography*, Vol. 66, pp. 1–21.

Stanback, T.M., 1985. The Changing Fortunes of Metropolitan Economies, in M. Castells (ed.), *High Technology, Space and Society*. Urban Affairs Annual Reviews, Vol. 28, Sage, Beverly Hills.

Wilson, A.G., 1981. *Catastrophe Theory and Bifurcation*, Croom Helm, London.

Index

301